The BEATLES
Finally Let It Be

Compiled by Bruce Spizer

With additional contributions by

Bill King,
Al Sussman,
Frank Daniels,
Piers Hemmingsen
and other Beatles fans

www.imagineandwonder.com

YOUR GUARANTEE OF QUALITY

As publishers, we strive to produce every book to the highest commercial standards. The printing and binding have been planned to ensure a sturdy, attractive publication which should give years of enjoyment. If your copy fails to meet our high standards, please inform us and we will gladly replace it. admin@imagineandwonder.com

www.beatle.net
498 Productions, L.L.C.
935 Gravier Street, Suite 707
New Orleans, Louisiana 70112
Fax: 504-299-1964
email: 498@beatle.net

Scan these QR codes with your phone camera for more titles from Imagine and Wonder and 498 Productions.

The Billboard, Cash Box and Record World chart data used in this book was taken from books published by Record Research, including Billboard Pop Album Charts 1965-1969, Billboard Pop Album Charts The Seventies and The Comparison Book 1954-1982. Photos provided by: Minnie Yorke for the Ritchie Yorke Project (page 61); Lizzie Bravo (page 106); Yaakov Edisherashvili (page 108); and Horacio Dubini (page 117). Most of the collectibles shown in the book are from the collections of Bruce Spizer, Frank Daniels, Gary Hein, Perry Cox, Scott "Belmo" Belmer, Piers Hemmingsen and Jeff Augsburger.

FSC
www.fsc.org
MIX
Paper from responsible sources
FSC® C017606

Paperback edition ISBN 9781637610015
Library of Congress Control Number 2021906710
Printed in China by Hung Hing Off-set Printing Co. Ltd.
123456789

PRINTED WITH
SOY INK
Trademark of American Soybean Association

I've Got A Feeling

The 1969 Christmas holiday season began for me at 3:00 PM on Friday, December 19. That evening I most likely played *Abbey Road* on my bedroom's stereo record player that my mother bought me for my birthday the previous summer. She realized how important music was to me and she had taken me to a high-end audio store before I headed to summer camp.

On my first day off from school, my mother brought me back to the Radio Center, a local New Orleans appliance store that sold televisions and radios. Once again, I asked the owner if I could buy the store's display RCA Nipper dog. And once again, he declined. After looking at various radios and 8-track players, I picked out a Philco portable combination radio/cassette player. My cousin had an 8-track player and I remembered that I didn't like how it changed channels, sometimes mid-song. I decided to give the smaller cassette format a try. My next stop was to Radio Shack to buy some Realistic blank cassettes so I could record directly off the radio.

On Christmas Eve, I tuned in to a Slidell, Louisiana radio station that broadcast in Spanish during the day, but, as my Spanish teacher described it, "went hippie" at night. The disc jockey announced that he was going to play some songs from an unreleased Beatles album titled *Get Back*. By this time I was buying Rolling Stone magazine at my neighborhood record store, Studio A, so I was aware of the *Get Back* LP. I excitedly recorded the new Beatles songs on my radio/cassette player, instantly falling in love with "Let It Be" and "The Long And Winding Road." After the DJ finished playing the Beatles songs, most likely from a bootleg LP, he played Barry McGuire's "Eve Of Destruction." It was a jolting reminder that the Vietnam War was still going strong.

When it was all over, I rewound the cassette tape and listened to the unreleased Beatles songs over and over again as if they were forbidden fruit. I thought, "I've got a feeling this is something really special."

Every two weeks I would get the next issue of Rolling Stone and read about the release of the *Get Back* album being delayed again. Although I was disappointed, I could still play my *Get Back* cassette. As February came to a close, I bought the "new" Beatles album, *Hey Jude*. Even though it did not have any new songs, it was a convenient way to hear the singles.

On Sunday evening, March 1, I watched The Ed Sullivan Show tribute to the Beatles. While some of the performances by other artists singing Beatles songs were interesting, the only things that mattered to me were the films of the Beatles singing "Let It Be" and "Two Of Us." Although I had heard both songs on my homemade *Get Back* cassette, it was great hearing them in improved sound quality and seeing my heroes in action. I taped the Beatles songs off the TV.

A week or so later I bought the "Let It Be" single at Studio A. I played the ballad over and over again, with "You Know My Name (Look Up The Number)" getting only a handful of spins. Within a few weeks of the disc's release, the top three songs on WTIX-AM in New Orleans were "Let It Be," Badfinger's "Come And Get It" and "Instant Karma" by John Ono Lennon.

That spring was my ninth-grade class trip to Washington, D.C. For the long bus ride from New Orleans to the nation's capitol, I brought my cassette player and a stash of cassettes. I was sitting with my friends who were also Beatles fans. Everyone enjoyed hearing the still unreleased songs from the *Get Back* album.

Shortly after we got back to New Orleans, I bought the new Beatles single "The Long And Winding Road." I remember how disappointed I was with the record. The song was one of my favorites on the cassette — a simple piano ballad with words of lost love. But the single was cluttered with strings, horns and a chorus.

A week later I went to Studio A and purchased the *Let It Be* album. I thought the red label was cool, but had mixed feelings about the recordings. "Two Of Us," "I've Got A Feeling," "One After 909" and "For You Blue" sounded great, but I was horrified with the new version of "Let It Be." It was a mess of blaring brass and out-of-place raunchy guitar. I loved the lyrics to "Across The Universe" but wished it did not have the strings and female chorus.

A few weeks later I went to see the *Let It Be* movie. It was a bittersweet experience knowing that the group had broken up by then. Some of the scenes, particularly the argument with Paul and George, pulled back the curtain on why the group was no more. But all was not depressing. I loved seeing and hearing "The Long And Winding Road" as a stripped-down piano ballad. And the rooftop concert was a gas!

That summer I went to East Africa with my parents. We had a six-hour layover in London, so we took a cab into the city. I went to a record store to buy the British version of the *Let It Be* album because it came with a special book that was not included with the U.S. album. My parents thought it was expensive and wondered why I wanted to lug it around Africa, but I insisted that I wanted the LP as a birthday present. At the time, I did not pay much attention to the disc's Parlophone labels. Twenty-five years later I learned that, by luck, I had bought the rare export edition of the LP. My parents were shocked to learn it was worth over $2,000!

Speaking Words of Wisdom

As promised in the acknowledgments page of my *Abbey Road* book, I'm back to tell the story of the Beatles January 1969 rehearsals and recording sessions that became known as the *Get Back/Let It Be* sessions. The title of this book, *The Beatles Finally Let It Be*, is a bit of an ironic pun. Throughout 1969 and the first few months of 1970, Apple kept postponing the release of the *Get Back* LP. By the time the album was finally released in May 1970, it had been retitled *Let It Be*. When Apple reactivated in 1994 with the release of *The Beatles At The BBC*, Apple was asked by fans time and time again, "When will *Let It Be* be released on video?"

Well, finally, Apple excited fans with the news that it would be re-releasing the *Let It Be* film, both in its original edit and a spectacular new version by Peter Jackson, titled *The Beatles: Get Back*, on September 4, 2020. Beatles fans rejoiced! The Beatles Finally Let It Be. But then Covid-19 intervened, pushing the film back a year until August 27, 2021. So much for finally!

This fourth installment of my Beatles album series was a bit more work than the previous books. Although most of the songs appearing on the *Let It Be* album were rehearsed and recorded during a one-month period in January 1969, the story behind the unreleased and the official compilations was truly a long and winding road that left us waiting a long, long time.

In addition to listening to 83 CDs worth of music and chatting from the sessions, I reread the classic books on *Get Back* sessions, including Doug Sulpy and Ray Schweighardt's *Get Back, The Unauthorized Chronicle of The Beatles Let It Be Disaster* (originally published as *Drugs, Divorce and a Slipping Image*) and John C.

Winn's *Lifting Latches, The Beatles' Recorded Legacy, Volume Three, Inside the Vaults*. These books are highly recommended for those seeking more details about the sessions. And, as always, I returned to Mark Lewisohn's *The Beatles Recording Sessions* time and time again.

I assembled the same team utilized in the previous volumes in this series. Piers Hemmingsen provides the Canadian perspective. Beatlefan editor Al Sussman writes about what was going on in the year 1970 to place the *Let It Be* album in historical context. Frank Daniels takes us through the songs and films of Early 1970. Beatlefan publisher Bill King returns with more fan notes. And, because so much of the music recorded during the *Get Back* sessions first appeared on bootlegs, I recruited Beatles bootleg guru Scott "Belmo" Belmer to tell that side of the story.

The Fan Recollections chapter has always been an important part of the books in the album series. This time I was able to provide memories from a few of the lucky individuals who were up on the roof or in the streets for the Beatles final public performance.

On the technical side, Diana Thornton worked her magic to make the book look terrific as always and Kaye Alexander coordinated the interactions with our new printer in Clarksville, Tennessee. (I could talk about that last train, but that's a tie-in to another of my favorite groups!) Proof readers included Diana, Frank, Al and Beatle Tom Frangione. In the tradition, my thanks to my family, Sarah, Eloise, Barbara, Trish, Big Puppy and others too numerous and crazy to name.

Finally, to paraphrase the ending credit of those early Bond films, The Beatles Album Series Shall Return...

words About Author

Bruce Spizer is a lifelong native of New Orleans, Louisiana, who was eight years old when the Beatles invaded America. He began listening to the radio at age two and was a die-hard fan of WTIX, a top forty AM station that played a blend of New Orleans R&B music and top pop and rock hits. His first two albums were *The Coasters' Greatest Hits*, which he permanently "borrowed" from his older sisters, and *Meet The Beatles!*, which he still occasionally plays on his vintage 1964 Beatles record player.

During his high school and college days, Bruce played guitar in various bands that primarily covered hits of the sixties, including several Beatles songs. He wrote numerous album and concert reviews for his high school and college newspapers, including a review of *Abbey Road* that didn't claim Paul was dead. He received his B.A., M.B.A. and law degrees from Tulane University. His legal and accounting background have proved valuable in researching and writing his books.

Bruce is considered one of the world's leading experts on the Beatles. A "taxman" by day, Bruce is a Board Certified Tax Attorney with his own practice. A "paperback writer" by night, Bruce is the author of 12 critically acclaimed books on the Beatles, including *The Beatles Are Coming! The Birth of Beatlemania in America*, a series of six books on the group's American record releases, *Beatles For Sale on Parlophone Records*, which covers all of the Beatles records issued in the U.K. from 1962- 1970, and his new series of books on the Beatles albums. His articles have appeared in Beatlefan, Goldmine and American History magazines.

Bruce Spizer at the controls of St. Charles Avenue streetcar No. 910 in New Orleans, Louisiana.

He was selected to write the questions for the special Beatles edition of Trivial Pursuit. He maintains the popular website www.beatle.net.

Bruce has been a speaker at numerous Beatles conventions and at the Grammy Museum, the Rock 'N' Roll Hall of Fame & Museum and the American Film Institute. He has been on ABC's Good Morning America and Nightline, CBS's The Early Show, CNN, Fox and morning shows in New York, Chicago, Los Angeles, New Orleans and other cities, and is a frequent guest on radio shows, including NPR, BBC and the Beatles Channel.

Bruce serves as a consultant to Universal Music Group, Capitol Records and Apple Corps Ltd. on Beatles projects. He has an extensive Beatles collection, concentrating on American, Canadian and British first issue records, promotional items and concert posters.

contents

The Beatles New Record's a Gas!
An American Perspective of *Let It Be*

As 1970 began, the Beatles *Abbey Road* sat atop the Billboard Top LP's chart for the final two of its ten weeks at number one. By this time, many Beatles fans in America knew the group had already recorded an album the previous year that would likely be issued in early 1970. Two of the songs from the sessions, "Get Back" and "Don't Let Me Down," had been issued as a single way back in April 1969. Some fans had even heard songs from the album that was going to be called *Get Back* on the radio or on a bootleg. When the "Let It Be" single was issued on March 11, those in the know recognized the song, having already heard a different version of the tune months earlier. Others had seen a color promo film of the group performing the song on The Ed Sullivan Show. But for most Americans, "Let It Be" was just the next Beatles single, the follow-up to the disc containing "Something" and "Come Together."

The new Beatles record came in a picture sleeve (shown previous page) featuring color photos of the faces of John, Paul, George and Ringo. The A-side was a beautiful ballad with a soothing message that, for some, had religious connotations in the line "Mother Mary comes to me." Paul's song was in many ways the opposite of John's 1969 retro-rocker, "The Ballad Of John And Yoko," with its "Christ you know it ain't easy" and "they're gonna crucify me" refrains. The B-side seemed like a throw-away effort, a burlesque-sounding tune titled "You Know My Name (Look Up The Number)."

"Let It Be" reached the top of the Billboard Hot 100 on April 11, holding off "ABC" by the Jackson 5 for two weeks before slipping to number two. John Ono Lennon held down the third spot with his instant classic, "Instant Karma (We All Shine On)." The top five was rounded out by Norman Greenbaum's religious rocker "Spirit In The Sky" and Simon & Garfunkel's "Bridge Over Troubled Water," which had spent the previous six weeks at number one. Apple had a third song in the top ten with Badfinger's "Come And Get It," written and produced by Paul McCartney. "Let It Be" was number one for four weeks in Cash Box and three weeks in Record World. The song charted for 14 weeks in Billboard, 13 in Cash Box and 12 in Record World. Its goofy flip side baffled program directors and failed to chart.

Americans first learned of the Beatles 1969 recordings that would ultimately be known as the *Get Back/Let It Be* sessions in TV Guide. The magazine's issue cover-dated April 19-25, 1969, contained a two-page spread informing readers of a TV documentary detailing the making of a new Beatles album. Shortly after the magazine was issued, radio stations began playing the new Beatles single, "Get Back," which topped the charts for five weeks. On April 30, the TV Guide image of the Beatles on the rooftop came to life when the Glen Campbell Goodtime Hour broadcast film of the band performing "Get Back" and its flip side, "Don't Let Me Down."

That summer, those who had discovered Rolling Stone magazine learned that the next Beatles album was due in July and was named *Get Back, Don't Let Me Down, and 12 Other Titles*. The July 12 issue (on sale two weeks earlier) indicated that the group was considering making a TV film for the LP. The songs on the album flowed together and were often interspersed with studio banter left in to give a "live" effect. One of the first tracks on the album is a jam on "Save The Last Dance For Me" turning into "Don't Let Me Down." Throughout the album, "The talk goes on, the chatter, the loose chords, the out of tune notes, the flat singing. But they are clearly having fun." The album includes a beautiful Paul McCartney ballad, "Let It Be," which was expected to be the single from the album. The song's melody is pure McCartney, with simple lyrics and a pretty guitar solo played through a Leslie speaker. Rolling Stone reported that the album, recorded at London's Twickenham Film Studios, was "done live with no baffles or intricate miking" and had minimal overdubbing. Its sound is dominated by acoustic guitars. We would later learn that although rehearsals took place at Twickenham, the album was actually recorded at Apple's Savile Row headquarters.

The September 6 Rolling Stone informed readers that the new Beatles album, tentatively titled *Get Back*, had been delayed from a September release until December. The album would come with a large book with color photographs taken by Ethan Russell during the recording of the LP and extensive text written by Johnathan Cott and David Dalton (all three contributors to Rolling Stone). The text was described as "an immense edited transcript" of the studio discussions during the recording of the album mixed with words from the authors to form "an oblong look at the history of rock and roll consciousness." The magazine lamented that EMI had ordered the earthy language removed from the "brilliant text" and that the Beatles wanted the book to be more in line with fan expectations.

Four cats on a London roof

A TV documentary will detail the making of the Beatles' new record album

The cats on the roof are, of course, the Beatles. And what they're up to up there is a recording session, the entire proceedings of which were, coincidentally, filmed for a television documentary.

In the panel of pictures at top are, from left to right: Ringo Starr, George Harrison, a hirsute Paul McCartney and John Lennon. In the bottom photo, the Beatles en masse in a *furor poeticus*.

The reason for making an album is obvious. The reason for filming the session is to let the world—all over which the Beatles hope to sell the documentary in a few months—know just how the Beatles go about their work. At least part of the world, however, was less than enchanted with the opportunity. Their neighbors (the recording studio just happens to be in London's elegant Savile Row) dispatched bobbies to quell the noise. Even bobbies couldn't do that.

14

The next issue of Rolling Stone, dated September 20, contained a track by track description of the *Get Back* album. The album was called a "model of simplicity—in concept, music, philosophy, and politics." Regression was a main theme, down to the album's cover with the group recreating their pose in the staircase well at EMI's Manchester Square headquarters used on the cover of their first British LP, *Please Please Me*. The album's opening track, "One After 909," was written by John and Paul in the late fifties. The group, augmented by keyboardist Billy Preston, plays by themselves with no orchestrations, electronic effects or overdubs. The album has no Indian instruments for George, no Ringo vocal and no peace-plug by John. The LP was engineered by Glyn Johns and recorded in Apple's Savile Row basement studio after rehearsals at Twickenham. The album was "noticeably informal, looser than *The Beatles*" and "freer" than any previous Beatles record, allowing the group to "kick out the jams."

The disc opens with "One After 909" recorded on Apple's rooftop. The song is followed by applause and a brief rendition of "Save The Last Dance For Me." After discussion, John says "Give me the courage to come screaming in," which he does in the next song, "Don't Let Me Down," a different take than the single. The next selection is a John Lennon blues-tinted number "Dig A Pony," whose theme is "you can do anything you want to do." This is followed by a McCartney screamer "I've Got A Feeling," with answer lines from Lennon, who messes up towards the end and admits "I cocked it up trying to get loud." The first side ends with the single version of "Get Back." Side Two opens with a George love song, "For You Blue," with some nice bits of music. "Teddy Boy" is a weird number about a mother comforting her son complete with square dance tempo and calls and left-in feedback from George's guitar. "Two Of Us On Our Way Home" is an easy-paced number with John and Paul singing harmony. After Paul says "So we leave the little town of London, England," the group gets back to their Liverpool days with the link track "Maggie May." The next song is "Dig It," a loose number with John shouting "I can hardly keep my hands still" and "dig it." "Let It Be" is a pretty and simple song with Paul on vocal and piano, whose message is "When all the heart-broken people in the world agree, there will be an answer, let it be." The album ends with another McCartney piano ballad "The Long And Winding Road" leading into a "Get Back" mini-encore. We are told that there are enough old gold finished pieces such as "Shake, Rattle And Roll," "Blue Suede Shoes" and a remake of "Love Me Do" that could make up a fantastic album. The Beatles have gotten back and they're more together than they've seemed in a long time.

4

Beatles Get Back, Track by Track

LONDON—*The Beatles, Get Back* album, now set for a December release in the U.S., is a model of simplicity — in concept, music, philosophy, and politics.

Regression appears to be one main theme for this album, beginning with the cover photo. The Beatles are posed at the offices of EMI records in Manchester Square, grouped over the staircase, just as they were for their first English album, *Please Please Me*, in 1963. The photograph is by Angus McBean, who took the original cover photo six years ago. And the first song on the album, "One After 909," is a 1959 Lennon-McCartney composition, written when the Beatles were still the Quarrymen roaming around Liverpool.

On the technical side of the music, the Beatles for the Get Back package are by themselves: No 40-piece orchestra, no special electronic effects — not even over-dubbing of instruments. There is no Eastern or Indian instrument for George, no vocal for Ringo, no peace-in plug for John. The only non-Beatle on the record is keyboard man Billy Preston. The LP, engineered by Glyn Johns, was recorded in Apple's new studios in the basement at 3 Savile Row, following rehearsals at Twickenham.

Beatles Get Back is a noticeably informal album, looser than *The Beatles;* freer, in fact, than any record the group has ever made. In a phrase, they kick out the jams. The reason is in the rehearsals. There, all composing was completed and arrangements worked out for songs, to that at Apple, there were no last-minute patchup jobs and changes on tunes. At Apple, in fact, the Beatles literally ran through the entire album, so that the results simulate a recorded concert or a bugged rehearsal session. Between songs, the Beatles are heard discussing upcoming numbers, criticizing their work in progress, and shouting comments up to Johns. Other sounds and voices heard between cuts are those of the film crew who made a movie of the Beatles working, both at Twickenham and at Savile Row. The film and the LP, along with an impressive book of session photos and reportage, will be released together in December.

Eleven songs, including "Get Back" and "Don't Let Me Down," make up the LP, with a short reprise of the "Get Back" theme at the end of the second side. Mini-jams serve as bridges between several numbers. One is a John and Paul rendition of the Drifters' "Save the Last Dance for Me," the other a Mersey Beat hoedown called "Maggie May."

Track by track, the Beatles "Get Back" this way:

[SIDE ONE]

1. "One After 909"—One of the five numbers recorded on Apple's rooftop (and the only one included on the album), this ten-year-old composition ("One of the first songs we ever wrote," says Paul) opens with a piano-run, guitar chorded false start. Then, with Harrison on lead guitar, Lennon and McCartney handling the vocals and with screaming Paul on lead, it is—how you say—a rave-up. The lyrics:

My baby said she's traveling on the one after 909
Move over honey, I'm traveling on that line
Move over once, move over twice
Come on baby don't be cold as ice
Said she's traveling on the one after 909 . . .
Pick up your bag, run to the station
Railman said you've got the wrong location
Pick up your bag, run right home
Then you will find you got the number wrong.

*

Light applause—mostly from Ringo's wife Maureen (for which she gets thanks from Paul)—then into the "Save the Last Dance" bridge. The short John-Paul duet is cut short; they chat, and John says "Give me the courage to come screaming in." He does, on—

2. "Don't Let Me Down"—The LP version includes Paul helping on the vocals and the same instrumental lineup as on "909"—Lennon on rhythm, Harrison on lead guitar. Preston is not on tap this time around.

3. "Dig a Pony"—John on lead again, with electric piano from Preston and rim shots from Ringo. The song is tinted by blues but is the first non-romance number on the LP. The theme: You can do anything you want to so long as you put your mind to it. In other words, you can work it out (to the point, even, that you could dig a pony). Random comments follow, and Ringo slams a cymbal, plowing into

4. "I've Got a Feeling"— Another screaming McCartney effort with answer lines from Lennon who does a verse, screws up, and mutters, barely audibly: "I cocked it up trying to get loud." Ringo again ties successive numbers together with a thump on his tom-toms and a question: "What does that sound like?"

5. "Get Back"— The theme stated. John is on lead; Preston on piano. This is the version released as a single.

[SIDE TWO]

1. "For You Blue"—George wrote it and sings it, playing a soft acoustic guitar and backed by John on steel and Paul on piano. No bass. "For You Blue" is a love song about that one chick you know is out there—the one you think and dream about, the one who haunts you—and the one you never quite got to meet. Some nice bits of music, done the blue jay way.

2. "Teddy Boy"—A weird number, the story being about a mother comforting her boy, saying I'll see you through. The message: We all need someone to turn to. All you need is love. "Teddy Boy" then moves into an outright hay-kicking square dance tempo, including calls. George's guitar causes some feedback, and it's kept in for posterity. John handles acoustic, and Paul sings. Again, no bass.

3. "Two of Us on Our Way Home"—The theme restated. Two of us riding nowhere, lazily, with hazy memories in our heads, heading back home. Lennon and McCartney harmonize on this easy-paced almost waltzy number, with bass affected by George on rhythm guitar.

. . . On our way back home.
You and I have memories
Longer than the road that stretches out of hand . . .

Paul the MC: "So we leave the little town of London, England . . ." and the group pours it on, getting back to their Liverpool days for "Maggie May." This bridge sets the pace for the next cut.

4. "Dig It"—Now Lennon's on bass for the rest of the side. McCartney is on piano, with George back to acoustic guitar. A loose number, Paul singing and gospelly John shouting encouragement: "I can hardly keep my hands still!" George joins in to chat it up with John. "Dig It" dips into politics but oh so gently: You can't really knock anything—BBC or Doris Day (or Richard Nixon, cops, or Al Capp), anything — because somebody can "dig it" even if you don't happen to.

5. "Let It Be"—As pretty and simple as the title makes it sound. Paul, singing like he did yesterday on "Yesterday," backs himself on piano, with Paul and John harmonizing behind him. George is on a Lesley-amplified guitar, so that his picking comes out like organ-playing. The lyric message: When all the heart-broken people living in the world agree, there'll be an answer, a final solution: Let it be.

6. "The Long and Winding Road"— McCartney wraps it up with another piano- dominated ballad meshed with the "Get Back" mini-encore. Here, he is singing to a girl who has left him standing, crying, "You'll never know the ways I've tried," he says, so don't leave me stranded; lead me down the long and winding road back to your door.

*   *   *

There's more—but not on *Get Back*. With a 160-page book full of words and color photos on the recording sessions to be packaged with the LP, the Beatles decided against another double-record set. Finished pieces in the can could make up an incredible separate album. Included are old gold pieces like "Shake Rattle and Roll" and "Blue Suede Shoes," along with a re-make of a Beatles oldie-but, "Love Me Do." Ringo has a vocal among the dozen or so other numbers stashed away. His composition—shades of *Candy*—is called "Octopussy's Garden."

All of this will out eventually, but exactly when is uncertain. The Beatles are reportedly working on yet another LP to be released before the film, book, and *Get Back* package, which was finished at the end of May (with the cutting of "One After 909").

The Beatles have gotten back and they're more obviously together than they've seemed in a long time.

John and Yoko On a Peace Cruise

LONDON—John and Yoko Lennon's plan to conduct their next peace effort from a private radio ship in the Mediterranean. Their hopeful audience will be countries of the Middle East.

The broadcasting ship is controlled by a Tel Aviv restaurateur, Abie Nathan who had tried several "peace flights" to Egypt and elsewhere, with no success. He met with Lennon August 21st in London to work out plans.

According to Lennon, "Yoko and I will broadcast live from the ship, and Mr. Nathan is anxious for our song, *Give Peace a Chance*, to be the signature tune of the radio station."

John and Yoko plan to join the ship sometime this month. The ship, a 70-tonner, is in New York.

The October 4 Rolling Stone indicated that the Beatles next LP would be *Abbey Road*. The record would precede the *Get Back* package and be issued in October. The *Get Back* LP was still scheduled for December. As this issue went on sale, Buffalo's WKBW-AM played tracks sourced from an early May acetate of the *Get Back* album on September 20. Two nights later, Boston's WBCN-FM broadcast a tape of a January 1969 acetate, erroneously describing it as the *Get Back* album. On September 24, Cleveland's WIXY-AM played six tracks from the same source as those heard on WKBW. The Plain Dealer's Jane Scott described the songs as "each good, each different. All in an early Beatles bag."

By the time the October 18 Rolling Stone went on sale, *Abbey Road* began to appear in stores. The issue contained an interview with George Harrison about the new LP. Harrison noted: "We had *Get Back* in the can, but one day we just decided that we'd like to do a newer album. There was no particular reason—we just wanted to use some of our newer songs." Rolling Stone reviewed *Abbey Road* in its November 15 issue.

The November 29 Rolling Stone reported that the *Get Back* album had been delayed again, this time to February, when the Beatles would be honored on The Ed Sullivan Show and appear in a feature-length film on the recording sessions. The Sullivan program would show film clips of Beatles performances and feature other artists performing Beatles songs. The group would drop by the show for handshakes, but would not perform. The Beatles would then attend the opening of the film, which had been renamed *Let It Be* after the McCartney ballad. The article explained that the film was shot in 16 mm for a planned TV special to promote the album and had been blown up to 35 mm for theatrical release by United Artists, the distributor of the group's previous films. (*Let It Be* would be the third and final film under the Beatles contract with United Artists.) The film soundtrack, essentially the still unreleased *Get Back* album, would be on Apple, but distributed by United Artists Records in the U.S. (as per its film contract, which entitled UA to two soundtrack albums). There would also be a one-hour edit of the film for television broadcast.

Not all of these grandiose plans would take place. While the Ed Sullivan Beatles tribute show was broadcast on March 1, 1970, the group did not attend. Nor would they attend the American theatrical debut of the film. The TV broadcast idea was scrapped. And, of course, the LP was delayed beyond its re-scheduled February release date.

The January 21, 1970, Rolling Stone reported that the *Get Back* album was delayed again to coincide with the release of the Beatles movie. In its place would be an album of "rare Beatles oldies" titled *The Beatles Again*, which would contain tracks previously unavailable on albums such as "Rain" and "Hey Jude." (The oldies album would be re-named *Hey Jude* and issued on February 26, 1970, as detailed on pages 122-125.) The magazine's Random Notes section mentioned that manager Allen Klein was itching to get the Beatles to tour the U.S. after the premiere of their movie, but cautioned that John did not seem interested in doing anything with his bandmates. This was backed up by a separate story on John telling the British press that he didn't know if he wanted to record together again with the Beatles. Lennon indicated that arguments had now grown from how an album should be done to differences of opinion on how things should be run, with major disagreements over Allen Klein. As for never cutting another record with the Beatles, John said he could see it happening. He then took a shot at Paul, saying "The Beatles can go on appealing to a wide audience as long as they make albums like *Abbey Road*, which have nice little folk songs like 'Maxwell's Silver Hammer' for the grannies to dig." He also talked about putting out "Cold Turkey" himself (as the Plastic Ono Band) after the Beatles balked at recording the song for the group's next single.

Another article told the tale of the other Beatles nixing John's plan to issue "You Know My Name (Look Up The Number)" and "What's The New Mary Jane?" as a Plastic Ono Band single because both were really Beatles recordings. Lennon indicated that "You Know My Name" would probably be the B-side to the next Beatles single, "Let It Be." The new disc was confirmed in the February 7 Rolling Stone, which provided a tentative release date of February 20 "just before the *Get Back*/*Let It Be* set is finally put out" along with the film.

In an article appearing in the March 7 Rolling Stone, Ringo doubted that the Beatles would attend the premiere of their film in America because John and George were not able to enter the U.S. as a result of their prior drug convictions. The magazine also reported the sale in Minnesota of a bootleg titled *Come Back*, which it described as a "poor-quality copy of the Beatles' *Let It Be* album, due to be released God only knows when by Apple." There was also a poor quality cassette of the recordings for sale in Buffalo, which seemed to have been recorded by a mike off a radio speaker (perhaps of the September 1969 broadcast of the early May 1969 acetate).

On March 1, Ed Sullivan presented "The Beatles Songbook" with performances by Dionne Warwick ("We Can Work It Out" and "A Hard Day's Night"), Peggy Lee ("Something" and "Maxwell's Silver Hammer"), the Muppets ("Octopus's Garden"), Steve Lawrence and Eydie Gorme (a medley of "Can't Buy Me Love," "The Fool On The Hill," "All You Need Is Love," "With A Little Help From My Friends," "When I'm Sixty-Four," "And I Love Her," "Michelle," "Ob-La-Di, Ob-La-Da" and "All My Loving") and Duke Ellington (a medley of "She Loves You," "All My Loving," "Eleanor Rigby," "She's Leaving Home," "Norwegian Wood" and "Ticket To Ride"). There were also dance and ballet numbers and a clip of Paul singing "Yesterday" from the group's 1965 appearance on the show, with Warwick and Lee singing along. But for Beatles fans, the highlights were the films of the Beatles performing "Two Of Us" (from the movie) and "Let It Be" (a segment from the film synced to the single). In reviewing the program in its April 2 issue, Rolling Stone called "Let It Be" a fantastic new single, noting that "Paul has rarely been in better form, pleading softly with his eyes, feeling around with the vocal in his restrained Little Richard way, keeping the number a long way from pretentiousness."

The March 19 Rolling Stone contained the "latest progress report on *Let It Be*, the forthcoming Beatles album which has *been* forthcoming for almost a year." According to Allen Klein, the release date would be in April. The "Let It Be" single was slated for March 2 release (although it would not be in stores until the following week). The Record Notes section mentioned that Paul McCartney had been working at home on a solo album. No details were available. McCartney's LP was "not expected to be released until after the next Beatles' LP is released in late March, early April, etc., etc., etc." The magazine noted that "Apple didn't say late March or early April of what year, however."

The "Let It Be" single was finally released by Capitol on March 11. The three music trade magazines reviewed the single in their March 14 issues. Billboard recognized the greatness of the song in a Pop Spotlight review: "With solo by McCartney, this ballad beauty with compelling lyric is among their finest." Cash Box described "Let It Be" as "One of the most powerful ballads from the team since 'Yesterday,'" noting that the single had arrived with "a flash of sales and play that has already placed it high on the charts this first week in release." Record World stated that "The Beatles were sure to blow the lid of the charts with 'Let It Be,'" further noting that the song "could be their biggest ever." The April 18 Billboard reported that the single had gone gold. The RIAA later certified sales of two million.

Leah McIver ......Patricia Crowley
Poss Timberlake ......Albert Salmi
Mark McIver ....Eric Shea
Suellen McIver ....Jodie Foster

7:00 2 ED SULLIVAN Ⓒ
"The Beatles' Songbook," featuring an all-star line-up. See the Close-up below. (60 min.)

7 FBI Ⓒ
A puzzler for the FBI: the kidnaping of Mary Cochella, a woman of modest means. An erroneous report that the victim was Mary's sister delays the G-men as the abductors demand ransom from Mary's husband —the cashier at a large sports arena. Erskine: Efrem Zimbalist Jr. Colby: William Reynolds. Ward: Philip Abbott. (60 min.)

Guest Cast
Frank Moonan......Robert Drivas
Mary Cochella ......Zohra Lampert
Shelly Brimlow ......Anne Francis
Ronnie Brimlow ....Wayne Rogers
Fred Cochella ....Paul Picerni

9 COLLEGE TALENT Ⓒ
Guests are producer Sam Lutz, and

recording executives James Hilton and Dave Alpert. Talent: the Jazz Quintet (San Fernando Valley State College); vocalist Gail Farrell (University of Tulsa); the Sound Staff Quartet (University of Utah); and vocalist Michele Downey (University of California). Arthur Godfrey is host.

11 THE SHOW—Variety Ⓒ
Guests: singer O.C. Smith, ABC News commentator Marlene Sanders and McKendree Spring, blues-rock group. Topics include the women's liberation movement; Vice President Agnew's criticism of the broadcasting industry; and pressures facing successful performers. Donal Leace, Bob Walsh. (60 min.)

Highlights
"Little Green Apples," "Your Own Back Yard" ..............O.C.
"No Regrets," "Should've Known Better" ....McKendree Spring

26 FILM

32 RAWHIDE—Western
"The Fish Out of Water." Favor decides to return to Philadelphia and

help ...
Favor... ...ers.
ley: ...Brad-
Cand... ...Favor:

7:15 26 ...
7:30 5 ...
Cic... ...love in-
tere... ...." Chet's
fit ... ...e allowed
him... ...a blind
date... ...girl, it's a
whol... ...really
digs ... ...Verna:
Olga ... ...Mil-
dred:

9 NEW ...
26 JERR ...
7:45 9 YOUR C ...
8:00 2 GLEN C ...
Guests: Raym... ...
ald, singer Neil...
Charlie Manna...
his talent for whistl...
super-inquisitive sales...
lashes out at marriage; ...
features the cast as famous ...
duos. (60 min.)

Highlights
"Watch What Happens" ......Ella
"Nikl Hoekey" ....Neil
"The Straight Life," "Moon River," "Home Again" ....
"Hey, Jude" ....

5 BONANZA Ⓒ
"Return Engagement..."
Crabtree arrives i...
sets off a ruck...
is murdered, a...
cused of th...
Greene. H...
Michael U...

Lotta ...
Stanho... ...e
Fallon ... ...ean
Bonn... ...uilfant
Howe... ...binson

7 N ...
"The... ...a brawl-
ing ... ...geance.
In t... ...funeral,
the ... ...brothers
dism... ...ying on
to p... ...h and
the I... ...John
Wayne... ...di-
rector ... ...ed

---

close up

ED SULLIVAN Ⓒ
7:00 2

THE BEATLES' SONGBOOK

Ed Sullivan salutes the Beatles.
The Beatles will be seen via sequences taped in London, where they talk about their music and introduce "Let It Be," the title song from their upcoming movie.
The Beatles' sound is being adapted to a variety of styles and genres. Ed's scheduled guests show how it's done: Dionne Warwick; Steve Lawrence and Eydie Gorme; Peggy Lee; Duke Ellington and his orchestra, with a new concerto based on Beatle compositions; Peter Gennaro as Sergeant Pepper in a dance production; Edward Villella of the New York City Ballet; and the Muppets puppets. Ray Bloch conducts the orchestra. (As we went to press, there was a a slim chance that the Beatles would appear in person.) (60 min.)

Langdon Winner reviewed the single in the April 16 Rolling Stone. He viewed "Let It Be" as part of the Jesus rock craze, with its "soothing 'Rock of Ages' piano right out of a Presbyterian Sunday school," but with lyrics that are "strictly Catholic." He thought the song was about the Virgin Mary returning to Earth in a time of torment and darkness with her simple message of deliverance: "There will be an answer. Let it be. Let it be." Its music conveyed a "feeling of peace and reassurance." He described the song as "rock and roll's first musical icon." Winner called the flip side, "You Know My Name (Look Up The Number)," an "outlandish show biz parody" and a "marvelous song which focuses on the absurd coyness of people who go to night clubs to be picked up" and get laid.

The Random Notes section of the April 2 Rolling Stone reported that the Beatles would be releasing two films: *Let It Be*, expected since last summer, and *The Long And Winding Road*, a "record of their travels and adventures over a period of two years." The initial word on the *Let It Be* movie was somewhat negative. Although it had been called "embarrassing," apparently the Beatles don't care anymore. The Record Notes section told of several bootleg albums containing songs from the new Beatles LP ranging from fair to poor quality. Titles included *Come Back*, *Get Back*, *Get Back to Toronto* and *Let It Be*. Some of the albums also included the song "Across The Universe." While the writer questioned the point of bootlegging something that would be officially released, fans would soon learn that the official *Let It Be* album would differ in many ways from the bootlegs, and not just in sound quality.

The April 18 Cash Box ran a picture on page 10 of Phil Spector, Ringo Starr, ABKCO promotion man Pete Bennett and a violin player taken at EMI Studios in London. The caption indicated that Spector was "engaged in the production of the Beatles upcoming LP, which will be released by United Artists Records under the label tag of Red Apple."

The May 14 Rolling Stone contained an article about the breakup of the Beatles written by editor Jann Wenner. In it, he mentioned that although a completed album had been edited and mixed last year, none of the Beatles were happy with it. Producer Phil Spector was brought in. According to John: "Phil pulled it together, remixed it, added a string or two here and there. I couldn't be bothered because it was such a tough one making it. We were really miserable then. Spector has redone the whole thing and it's beautiful."

On May 11, 1970, two months after the release of the "Let It Be" single and one week prior to the release of the *Let It Be* album, Capitol pressed a 45 with two songs from the LP: "The Long And Winding Road," a piano ballad by Paul in the same style as "Let It Be;" and "For You Blue," an upbeat love song by George. The disc was packaged in a picture sleeve (see page 101). The labels to the disc did not have the usual "Produced by George Martin" credit, but rather proclaimed "Reproduced for disc by Phil Spector." On the A-side, Spector did much more than add a string or two. He added a "wall of sound" of 18 violins, four violas, four cellos, a harp, three trumpets, three trombones, two guitars, a choir of 14 singers and Ringo on drums. Whether it was beautiful or not was a matter of opinion.

Spector's augmented remix was a far cry from the simple piano ballad found on the bootlegs. While some, including John Lennon, believed that Spector had made necessary improvements to a dull and plodding song, others thought he grossly overproduced the track. George Martin and Glyn Johns were shocked and disgusted. Paul McCartney was particularly upset with the use of the choir. Although Paul had previously considered adding strings and brass to the song, Spector went way beyond the tasteful brass and strings George Martin had added to the "Let It Be" single.

The three music trades reviewed the disc in their May 16 issues. Billboard wrote that the Beatles had "come up with another ballad beauty with Paul solo backed by a large lush orchestra and choir." The flip side was described as an "easy beat rhythm item" written by George. Record World kept it simple, calling its hit potential "a foregone conclusion" and added "Keep it up, boys" even though the group had broken up. Cash Box observed: "If this ballad turned out to be the Beatles' swan song, they could hardly choose a more potent selection. Strings, chorus for satin setting, brass, a Phil Spector (though not Spector-like) production. Who could ask for more from the new LP?" The flip side showed the "team's lighter side with less emotion and more humorous charm."

While Paul's ballad was the A-side and received the majority of air play, George's tune was popular enough to cause Billboard to track the 45 as a double-sided hit record. "The Long And Winding Road"/"For You Blue" entered the Billboard Hot 100 at number 35 on May 23, while "Let It Be" was still in the top ten at number six. After moving up to 12 and then to 10, the record topped the charts in its fourth week on June 13. It replaced Ray Stevens' "Everything Is Beautiful" and thankfully kept "Which Way You Goin' Billy" by the Poppy Family from becoming a number one hit. After two weeks at the top, the single dropped to number four behind "The Love You Save" by the Jackson 5, "Mama Told Me (Not To Come)" by Three Dog Night and the Temptations' "Ball Of Confusion," with its line "The Beatles' new record's a gas." The Beatles new record spent two more weeks in the top ten before running out of gas and dropping to numbers 20 and 21 in its final weeks in The Hot 100. All told, the single charted for ten weeks, including six in the top ten. Although "For You Blue" received co-billing, it has never been considered a number one hit.

Record World also listed the single as "The Long And Winding Road"/"For You Blue," reporting the disc for ten weeks, with two at number one. Cash Box charted "The Long And Winding Road" for 11 weeks, including two at number one. It charted "For You Blue" for two weeks, with a peak at 71. The RIAA certified sales of one million units.

"The Long And Winding Road" would be the last single containing previously unissued performances by the Beatles until the mid-nineties. From 1964 through 1970, the Beatles had 20 number one hits in Billboard, 22 chart toppers in Cash Box and 23 number ones in Record World (previously Music Vendor). The single was not issued in the U.K.

Apple Records

THE BEATLES

THE LONG AND WINDING ROAD

From The Beatles' Motion Picture "Let It Be"

2832   Manufactured by Apple Records Inc., 1700 Broadway, New York, N.Y. 10019   An abkco managed company

The *Let It Be* album, with its red apple label, was finally released in America on May 18, 1970, more than 15 months after the conclusion of the *Get Back* sessions held at Apple's Savile Row headquarters. The disc opens with John's dialog: "'I Dig a Pygmy' by Charles Hawtrey and the Deaf-aids. Phase one in which Doris gets her oats." This is followed by Ringo hitting his snare drum leading into the album's first song, "Two Of Us." This song, featuring Paul and John harmonizing over acoustic guitars, was one of the two Beatles songs broadcast a few months earlier on The Ed Sullivan Show. The next track, "Dig A Pony," has John on lead vocal in a performance vastly superior to the ragged version of the song previously available on bootlegs. "Across The Universe" has thoughtful lyrics and a dreamy vocal by John, although Spector's added brass, strings and choir come across as superfluous. This song was not from the 1969 sessions and had been previously issued in the U.K. as the Beatles contribution to a charity LP. George's "I Me Mine" alternates from a waltz to an all-out rocker with biting guitars on the chorus. The song, which was rehearsed at Twickenham and appears in the film, was not recorded until January 3, 1970, and thus was not available for the bootlegs. The next track, a 51-second edit of "Dig It," fades in with John singing "Like a rolling stone" three times, followed by "Like the FBI, and the CIA, and the BBC, B.B. King, and Doris Day, Matt Busby, dig it, dig it, dig it...."

John's free-form jam is linked to the title track with Lennon's "That was 'Can You Dig It' by Georgie Wood. And now we'd like to do 'Hark, The Angels Come.'" Although the first verse and chorus of "Let It Be" sound like the single, the remainder of the album version of the song has a totally different feel. Spector brought the brass more to the front of the mix and replaced George's beautifully restrained guitar solo with a distorted gritty effort recorded by Harrison on January 4, 1970. By the end of the song, Paul's voice is competing with the blaring brass and George's raunchy guitar. The side ends with 39 seconds of the Liverpool skiffle tune "Maggie Mae" (spelling changed from "May").

Side Two opens with "I've Got A Feeling," a blues-driven rocker sung primarily by Paul, with John singing the "Everybody had a hard year" segments. This version of the song is a significant improvement of the rough take heard on the bootlegs, which breaks down towards the end. The song builds to a thrilling final verse where the vocals of Paul and John weave in and out of each other. At the end of the song, John says, "Oh my soul...so hard." The next track, "One After 909," is a fun rocker with unsophisticated lyrics sung by John and Paul, including the wonderfully silly line, "Move over once, move over twice/Come on baby, don't be cold as ice." The take is the same as the one on the bootleg, but in superior sound. At the end, John adds a brief rendition of "Danny Boy." The next two tracks, "The Long And Winding Road" and "For You Blue," were issued on a single a week ahead of the album. In between the two songs, John says "Queen says 'no' to pot-smoking FBI members." During "For You Blue," George encourages Lennon's guitar playing with "Go, Johnny, go" and "Elmore James got nothin' on this baby." The album closes with "Get Back," preceded by instrumental and vocal warm-ups and banter, including John's "Sweet Loretta Fart, she thought she was a cleaner, but she was a frying pan," and Paul practicing his opening words, "Sweet Loretta Mar...." The single's ending coda is missing, replaced with Paul's "Thanks, Mo" (to Ringo's wife, Maureen) and John's "I'd like to say 'Thank you' on behalf of the group and ourselves. I hoped we passed the audition."

Allen Klein was confident that the *Let It Be* album would be one of the Beatles biggest sellers. As Klein told Billboard, the album had "two top singles and a film to help it along." Although United Artists distributed the album, Capitol was hired to press four million copies of the record. Its initial shipment was 2.7 million units, which grew to 3.2 million in just 13 days. The album was certified gold on May 26, 1970. The RIAA certified sales of four million.

Cash Box and Record World ran brief reviews of the *Let It Be* album in their May 16 issues. Cash Box observed that the most powerful songs on the album were the singles "Get Back" and "Let It Be" and that "The Long And Winding Road" had just hit the singles chart. As for the rest of the LP, the songs did not hit hard at first, but knowing the Beatles, would most likely "enchant after a few listens." The magazine pragmatically noted, "Whatever we do or do not think, the LP will be #1." Record World stated that the long-awaited package showed "every sign of being their biggest, with the movie as a sales aid." The following week Billboard featured the album as a pop spotlight, noting that the album gave the "impression of a 'live' performance." After mentioning the singles on the disc, Billboard listed "I Me Mine," "I've Got A Feeling" and "Across The Universe" as the best of the previously unheard material.

Let It Be made its debut on the Billboard Top LP's chart at number 104 on May 30. The following week it moved up to the second spot behind Paul's solo album *McCartney.* On June 13, *Let It Be* began its four week run at the top before being replaced by the soundtrack to *Woodstock.* Billboard charted the new Beatles album for 59 weeks, including ten weeks in the top ten. *Let It Be* topped the Cash Box album chart for six weeks and was in the top ten for 14 weeks. Record World reported the album at number one for five weeks and in the top ten for ten weeks.

While the music trade magazines had focused on the album's hit singles and sales potential, the music critics found plenty to criticize, starting with Phil Spector. Time magazine's review of the *Let It Be* album appeared in its May 18 issue under the title "Spector of the Beatles." It opened with praise for the "Let It Be" single, calling it "sturdy, unadorned and honest as a country church...one of the most moving pop songs of this or any other year." Time noted that the song had just come out again on a new Apple album, but this time with brass and secular maracas courtesy of "yesteryear's teen tycoon of rock," Phil Spector, who had been brought in by Allen Klein "to give the album a little commercial passion." Spector's "broad-brushed addition of strings, harp and choir" to "The Long And Winding Road" was "outright embarrassing." Out of the 19 [American] album's released by the Beatles, *Let It Be* was one of the worst. However, no Beatles album could be dull. Highlights included: "Get Back" ("topnotch"); "For You Blue" ("a small gem featuring a moonlit slide guitar that twangs all the way from Nashville to Waikiki"); and "One After 909" ("authentic...oldtime rock 'n' roll"). Time predicted the album would be roundly panned and sell millions.

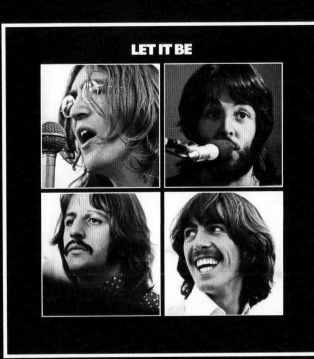

NOW AVAILABLE

THE BEATLES
LET IT BE

ORIGINAL MOTION PICTURE SCORE
AVAILABLE ON APPLE RECORDS,
CARTRIDGES & CASSETTES

LET IT BE

Manufactured by Apple Records, Inc.
an abkco managed company

John Mendelsohn reviewed the album for the June 11 Rolling Stone, immediately commenting on what might have been. Those who had found the Beatles recent work to be technically breathtaking but emotionally vapid were encouraged by the news that the group was about to release "an album full of gems they'd never gotten around to polishing beyond recognition." Who wouldn't prefer a slipshod take of "Save The Last Dance For Me" over a "self-conscious and lifeless" recording such as "Oh! Darling"? Mendelsohn then summed up his feelings of the entire saga. "Well, it was too good to be true—somebody apparently just couldn't Let It Be, with the result that they put the load on their new friend P. Spector, who in turn whipped out his orchestra and choir and proceeded to turn several of the rough gems on the best Beatle album in ages into costume jewelry."

Mendelsohn wondered why Spector thought that "lavish decoration of several of the tracks would enhance the straightforwardness of the album." Spector had rendered "The Long And Winding Road" to be "virtually unlistenable with hideously cloying strings and a ridiculous choir." The song could have grown on listeners as charming had Spector not transformed "an apparently early take into an extravaganza of oppressive mush." Mendelsohn felt that "I Me Mine" might have benefited from the strings had Spector obscured its raunchy guitar. But as it stood, the song was sickeningly sweet but not funny enough to laugh at. Mendelsohn also wondered why Spector deviated from the "Let It Be" single. The album version's "jagged guitar and absurdly inappropriate percussion almost capsize the entire affair," with its blaring brass about as appropriate as piccolos being added to "Helter Skelter."

He thought most of remaining songs were splendid. "Across The Universe" was "dreamy, childlike, and dramatic" with "an unusually inventive melody and tender devotional vocal." "I've Got A Feeling" and "One After 909" were "rough-honed rockers" that were "as much fun to listen to as they apparently were to make." He enjoyed John's "crossword-puzzlish" "Dig A Pony." His favorite tracks were the infectiously rhythmic "Two Of Us" and "Get Back." Mendelsohn's concluding paragraph responded to John's humorous comment, "I hoped we passed the audition," that ended the album. "Musically, boys, you passed the audition. In terms of having the judgment to avoid either over-producing yourselves or casting the fate of your get-back statement to the most notorious of all over-producers, you didn't. Which somehow doesn't seem to matter much any more anyway."

RECORDS

LET IT BE, The Beatles (*Apple AR 3400*)

To those who found their work since the white album as emotionally vapid as it was technically breathtaking, the news that the Beatles were about to bestow on us an album full of gems they'd never gotten around to polishing beyond recognition was most encouraging. Who among us, after all, wouldn't have preferred a good old slipshod "Save The Last Dance For Me" to the self-conscious and lifeless "Oh! Darlin'" they'd been dealing in?

Well, it was too good to be true—somebody apparently just couldn't Let It Be, with the result that they put the load on their new friend P. Spector, who in turn whipped out his orchestra and choir and proceeded to turn several of the rough gems on the best Beatle album in ages into costume jewelry.

Granted that he would have preferred to have been in on the project from its inception rather than having it all handed to him eight months after its announced release date (in which case we would never have been led to expect spontaneity and his reputation would still be intact), one can't help but wonder why he involved himself at all, and wonder also, how he came to the conclusion that lavish decoration of several of the tracks would enhance the straightforwardness of the album.

To Phil Spector, stinging slaps on both wrists.

He's rendered "The Long and Winding Road," for instance, virtually unlistenable with hideously cloying strings and a ridiculous choir that serve only to accentuate the listlessness of Paul's vocal and the song's potential for further mutilation at the hands of the countless schlock-mongers who will undoubtedly trip all over one another in their haste to cover it. A slightly lesser chapter in the ongoing story of McCartney as facile romanticist, it might have eventually begun to grow on one as unassumingly charming, had not Spector felt compelled to transform an apparently early take into an extravaganza of oppressive mush. Sure, he was just trying to help it along, but Spectorized it evokes nothing so much as dewey-eyed little Mark Lester warbling his waif's heart out amidst the assembled *Oliver* orchestra and choir.

"I Me Mine," the waltz sections of which reminds one very definitely of something from one of *The Al Jolson Story's* more maudlin moments, almost benefits from such treatment—it would have been fully as hilarious as "Good Night," after all, had Spector obscured its raunchy guitar with the gooey strings he's so generously lavished on the rest of it. As he's left it, though, it, like "Winding Road," is funny enough to find cloying but not funny enough to enjoy laughing at.

Elsewhere, Spector compounds his mush fixation with an inability to choose the right take (it is said that nothing on the "official album" comes from the actual film sessions, mind you). Inexplicably dissatisfied with the single version of "Let It Be," for instance, he hunted up a take in which some jagged guitar and absurdly inappropriate percussion almost capsize the whole affair, decided that it might be real Class to orchestrally embellish the vocal, and thus dubbed in—yes!—brass. Here the effect isn't even humorous—Spector was apparently too intent on remembering how the horns went on "Hey Jude" to listen closely enough to this one to realize that they're about as appropriate here as piccoloes would have been on "Helter Skelter."

Happily though, he didn't impose himself too offensively on anything else, and much of what remains is splendid indeed:

Like John's "All Across The Universe," which, like "Julia," is dreamy, childlike, and dramatic all at once and contains both an unusually inventive melody and tender devotional vocal.

Like the two rough-honed rockers, the crudely revival-ish "I've Got A Feeling" and "One After 909," both of which are as much fun to listen to as they apparently were to make. "C'mon, baby, don't be cold as ice" may be at once the most ridiculous and magnificent line Lennon-McCartney ever wrote.

Like John's crossword-puzzlish "Dig a Pony," which features an urgent old rocker's vocal and, being very much in the same vein as such earlier Lennonisms as "Happiness Is a Warm Gun," nearly makes up for the absence of "Don't Let Me Down" and "The Last Dance."

And especially like everyone's two favorites, "Two of Us," which is at once infectiously rhythmic and irresistibly lilting in the grand' tradition of "I'll Follow the Sun," and the magnificent chunky, thumping, and subtly skiffly "Get Back," which here lacks an ending but still contains delightful comping by John and Billy Preston.

All of these are, of course, available on the bootleg versions of the album, a further advantage of which is their pure unSpectoredness and the presence of various goodies that didn't quite make it to the official release.

Musically, boys, you passed the audition. In terms of having the judgment to avoid either over-producing yourselves or casting the fate of your get-back statement to the most notorious of all over-producers, you didn't. Which somehow doesn't seem to matter much any more anyway. JOHN MENDELSOHN

Well, by now you've probably heard the official album, admired the production, and scowled at its lack of balls. The bootlegs are of varying quality, have different takes, and cost about the same. The one here is the best we've heard, as well as one of the most complete, and it'll do until George Martin gets around to putting out a bootleg of what it *should* have sounded like. ED WARD

GET BACK

The review was followed by Ed Ward's recommendation of the *Get Back* bootleg (see page 195, last paragraph) for those who had admired the production of the official album, but "scowled at its lack of balls." Ward commented that it would do until "George Martin gets around to putting out a bootleg of what it *should* have sounded like."

Robert Hilburn reviewed the album in the May 31 Los Angeles Times. Hilburn noted that *Let It Be* was not a soundtrack album in the traditional sense, pointing out that only a few of the album's songs were shown in their entirety in the film and that some of the album's songs were "reproduced for disc" by Phil Spector. He ranked *Let It Be* in the middle of the pack of Beatles albums, lacking the ambition of *Revolver*, *Sgt. Pepper* and *Abbey Road* and the raw enthusiasm of early releases such as *Beatles '65* and *Yesterday And Toady*. Hilburn singled out four songs as the album's best: "Get Back," "Let It Be," "The Long And Winding Road" and "One After 909" (the first three having already been issued on singles). The latter song was called a "lively selection, full of fun and enthusiasm." "Two Of Us" and "For You Blue" were called "nice, modest efforts." Although Hilburn called *Let It Be* a "semi-disappointment by Beatles standards," it would be praised if done by most any other group, thus demonstrating how far ahead the Beatles were compared to nearly all of their contemporaries.

Craig McGregor's article in the June 14 New York Times was not so much a review of *Let It Be*, but rather a put down of the Beatles and other "white imitators...who exploited the black man's music and finally betrayed it." The title, "So in the End, the Beatles have Proved False Profits," set the tone as did the opening lines: "So the Beatles have broken up. Judging by their latest album, *Let It Be*, it's about time." McGregor acknowledged that the Beatles had been the "most imaginative and most influential of all rock groups," but felt there comes a time when an artistic group reaches a creative impasse and either finds a new direction or splits up.

Let It Be was the group's "least together album" since *The Beatles*, which McGregor described as a "two-record conglomerate of pop sounds" indicating that the group's creative energy was on the wane. He viewed parody as the "most accessible and least demanding of all forms" because parody is easier than attempting something new. He named three songs as parodies: "For You Blue" (a "put-down of country blues"); "Dig It" (a parody of the Rolling

Stones, most likely due to John singing "Like a rolling stone"); and "Maggie Mae" (a satire of the group's skiffle past). The album was a "mish-mash of different musical styles" with little feeling for development or structure as was evident in *Abbey Road* and made *Sgt. Pepper* a "brilliantly unified masterpiece." While he could forgive the Beatles for being eclectic, he was troubled that "their final statement should be so counterrevolutionary" with a "spiritual weariness, a sense of resignation" extending to the lyrics of songs such as "Across The Universe" and "Let It Be."

McGregor characterized "The Long And Winding Road" as a "Phil Spector mellow-drama" with "overripe harmonies and MGM melody" that belonged "back with Cole Porter and the thirties." He found significance that the Beatles changed the title of the album from *Get Back* to *Let It Be*, for the latter song defines where the Beatles are now: the end of the road, returning to the music of "Before The Revolution." Rock had rebelled against the tradition that "Let It Be" stood for: the tuneful, sentimental Tin Pan Alley ballad.

McGregor acknowledges that the Beatles had helped with the revolution. Although they were "white imitators of black music," their imitations were unique. He provides some examples, but gets his facts wrong. He calls the group's recording of "Money" a classic, but falsely credits the song to John Lee Hooker and incorrectly states the song is from their first album. He praises the "driving purity of 'My Babe'" (perhaps meaning "She's A Woman," whose opening line "My love don't bring me presents" is sung by Nilsson as "My babe don't bring me presents"). He also likes the "rich, multitextured expressionism" of "I Am The Walrus" and "A Day In The Life." Those and forty other songs represent the "revolutionary stream in the Beatles' music." The Beatles also have a softer, more conventional side demonstrated by songs like "Michelle" and "Julia." With *Let It Be*, the soft, romantic tone has become the dominant one. It was this perceived move to softer songs that led McGregor to label the Beatles as "false profits."

He found it a cruel paradox that "the most important group in rock should have been white instead of black, and English instead of American, and should finally have turned its back on the revolution." The remaining paragraphs of his article deal more with race and culture than music, save for his mention of the Beatles following Elvis' pattern of starting off "hot" and then cooling down.

The *Let It Be* movie made its world premiere in New York City on May 13, 1970. The film began opening in other American cities a week later. Due to the persisting delays of the movie's release, by the time it arrived in theaters, the public had learned that the group had broken up. This made watching the film more difficult as audiences searched for clues as to what went wrong. Many noticed Yoko's constant presence at John's side and wondered if she was responsible. Others observed that Paul seemed to be running the show, unintentionally causing resentment. Most telling was Paul's discussion with George regarding one of Harrison's guitar parts. When George disagrees with Paul's assessment, McCartney says "I'm trying to help you, but I always hear as though I'm annoying you." After further remarks from Paul, George replies, "Yeah, OK, well I don't mind. I'll play, you know, whatever you want me to play, or I won't play at all if you don't want me to play. Whatever it is that will please you, I'll do it." But as disconcerting as that scene was, the elegance of "Two Of Us," "Let It Be" and "The Long And Winding Road" shown through. Unlike the "soundtrack" album, the film's actual soundtrack was left alone, providing pure versions of "Let It Be" and "The Long And Winding Road." And the joyous excitement of the rooftop concert allowed fans to leave the theater in a relatively good mood. As was the case with the album, reviews of the film were mixed.

Charles Champlin, writing in the May 20 Los Angeles Times, found the *Let It Be* documentary to be "every bit as interesting" as their classic films *A Hard Day's Night* and *Help!* The camera work was described as "observant" and "keenly alert," giving the movie warmth and energy. *Let It Be* was "an immensely interesting glimpse at these four pleasant and talented young men who constitute so large a hunk of social history."

Cash Box praised the film in its May 23 issue, calling it a "completely honest, un-contrived, crude, open camera view of how the boys create the great music they have been producing for almost a decade." During the film's "very inside" first hour, we see the group rehearsing and kidding around, giving the feeling that "you're peeking in on something private." Paul McCartney stands out and delivers a hilarious performance of "Besame Mucho." The ending rooftop segment is amusing, showing great musicians performing and having fun, while still being "really together." *Let It Be* provides "an opportunity…to watch and hear how the hottest group the record industry has ever know[n] gets its music together. And from that standpoint it's marvelous."

In his Tomorrow column in the May 23 Billboard, Ed Ochs sums up the movie as follows: "It is human and beyond review. *Let It Be* just is." Ochs sees the resulting album as the true ending of the movie: "the film manages to end brilliantly with the album, unseen by the Big Brother eye of the camera, as all the many edited songs and broken, seemingly hopeless communications are healed together in one svelte action." The movie is revolutionary in two ways. Its last act takes place outside the cinema, lingering with the ritual associated with every new Beatles record. In addition, it "signals the day of filmed rock concerts," the birth of a new movie rage (example, *Woodstock*). The film opens with a peaceful high of the Beatles enjoying their music, but "Tension gathers like a distant storm." Ochs then gives his observations of each Beatle's on-screen personality. He is sure that "the making of film changed them." If it contributed to their break-up, then a routine event that "had resulted in 19 albums...this time ended in tragedy."

The message of Bob Moore Merlis in the May 23 Record World is simple: If you love the Beatles you will love their *Let It Be* film/concert. It is a "simple story of how four simple musicians get it together musically." Highlights include Paul's step-daughter, Heather, scaring Ringo; Paul singing "Besame Mucho;" the group rocking out on some oldies; George and Ringo working out "Octopus's Garden;" and the rooftop concert. Although not a deep film, *Let It Be* is a "unique exposition of musical talent and provides a few glimpses of four surprisingly amiable personalities."

The New York Times reviewed *Let It Be* in its May 29 edition. Although the film is "none too artfully made....The very helter skelter, unstudied nature of the picture provides a revealing close up of the world's most famous quartet, playing, relaxing and chatting." Musical highlights include the beautiful tunes "Let It Be," "I Me Mine" and "Get Back." The faces of the group's members have changed, with all showing more assurance and ease. The film's most intriguing figure is Yoko Ono, who, except for a brief waltz with John, stays by his side, with her eyes focused on him.

That same day, New York's Daily News ran a review of the movie by Ann Guarino titled "The Beatles Just Play It Relaxed-Like." Guarino assures readers that if you like the Beatles, you'll dig their new film, which has no story line and comes across as a documentary or home movies. She describes the film's contents and warns fans not to miss "this glimpse of them in relaxed fashion" since the group is splitting up and may not appear together again.

Time magazine, in its June 8 issue, described the film as "instant history," noting that "Rock scholars and Beatles fans will be enthralled with the film," while others might find it a "mildly enjoyable documentary newsreel." Time notes that the film concentrates on Paul to the extent that its billing could be changed to "*Let It Be*, starring Paul McCartney and some other Beatles." Although the others have their moments (John and Yoko dancing to "I Me Mine" and Ringo and George working out "Octopus's Garden"), Paul seems to be in charge of the recording sessions and sings the best songs such as "Let It Be" and "Get Back." The music is the film's strength: "There are no more charismatic performers or immaculate musicians on the rock scene today than the Beatles." While *Let It Be* might not be much of a film, it is a fine concert.

Michael Goodwin did not waste any time telling readers what he thought of the movie in the June 25 Rolling Stone, opening up his review with: "*Let It Be* is a bad movie. Although the music is groovy, the film itself is so formless and badly made that the final effect is simple, crashing boredom." He laments that *Let It Be* could have been a fine flick if it had a better director. Goodwin wonders what Michael Lindsay-Hogg did beyond making sure the cameras were loaded with film and the tape recorders were running. Beyond that, he found Lindsay-Hogg's work to be a disaster. Goodwin believed that Lindsay-Hogg had failed to do his basic directorial responsibilities such as cutting the bad stuff, properly arranging the good stuff and properly placing the cameras. "You have to use so much energy doing his job for him, that by the end of the film you've put in your hard day's night and ought to be paid." He criticizes the director's constant use of facial close-ups, which miss the point that music is a "*collective* activity in which musicians work together." In the Beatles first two films, director Richard Lester's use of the close-up technique was effective because it was used sparingly, while Lindsay-Hogg was attempting to be "cinematic." Goodwin also objected to "pointless editing," which "rapid, rhythmless cutting for lack of anything else better to do."

Goodwin admits that "it isn't *all that bad*." The rooftop sequence is a treat: "well shot, well edited and relaxed. It's a groove to dig the Beatles playing in front of an audience again—the people who come from adjoining rooftops to listen." As for the music, it definitely passes (a reference to John's "I hoped we passed the audition.") He enjoys the new songs and the oldies. Goodwin concludes, "If you can get past the movie and into the music, congratulations."

The 13th Annual Grammy Awards show for 1970 recordings was broadcast live on ABC-TV on March 16, 1971. "Let It Be" was nominated for Song of the Year, but lost out to Simon and Garfunkel's "Bridge Over Troubled Water." The Beatles song was performed on the show by Dionne Warwick, while "Bridge Over Troubled Water" was sung by Aretha Franklin, who had previously recorded "Let It Be." Other nominated songs included "Everything Is Beautiful" by Ray Stevens, "We've Only Just Begun" by the Carpenters and "Fire And Rain" by former Apple artist James Taylor. "Let It Be" also lost out to "Bridge Over Troubled Water" for Record of the Year. Other nominees for that award included "(They Long To Be) Close To You" by the Carpenters, "Everything Is Beautiful" and "Fire And Rain."

Let It Be was not nominated for Album of the Year. As expected, the award went to Simon and Garfunkel's *Bridge Over Troubled Water*, which won over *Sweet Baby James* by James Taylor, *Chicago* by Chicago, *Close To You* by the Carpenters, *Déjà Vu* by Crosby, Stills Nash & Young and *Elton John* by Elton John. *Let It Be* did win the Grammy award for Best Original Score Written for a Motion Picture or Television Special. Viewers of the program got a surprise treat when Paul showed up to accept the award on behalf of the Beatles. Earlier in the program, host Andy Williams joked about John being naked on the *Two Virgins* LP cover: "The cover proved that John isn't one of the Lennon sisters."

The next month the Beatles won another award at the 43rd Annual Academy Awards held on April 15. The Oscar for Best Original Song Score went to *Let It Be*, Music & Lyrics by the Beatles: John Lennon, Paul McCartney, George Harrison and Ringo Starr. *Let It Be* was not nominated for Best Documentary Feature, which went to *Woodstock*.

Let It Be would be the last traditional Beatles album. There would be repackages of previously-released recordings, discs containing the live Hollywood Bowl concerts and BBC performances, and collections of outtakes, remasters and remixes, as well as anniversary editions. The Beatles January 1969 recordings would be heavily bootlegged. The *Let It Be* album itself was deleted from the United Artists catalog after a few years, with counterfeit copies filling the void until Capitol obtained the UA catalog and reissued the LP in 1979. In 2003, the *Let It Be* tracks were reworked, remixed and released as *Let It Be... Naked*. As detailed throughout this book, the story of the Beatles January 1969 recordings was and still is a ball of confusion. But as the Temptations sang, "The Beatles' new record's a gas!"

Melody Maker

SEPTEMBER 14, 1968   1s weekly

BEATLES TO PLAY A 'LIVE' CONCERT?

Jagger is mad over LP sleeve ban

MICK Jagger is furious at a top-level decision to ban the sleeve design for their next album, "Beggars' Banquet," because it is alleged to be "offensive."

And the album won't be released in Britain or America until the dispute between the Stones and Decca Records is resolved.

On Monday Mick told the MM: "The front of the album looks like a low-down American toilet wall. It doesn't actually show the bowl, which is rude, like they do in the Harpic adverts, but you can just see the top.

"It's got Rolling Stones written on the wall and on the back the words are all about the record.

"There are no swear words at all, nothing obscene. But they've just said we can't use it as a record cover.

"Nobody who buys our records would object. And there aren't any political slogans, unless you call Lyndon loves Mao a political slogan.

"It's really terribly harmless sleeve notes written in graffiti style.

"We suggested that a solution would be to put the sleeve in a brown paper bag marked 'unfit for children' but they still wouldn't release it.

MICK: 'harmless'

"Theatre censorship and film censorship are slowly disappearing and the only worthwhile censorship is self-imposed by the artist.

"You can't have entrepreneurs making moral judgements.

"But I'm sure there are reasonable and God-fearing gentlemen at Decca, and that a final solution will be reached.

"The music on the album is of the sort we could play on stage and I personally think it is better than our last one and the one before.

"Street Fighting Man is not coming out as a single because we're too busy doing other things to promote a single."

A Decca records spokesman said on Monday: "We can make no comment on this at all."

Says Paul— 'Singing live is much more appealing to us now'

THE Beatles are planning a live TV show — and may even appear in concert.

Paul McCartney told the MM this week: "The idea of singing live is much more appealing now — we are beginning to miss it.

"We will be doing a live TV show later in the year, I don't know about a concert, but it might lead to that.

"I love the idea of playing again —and I know the others feel the same way."

NEW LP

The Beatles recorded a special film clip last week to be shown on Top Of The Pops tonight (Thursday).

Said Paul: "We recorded both 'Hey Jude' and 'Revolution.' We decided to do clips this time instead of zany films and that sort of thing. We all really enjoyed doing it."

"Hey Jude" is at number one in the Pop 30 for the second week and, in America, sales have already topped two million.

The Beatles hope to complete their new album, as yet untitled, by the end of this month.

Their Press Officer, Tony Barrow, told the MM: "It will probably be out in time to catch the pre-Christmas sales rush."

● Paul McCartney talks to the MM on page 5.

Louis makes Yorkshire return

● ARMSTRONG

LOUIS Armstrong and his All Stars will be back in Britain in December—for a two-week season at the new Wakefield Theatre Club, in Yorkshire.

Satchmo is just one of a host of star names booked for the new Yorkshire nightspot which opens on October 6 with Dusty Springfield as the star. The club is only a few miles from the Batley Variety Club where Louis starred for two weeks in June. He opens in Wakefield on December 1.

The Wakefield club is also presenting a week of Jazz Expo '68—selected star jazz names from the London Festival, opening on October 20. Among the names appearing during the week are the Horace Silver Quintet, the Muddy Waters Blues Band, the Stars of Faith, the Dizzy Gillespie Big Band Reunion, the Gary Burton Quartet, Red Norvo, the Dave Brubeck-Gerry Mulligan Quartet, the Newport All Stars with Benny Carter and Ruby Braff, Count Basie and His Orchestra and Earl Hines.

In addition, the club is negotiating to present Ella Fitzgerald for two weeks next spring and the Woody Herman Herd for a week around the same time. Johnnie Ray has been booked for a week from October 27.

Among the other stars who will appear are Charlie Drake (October 13); Matt Monro (November 2); O. C. Smith (17); Kathy Kirby (December 15).

EMPEROR ROSKO BLIND DATE—PAGE 9

A Very Special Collection
A British Perspective of *Let It Be*

As Summer 1968 came to a close, the British music magazines ran stories of the Beatles possible return to live performances. The September 14 Melody Maker ran the enticing front-page headline "BEATLES TO PLAY 'LIVE' CONCERT?" The magazine reported that the group was planning a live TV show and might even appear in concert. Paul McCartney told Melody Maker that "The idea of singing live is much more appealing now—we are beginning to miss it." He indicated that the group would be doing a live TV show later in the year and that it might lead to a concert. "I love the idea of playing again—and I know the others feel the same way." Paul explained that the group really enjoyed doing the performance clips for "Hey Jude" and "Revolution" instead of "zany films and that other sort of thing." McCartney was referring to the group's live vocal performances over backing instrumental tracks for the group's new single, which had been filmed before an audience at Twickenham Film Studios on September 4. New Musical Express (NME) reported that the color promotional clips were for broadcast in the U.K. and distribution on the international market. Although no one knew it at the time, these performances would be the Beatles first steps on the long and winding road that would lead to the release 20 months later of *Let It Be* album and movie.

The following week (September 21), Melody Maker ran an article titled "Beatles Plan For TV Show" which quoted Beatles press officer Tony Barrow. "They have realized that they could easily do a show for TV—like the live clips of 'Hey Jude' and 'Revolution'—only featuring perhaps 10 or 12 numbers." Barrow stressed that it was just an idea at this stage, with the venue undecided (TV studio or theater), but that they likely would do the TV show and might follow with some live concerts. That week Disc and Music Echo (Disc) ran the headline "Beatles Want 'Live' T.V. Show!" Disc reported that the group might soon be seen in a live television spectacular filmed by Apple before a studio audience and sold to TV networks throughout the world. Barrow explained that the group was pleased with the promotional films for "Hey Jude" and "Revolution" and that they thought a television concert would be the next logical step. He indicated that a 45 to 60-minute show was a "distinct possibility."

New Musical Express

EVERY FRIDAY 7 D

BEATLES 'LIVE' by PAUL
London appearance plan, Sub. LP

LONDON'S CHALK Farm Roundhouse is now the likely venue for a Beatles live TV special or other public performance, Paul McCartney told the NME this week. The Royal Albert Hall — reported last week — is OUT because of booking and other problems.

Added Paul, unshaven after day and night recording on the forthcoming Beatles' double LP: " What is probable is that before anything else, we will do our own TV show in which we'll perform the numbers from the new album. Mary Hopkin may take part and also people like Jackie Lomax and James Taylor."

It is now virtually absolutely definite that the Beatles will appear live again either by Christmas or early in the New Year.

BUT PAUL WISHES TO STRESS THAT NO DEFINITE ARRANGEMENTS HAVE YET BEEN MADE AND THAT A CONCERT OR OTHER SHOW— IF IT TAKES PLACE—COULD CONCEIVABLY BE AT ANY LONDON VENUE.

Plans are still in the discussion stage, and even the Beatles have not yet resolved details of the project.

The title of the group's long-awaited next album—as previously reported, the double set features 24 tracks—has still not been decided. But a spokesman said this week:

" The album title is almost certain to be something completely simple. After progressing from their early days to the intricacies of " Sgt Pepper," the Beatles want to be completely straightforward again. The title could be something as utterly simple as ' The Beatles '."

One track will be a Chuck Berry-style number, " Back Home In The U.S.S.R."

Although a price has not been set for the two-in-one set, it is thought it will be slightly less than the cost of two separate records. It is emphasised that there has been no " spreading " of tracks to cover two parts— many of the tracks are far longer than normal.

Mid-November release has been planned for the LPs, but the final work was not completed until Tuesday and this puts it at least 10 days behind schedule.

HOWEVER, DEFINITELY SCHEDULED FOR DECEMBER IS A SPECIAL CHRISTMAS " BONUS " BEATLES LP.

This is the " Yellow Submarine " set as released in America —four new numbers " All Too Much," " Hey Bulldog," " Altogether Now " and George Harrison's composition " Northern Song "; plus " All You Need Is Love " on one side; and instrumental contributions to the film by the George Martin Orchestra.

● Jackie Lomax was leaving for a " Sour Milk Sea " promotion tour of America on Wednesday with Beatles' aide Mal Evans, and will stay two or three weeks.

● National Beatles fan club secretary Freda Kelly gave birth to a son, Timothy, at Liverpool Sefton General hospital at the weekend.

BEATLES CONCERT REPORT

THE NME UNDERSTANDS THAT VIA THEIR APPLE COMPANY THE BEATLES HAVE BOOKED THE ROYAL ALBERT HALL, LONDON, FOR A LIVE CONCERT IN DECEMBER.

THERE ARE REPORTS THAT OTHER APPLE ARTISTS—POSSIBLY MARY HOPKIN—WILL ALSO TAKE PART.

IF FINALISED, THE LONDON DATE WILL BE THE BEATLES' FIRST PERFORMING PUBLIC APPEARANCE IN BRITAIN SINCE THE NME CONCERT AT WEMBLEY, ON MAY 1, 1966.

RECENTLY PAUL McCARTNEY HAS BEEN QUOTED AS SAYING HE WOULD LIKE TO PERFORM ON STAGE AGAIN, FOLLOWING THE REACTION TO THE IN-PERSON TV APPEARANCE OF THE BEATLES SINGING " HEY JUDE ".

NO CONFIRMATION OF THE CONCERT WAS AVAILABLE FROM APPLE AS THE NME WENT TO PRESS THIS WEEK, HOWEVER.

Issue No. 1134
Week ending October 5, 1968

By October, rumors spread throughout England that the Beatles had booked the Royal Albert Hall in London for a December concert. The October issue (No. 63) of The Beatles Book quoted Tony Barrow saying that he could see the group "playing somewhere like the Royal Albert Hall...where they can install really good sound systems." The October 5 NME stated its understanding that the group had booked the Royal Albert Hall and mentioned reports that other Apple artists, possibly Mary Hopkin, would also be on the bill. This would be the Beatles first U.K. concert since May 1, 1966. Paul had been quoted saying he wanted to perform on stage again based on the reaction to the promo video of the Beatles performing "Hey Jude." NME cautioned that it had not confirmed the story with Apple.

The next week, readers of the October 11 music magazines learned that the story of the Albert Hall concert was full of holes. Disc shot down the rumor quoting Tony Barrow and Apple press officer Derek Taylor. Barrow called the Royal Albert Hall an unlikely venue, adding that "if the boys do decide to do a show, it would be in a studio on the lines of the appearances they made to promote 'Hey Jude.'" Taylor also drew comparisons to the "Hey Jude" TV film, adding that "The Beatles will appear live, but not before the New Year." Melody Maker reported that the Beatles wanted to play before a live audience again, with the most likely format being a TV special. This was confirmed by Barrow, who indicated that they would most likely play before a "special audience of perhaps five hundred" and that the TV film required a "more intimate venue than the Albert Hall." In NME, Paul said that Albert Hall was out due to booking and other problems. He indicated that the likely venue would be London's Chalk Farm Roundhouse for a live TV special or other public performance. Paul said it was probable that "we will do our own TV show in which we'll perform the numbers from the new album" (meaning the then-yet-to-be-released double album The Beatles). It was also possible that Apple artists Mary Hopkin, Jackie Lomax and James Taylor would be involved.

The November 16 mags provided more details. Disc reported that the Beatles would be at the Roundhouse from December 14 to 21 to rehearse and perform live for a television special based on their new album. There would be three shows, each attended by 1,000 people. Melody Maker added that there would be a run-through, dress rehearsal and final show. Derek Taylor said "The group will be playing tracks from their album, old rock and roll tunes, anything they feel like or can play." In NME he said the concerts would probably be filmed by Michael Lindsay-Hogg.

The November 22 Disc reported that the Roundhouse concerts would be free of charge, but probably delayed until January as the group's members were involved in various projects. Derek Taylor confirmed the likelihood of the shows being delayed in the November 30 Melody Maker. "It's likely they will be postponed until mid-January. But they will take place and that's a promise." The next week Melody Maker told of the "Mystery Over Beatles 'Live' Venue." Derek all but ruled out the Roundhouse or a Liverpool location for the concert, which was now scheduled for January 18, 1969, noting that it would most likely be in London because the show would be taped in color for TV and that all the color equipment was in London. The December 14 Disc speculated that the Beatles might play a concert in 1969 at Liverpool's Cavern Club, quoting its owner saying Paul expressed a desire to play there again. McCartney joked that "it would be for all the Coke we can drink. We're in the big time now. We'll want £15!"

The December 1968 issue (No. 65) of The Beatles Book informed readers that the group was finalizing details for its one-hour color television show. After rehearsals, the band would perform three separate live shows in front of invited audiences. The sets would be recorded on color videotape with the final TV show consisting of the best parts of the three. Most of the songs would be from the group's new 30-track double LP, with a few oldies thrown in. Apple could not yet confirm if the show would include guest appearances by other Apple artists such as Mary Hopkin and Jackie Lomax. No details regarding the TV broadcast were available, but it was unlikely that the show would air before February or March. The group had considered selling tickets and giving the proceeds to charity, but that idea was dropped because seats for TV shows must be distributed for free. Apple urged fans not to write in for tickets as they had already received over 20,000 requests for the small number available. The Beatles Book announced that readers could send in a coupon for a "lucky dip" that would award 50 pairs of tickets to see the live performance.

The magazine's January 1969 issue (No. 66), published around December 20, 1968 due to the Christmas holidays, reported that "Camera and technical crews have been booked for the week of January 17-24," but that no final decision could be made until Paul returned from Portugal. The magazine dispelled rumors that the program would be filmed in Liverpool and that singer Andy Williams would make a guest appearance. Readers were told that editor Johnny Dean would draw the winning names for the tickets to the Beatles TV show from a drum on New Year's Day.

BEATLES TV SHOW

The Beatles are shortly to finalise details for their own one-hour colour television show. It will NOT now take place at the Roundhouse as announced.

After rehearsals they will give a set of separate "live" performances before invited audiences. All three shows will be recorded on colour videotape and the final television programme will be made up from the best parts of the three. Much of the material will be songs from the Beatles' current bundle of 30 LP tracks but a few oldies will be included too. Songs selected for each of the three performances may vary slightly. At press time nobody at Apple could say for sure whether or not a late decision would be made to include guest appearances by other Apple recording artists such as Mary Hopkin and Jackie Lomax.

An early idea to sell audience tickets and give the money to charity was dropped because seats for television show performances cannot be sold but must be given away without charge.

An Apple spokesman asks us to emphasise that there is no point in people continuing to write in for tickets to the Apple offices. The letters already received there run to well over 20,000 ticket requests, far more than the number of available seats.

The only remaining opportunity for Beatle People to get TV show tickets is to take part in the *Beatles Monthly Book* Lucky Dip through which 100 seats will be allocated to regular readers. For full details please see page 30 of this issue.

No details of British screening date for the Beatles' show are set nor is it certain which TV channel will get the programme. Different TV companies will see the completed videotape when it is ready and Apple will receive their offers. It is unlikely that the show will be seen here or abroad before February or March next year.

"Beatles" LP Cover

From "The Beatles", Cliff
recorded "Back In The U.S.S.
Lewis with his Orchestra and
a N.E.M.S. single coupling "Ge
"Julia". New Czech girl singe
is recording "Martha My Dea
be her first single for N.E.M.S.
all Lennon-McCartney instru
Cyril Stapleton's Orchestra
"Goodnight" and "Ob-la-di, O
other tracks include "Fool O
"She Loves You", "Michelle"
day". Mercury Records are r
plete LP of instrumental ver
Beatles" LP numbers including
by Paul Mauriat. Marmalade
version of "Ob-la-di, Ob-la-da

BEATLES TELEVISION SHOW

As this issue of *Beatles Monthly* went to print—earlier than usual because of the Christmas holiday week—Apple and The Beatles had yet to announce new details for the making of The Beatles' much-publicised TV show to be videotaped in colour before an invited audience. Camera and technical crews have been booked for the week of January 17-24 but Paul's return from Portugal was awaited before a final decision on venue could be taken.

Rumours that the programme might be made in Liverpool instead of London have been denied. So has the idea that Andy Williams, who lunched with Apple executives a few weeks ago, might make a guest appearance in the show.

***Meanwhile 50 *Beatles Monthly* readers, winners of the Lucky Dip competition announced last month, are to receive pairs of free tickets for the TV show and will be able to watch The Beatles in "live" performance. The 50 winning names are to be drawn from a drum by *Beatles Monthly Book* Editor Johnny Dean on New Year's Day. Their names will be listed in the February issue and they will hear by post of their success no later than Saturday, January 11. Winners will get full details of performance date, time and venue along with their pairs of tickets. Unfortunately unsuccessful applicants cannot be notified but those who do not hear by post during the first 11 days of January should take it for granted that they were not amongst the lucky 50 readers.

JOHN-YOKO FILM FOR
AUSTRALIAN T...

John Joins Stones!

John heads an all-star quartet put together for a single, once-in-a-lifetime performance to be seen in the Rolling Stones' forthcoming TV show, "Rock 'n' Roll Circus". The group, known as A. N. OTHER, includes John as singer and rhythm guitarist, backed by ex-Cream star Eric Clapton, Hendrix Experience drummer Mitch Mitchell and Stone guitarist Keith Richard. In the show they will be seen playing *Yer Blues* with John as lead singer.

Yoko Ono accompanied John to the filming of the show and may be seen singing in the finished version of the TV film.

George had planned to join John as a guest on "Rock 'n' Roll Circus", but was prevented from doing so by urgent remixing sessions on material for Apple's first Jackie Lomax LP, produced in Hollywood.

Yes, It's Really Tiny!

As soon as Beatles Fan Club members began to receive their copies of the latest Fan Club Christmas Record, Freda Kelly's Liverpool offices were flooded with 'phone calls from all over the country. Main topic: "Is that REALLY Tiny Tim with George on Side Two?" Simple answer: "Yes!"

George's contribution to the longer-than-average eight-minute disc was recorded in the New York apartment of attorney Nathan Weiss. By chance Tiny Tim was visiting George at the time and is heard adding his own message as well as singing *Nowhere Man* to his own banjo accompaniment.

Ringo's quick-fire conversation with his own pre-recorded voice, Paul's piano playing and singing of his own *Happy Christmas* theme song and John's typically Lennonesque story-telling were taped in The Beatles' own homes. The final version of the disc was edited and put together for the first time this Christmas by a guest producer, deejay Kenny Everett.

NEW YEAR "SUB"

Further delays in the release of Apple's "Yellow Submarine" soundtrack LP have set back the issue date to mid-January.

As previously reported, Side One has The Beatles' six recordings. On Side Two George Martin's Orchestra presents *Pepperland, Sea Of Time, Sea Of Holes, Sea Of Monsters, March Of The Meanies, Pepperland Laid Waste* and *Yellow Submarine In Pepperland* (which is the Pepperland title tune). Catalogue numbers for the LP are PCS 7070 (stereo) and PMC 7070 (mono).

Sussex
26 Aberdour Street, London, S.E.1.   Telephone: Bermondsey 7074.

29

BEATLES BOOK EXCLUSIVE!
100 FREE BEATLES
SHOW TICKETS TO BE WON

50 Pairs of Beatle People will see the 'Live' Performances!

The Beatles will shortly be preparing the world's biggest concert. They'll be rehearsing and recording an hour-long show which will be seen on a hundred million television screens all around the world. Through *The Beatles Book*, 50 pairs of Beatle People will have the opportunity of watching John, Paul, George and Ringo in action making an historic TV programme. What's more the 100 lucky winners won't have had to solve puzzles or answer competition questions—this is an open-to-all costs-nothing-to-enter BEATLES LUCKY DIP!

If you would like to try your luck here's what you have to do:—
1. CUT OUT THE BEATLES SHOW COUPON from this page.
2. Fill in your NAME AND ADDRESS very clearly in BLOCK CAPITALS.
3. ENCLOSE the coupon in an envelope addressed to:—
   BEATLES SHOW TICKETS
   THE BEATLES MONTHLY BOOK
   58 PARKER STREET
   LONDON W.C.2.
4. YOUR COUPON MUST REACH *THE BEATLES MONTHLY BOOK* BY DECEMBER 31ST AT THE LATEST—so try to post it off as soon as possible.

At press time it is not possible to tell you the exact dates of the performances which will be videotaped in colour in the New Year. Neither the Beatles themselves nor their Apple helpers have sorted that out. But the dates will be sometime during January and the 100 special free seats reserved for *Beatles Monthly Book* readers will be allocated by Apple for one or more of the shows as soon as possible.

On January 1st all your applications will go into a drum. The first 50 pulled out will get A PAIR OF TICKETS. The tickets will show the date and time of the performance.

BEATLES LUCKY DIP COUPON

PRINT CLEARLY IN BLOCK CAPITALS

Name...

Address.......................................

....

Several final points—PLEASE DON'T telephone our offices about your application or the switchboards could be jammed all day and night!

—PLEASE DO remember that your application is not valid unless it is accompanied by a special BEATLES SHOW COUPON from this page.

—ONE COUPON puts you in the LUCKY DIP running for just ONE PAIR of show tickets.

—DO NOT enclose any other letter with your application, use a separate envelope.

AND LASTLY . . . if you ARE lucky enough to get a pair of tickets DO PLEASE write in to *Beatles Monthly Book* editor JOHNNY DEAN with your reactions. We'll print a full selection of readers' letters about the Beatles first "live" performances for almost three years in a future issue.

Close-up of George and Paul drinking from that fountain you saw on page 20. ▶

Printed by S. Tinsley & Co. Ltd., Lancing, Sussex
Distributors: Surridge Dawson & Co. Ltd., 26 Aberdour Street, London, S.E.1.   Telephone: Bermondsey 7074.

30

The start of the new year brought news of a live Beatles album. In the January 4, 1969 Disc, Derek Taylor stated that the songs would be new and fresh, with "no hangover numbers from a year ago." That same week Melody Maker provided additional details from Taylor: "The group started writing and rehearsing a number of songs this weekend. There is no shortage of material. Paul has eight or nine songs finished, John has a few, and George also has some material." The group would do a run-through, a rehearsal and then the live show taped for future TV broadcast. Although the concert was set for January 18, it would likely take place later. The Beatles would perform 12 to 14 songs for the LP. The January 11 Disc disclosed that the Beatles were at Twickenham rehearsing for the TV concert.

The January 18 Melody Maker reported that a documentary of the Beatles was being shot at Twickenham Film Studios. It would show the group writing, rehearsing and recording songs along with casual studio dialog and action. That week NME announced that the Beatles had called off their "'Live Album' TV." No reason was given; however, unknown to the press, George had quit the group on January 10 and had agreed to return only if the Beatles moved from Twickenham to their Apple headquarters to record an album and scrapped plans for the TV concert.

Although George's temporary departure from the band was, for the most part, successfully concealed, the January 21 edition of the Daily Sketch, a British tabloid, reported that "The awful tension of being locked up in each other's lives snapped the other night at a TV rehearsal and Beatles John and George swung, at very least, a few vicious phrases at each other." Michael Housego's article, "The End of a Beautiful Friendship?," was part of a Sketch special investigation series on the Beatles future. Housego observed that the group had been "drifting apart as buddies, seeking strange new thrills and, frankly, getting on each other's nerves." This was not surprising, as they had for years "been imprisoned and denied an ordinary life." A bitter George Harrison had told the reporter that he believed "the world wants us to take a tumble." Housego summed it up this way: "Drugs, divorce and a slipping image played desperately on their minds and it appeared to them all that the public was being encouraged to 'hate them.'" He predicted that the group would stay together out of economic necessity, but "They will never be exactly the same again." The following day, during rehearsals at Apple, Paul read parts of the article to the band as they jammed on "Good Rockin' Tonight." (The *Get Back* book packaged with the *Let It Be* LP documents Paul's reading of the article.)

The January 25 NME reported that the Beatles were still rehearsing new songs for their next LP, but plans for the TV concert were fading away. There would be a TV documentary of their rehearsals. That week Record Mirror told of Phil Spector's comeback and the release by Decca of some of his prior masterpieces in an article titled "Re-Produced Phil Spector!" Fourteen months later these Beatles recordings would be "Reproduced for disc by Phil Spector."

The end of January brought exciting news to Beatles fans who read the mainstream press. The January 30 edition of The Evening Standard contained an article titled "Police stop Beatles 'making a din'" in which Ray Connolly reported that the police halted the group's performance on the roof of their Savile Row Apple offices after receiving dozens of complaints about the noise (see page 105). A director of a neighboring business barked: "I want this bloody noise stopped. It's an absolute disgrace. You can't even hear your telephones, dictate a letter or have your windows open." Connolly explained that the Beatles were filming a TV spectacular built around a new album. Hundreds of people congregated on the streets looking up at the roof. Office girls hung out of windows. Listeners heard Paul singing "Don't let me down" and "I am to miss the train." A bank employee observed that "Everyone on the balconies and roof seemed to be enjoying the session." As for the complaints, "Some people just can't appreciate good music." An Apple spokesman added: "It was all supposed to be very hush-hush. But when you put the Beatles on top of a building in the middle of London and ask them to sing a song it is rather difficult to keep it secret."

The next day the Daily Mirror reported on the Beatles free lunchtime show in an article titled "Rooftop Beatles upset the neighbors." An accountant with the neighboring branch of the Royal Bank of Scotland was not impressed: "I am furious. We were trying to talk to our customers but couldn't hear them. I telephoned the police but apparently they are powerless to do anything." Although four police did show up at Apple, with two going inside, the session continued for about forty minutes, "drawing crowds to the streets and onto adjoining rooftops." An Apple spokesman indicated that the group played four or five numbers for an upcoming film. The Daily Express reported that Savile Row merchants were upset with the Beatles open-air rooftop concert in the article "Hitting the roof over the Beatles." Businessmen fumed and held-up drivers hooted as hundreds in the streets looked skywards and excited office girls leaned out of windows. The session, recorded for a TV spectacular, finished shortly after the arrival of the police.

The music weeklies failed to cover the concert, although it was mentioned in the February 8 NME in an article titled "Allen Klein to help Beatles." NME noted that rehearsals for the previously planned (and canceled) TV concert would be the basis for a TV documentary and that "some of the specially-written songs were heard by startled passers-by...when the Beatles gave a spontaneous performance on the roof of Apple and were filmed for the programme." The magazine reported that 12 tracks centered around the documentary were complete, with final recording to take place within the next fortnight (two weeks) and the resulting album to be released in April or May. That week Derek Taylor told Melody Maker that the Beatles had recorded 160 hours of film, which would be edited down for a documentary and their next album. He noted that they still had some recording to do. As for the music, it was "very tight, together and fantastic—even better than their last double LP." Disc speculated that the Beatles next single might be "Get Back," one of the songs recorded in the Apple basement studio. The article quoted Billy Preston, an American pianist, describing the session: "The track was called 'Get Back' and I played solo piano on it. They said then that it was good enough to become their next single."

The February issue (No. 67) of The Beatles Book reported on the "TV Show Mystery," telling readers that the Beatles much-delayed TV show, recently rescheduled for January 18, had been canceled. The Beatles had spent two weeks at Twickenham rehearsing for the planned 90-minute TV spectacular and had eight new songs for the show. Paul talked of possibly making the show in Africa or "somewhere just as sunny." The magazine believed that although the immediate production had been shelved, the group was still keen on doing the show.

Beatles road manager Mal Evans gave a detailed account of the January Beatles sessions at Twickenham and Apple in the March issue (No. 68) of The Beatles Book, which contained several pictures from the sessions, including ten black and white photos, a color center-spread and color pictures on the front and back cover. Evans described how the sessions differed from those of the past few years, with the group starting before noon rather than working at night and into the early morning. Also different was the extensive time the group spent rehearsing before the recording began. He explained that the initial idea behind the rehearsals was to prepare for a TV show concert. Possible locations included the Roundhouse, a flour mill on the Thames and an outdoor Roman theater in Tripoli.

TLE NEWS BEATLE NE

TV SHOW MYSTERY

After a magical mystery tour of on-and-off press stories, January 18 was finally cancelled as the latest and most frequently quoted date for the making of The Beatles' much-delayed TV show.

The Beatles spent more than a fortnight from January 2 in Twickenham Film Studios preparing for the colour videotaping of what promised to be a 90-minute TV spectacular in the form of a "live" performance given to an invited audience. Within the first 12 days at Twickenham the group had written and rehearsed eight new songs for the show.

Although an earlier plan to have a full-scale audience of up to 1,500 people present during the making of the programme was scrapped, special arrangements were made to provide seating for 50 pairs of Lucky Dip contest winners (readers of *The Beatles Monthly Book*) plus about the same number of Fan Club Area Secretaries and their guests.

During the first week of January Paul was talking about the possibility of making the show on location in Africa or "somewhere just as sunny". Indeed it was The Beatles' strong desire to make the show out of doors which led to the cancellation of the January 18 production date. Nowhere suitable could be found in good time. Various other possible locations abroad have been mentioned but *Beatles Monthly* understands that there is NO likelihood of the performance and TV show being recorded in America despite a wild spate o f rumours to that effect.

Even after the January date had been put off, The Beatles went on working at Twickenham, readying their eight new numbers and other TV show material. This suggests that whilst everything was shelved so far as an immediate production is concerned, the group continues to be keen on the theory of making such a show.

George's Apple Musical

At his home and at the Apple office G
January eveni

STOP PRESS

MARCH No. 68 2/6

The Beatles BOOK
MONTHLY

No. 68 MARCH 1969

ABOVE: Two Beatle girl-friends currently very much in the

BELOW: George and Ringo have recently been wearing clothes they could have bought three years ago

Evans dispelled reports of George having a fight with the other members of the band, providing his insights behind Harrison's "walk out" and the cancellation of the TV show. He explained that Paul was the most enthusiastic about the "live" show, with George being against it, still believing that the group should concentrate on perfecting recordings rather than churning out the same stage show. Evans claimed that George wasn't suggesting that the group break up and that singing and playing together would always be fine. Harrison left on January 10 because he "didn't want to stay at Twickenham rehearsing for a show he couldn't believe in." This made it impossible to continue with the original plan for a TV concert. Instead, the group would continue rehearsing and writing songs, but use them for an album that would be released before summer. The film shot at Twickenham and Apple would form a "Beatles At Work" semi-documentary, available for TV "at home and across the world." Evans noted that "It could even finish up as something just as suitable for cinema screening as for telly." Apple was also preparing a book with pictures taken during the sessions.

Evans described the group's activities at Twickenham, noting that they were familiar with the facility, canteen and crews, having worked there for *A Hard Day's Night*, *Help!* and the "Hey Jude" promotional clips. He told of playing the anvil on "Maxwell's Silver Hammer." The equipment was moved from Twickenham to Apple on January 16, with the group trying the Apple studio for the first time on January 20. He added that the group borrowed studio equipment from EMI. Evans covered up the mess Alex Mardas had made of their studio and mentioned his "amazing gadgets." He informed readers that the session's engineer was Glyn Johns, who had worked with the Rolling Stones [as engineer] and the Steve Miller Band [as producer]. George Martin served as the session's producer. Evans also told of the group "limbering up" with fantastic jam sessions of oldies to get the singing and playing flowing before recording their songs. The band would "go wild and roar" into songs such as "Lawdy Miss Clawdy." He suggested that the group might some day release a record of these jam sessions so fans could hear what goes on before they record their hits. He praised their treatment of the old skiffle song "Maggie May." George brought two presents to the sessions: a rosewood Telecaster from Fender and a Leslie Speaker from Eric Clapton. Keyboardist Billy Preston sat-in during the Apple sessions, serving as a "Fifth Beatle." Evans also wrote about the rooftop concert, which could be heard across Regent Street causing numerous calls from "puzzled and/or cross neighbors."

While Evans provided an upbeat summary of the January Twickenham and Apple sessions, John gave a darker view in the April 12 Melody Maker. "We filmed the whole thing showing all the traumas we go through. Every time we make an album we go through a hellish trip."

This was in sharp contrast to George's description of the sessions a week earlier in Disc, which reported that the group had completed eight songs, including one by George. The LP would be a "return to the John, Paul, George and Ringo of four years ago, but a bit better." Harrison added, "It's the old guitars, bass and drums bit again. We're doing it simply, but with great effect, after going through all those things like *Sgt. Pepper*. It'll be a regular, simple, single LP with 14 tracks." George also talked about the Beatles deciding on the script for a third film. "It will be at least as big as *2001* visually, with full stereo sound and cinema." He stated that they had the idea a year ago and that it was fantastic. "We agreed to let each other do exactly what he wants to do with it. By allowing each other to be each other we can become the Beatles again." It is not known what film George was talking about, as it never came to be.

In mid-April the Beatles rush-released a single that paired two songs from the January Apple sessions: Paul's "Get Back" and John's "Don't Let Me Down." The A-side was described by NME as unadulterated rock 'n' roll, while the flip was powerful blues. Although the disc was neither adventurous nor experimental, it was "honest-to-goodness pop-rock." Chris Welch in Melody Maker called the disc "a nice bit of rock and roll for the people." Disc's Penny Valentine stated that the group had gone back to basics and its roots and the Stones' roots. She felt that was a good thing, as "we might have all forgotten where we came from." Although there were some mutterings of disappointment with the single on the grounds that it was not progressive enough, such criticism did not affect sales. The single was awarded a Silver Disc by Disc on May 3, 1969, for sales of 250,000. Sales would soon reach 500,000. The disc topped the Record Retailer chart for six weeks and the NME and Melody Maker charts for five weeks. The "Get Back" promo clip was shown in black and white on Top Of The Pops on April 24 and May 8, 15 and 22. It featured the Beatles performing the song during their London rooftop concert with Paul on lead vocals and John playing the song's rockabilly-styled guitar solo. When the song was over, the camera panned to the crowd forming in the streets below. This was the first time that fans got to see film from the January sessions they had been reading about for months.

The April 19 NME informed readers of the group's upcoming plans: "BEATLES SUMMER TV, ALBUM AND BOOK." The article reported that 68 hours of film of the Beatles working on their new album had been edited into two television specials which would be broadcast on consecutive summer nights to coincide with the release of the Beatles next album. Additional tracks would be recorded in May. In addition, a paperback book containing a "transcript detailing behind-the-scenes incidents during the making of the film" would be published at the same time as the album's release. The book was edited by U.S. writers David Dalton and Jonathan Cott, with a foreword by Derek Taylor. It would be "a candid insight" that included notes of the arguments that occurred during the recording of the album. The following week Melody Maker reported similar, but less detailed, information.

John talked about the new album, which he dubbed "the next Great Beatle Event," in the May 3 NME. He stated that most of the tracks would be like "Get Back" and that they had done about 12 tracks, adding that some needed to be remixed. He was no longer interested in the production of the group's records. "For me, the satisfaction of writing a song is in the performance of it. The production is a bit of a bore.... All I want to do is get my guitar out and sing songs." John admitted that he fancied doing some live shows, but couldn't give any plans as the group was not even in agreement. That week John also told Melody Maker that 12 tracks had been recorded and that the group had two weeks to finish the LP. It would be out soon, as soon as "it takes to get the tracks together."

The May 10 Disc reported that the album's release had been pushed back from June to late summer because finishing touches were taking longer than expected. Disc explained that part of the problem was that most of the album had been recorded live in the studio, as it happened, with bits of dialog interspersed between songs. The album played continuously like *Sgt. Pepper*. Apple's Mavis Smith explained: "At the moment all the recordings are unedited and the plan originally was to release the LP like this. But they may decide to make some changes."

The June 1969 issue (No. 71) of The Beatles Book reported that Apple's Tony Bramwell was hopeful the next album would be released in mid-July, but cautioned that no release date could be confirmed "until all four Beatles have expressed full satisfaction with the re-mixed tapes."

DISC
and MUSIC ECHO 1s

MAY 10, 1969   EVERY THURSDAY

Is this man sick ?

'PINBALL WIZARD' STORM: BACK PAGE

BEATLES' next LP—the one made during rehearsals, recording and filming of the TV documentary about their Apple activities—has run into trouble.

A last-minute hitch means that release has been switched from next month to late summer. And the reason, according to Apple, is that the group is running behind schedule.

Last week John Lennon revealed that he and Paul McCartney were writing non-stop to meet a deadline. But now it seems that although the songs are finished final touches will take longer than expected.

Part of the problem is that most of the album has been recorded as it happened—"live" in the studio, interspersed with ad-lib comments and other sounds—and runs continuously, without breaks, similar to "Sgt. Pepper."

"At the moment all the recordings are unedited and the plan originally was to release the LP like this," explained Apple's Mavis Smith. "But they may

Beatles' album delayed

decide to make some new changes."

Meanwhile, the group's single "Get Back" remains at number one in the chart, with total United Kingdom and American sales soaring to two million.

Next week, Ringo Starr flies to New York for a week's final filming of "The Magic Christian," on location.

And this week, John Lennon bought for £150,000 a seven-bedroom Georgian mansion with 72 acres of land at Tittenhurst Park, near Ascot.

The purchase comes soon after John's claim that he was "down to his last £50,000." But, says Apple, this remark was made "for a joke!"

The Lennons move into their new home in August. Their neighbours will be Queen's dress-maker, Norman Hartnell, and Leapy Lee.

● The exclusive new colour picture (above) of the Beatles was taken aboard a boat on the Thames at Twickenham.

IS CARNABY STREET SWINGING OR HAS KINGS ROAD TAKEN OVER? SEE PAGE 13

While in Canada for his second Bed-In For Peace, John spoke with NME's Toronto correspondent Ritchie Yorke. His comments ran in the magazine's June 7 issue in an article titled "Beatles' LP in July, Lennon Peace Disc." John said that the album would be titled *Get Back, Don't Let Me Down And 12 Other Tracks*. Its cover would be just like the *Please Please Me* LP. "We had our picture taken in the same positions as on that early album, but looking like we do now. It looks great." The "Lennon Peace Disc" was released as "Give Peace A Chance" on July 4, 1969.

The June 14 Melody Maker told of a similar title for the LP and reported that the Beatles were considering preparing a promotional film for the album to air on TV. The following week the magazine indicated that the Beatles next album would include a special book with photographs. This was another change of plans for the *Get Back* project, as the book was originally supposed to be sold separately from the LP.

The July 1969 issue (No. 72) of The Beatles Book reported that the album might be released in late August. There was also a "chance that several additional tracks would be added to the finished production." John and Ringo were waiting for the return of Paul and George before deciding whether to add the newer numbers or hold them for a later album. Apple managing director Neil Aspinall confirmed that the new album was tentatively titled *The Beatles; Get Back*, but added that it might be expanded to have wording similar to the group's first album.

The most exciting article in the magazine was an exclusive report by Mal Evans on "*The Beatles Get Back*" LP. Evans reported that the album was finished at the end of May, with George being the only Beatle in the country to supervise the final re-mixing sessions that produced the master tape for the disc. The album was being held back for August release so that it could come out simultaneously with the special book of pictures from the recording sessions and the television broadcast of film shot during the sessions. Evans confirmed that the title was *The Beatles; Get Back*, which was appropriate, as the group did indeed get back with the recordings "all the way back to the simplicity of their earlier stuff." The photograph for the cover shows the group at the same location and pose as their first album, *Please Please Me*. Both pictures were taken by the same photographer, Angus McBean, at EMI's London offices in Manchester Square.

The Beatles Book MONTHLY

JULY No. 72 2'6

"THE BEATLES GET BACK"
August LP Surprises

★ 10-year-old song is included! ★ Skiffling Beatles do "Maggie May"! ★ No vocals from Ringo! ★ "The Beatles with their socks off" — and they've re-recorded "Love Me Do" but It's not on the LP!

NOW READ THIS EXCLUSIVE BEATLES MONTHLY ALBUM REPORT BY MAL EVANS

THE Beatles' next LP album was finished at the end of May—with George the only Beatle remaining in Britain at the time, supervising the last of the re-mixing and re-balancing sessions to produce the final tapes from which the LP record will be made.

Release of the album is being held back until August so that it can coincide with the publication of a special book full of recording session pictures. Apart from the LP and the book, there's the film which was made while the new numbers were being rehearsed at Twickenham and recorded in Apple's own new studio in the basement beneath 3, Savile Row, our London headquarters. The fellows would like the film to go on television in August so that everything comes together at the same time.

Before I go into the new LP in track-by-track detail let me set down some of the background information.

The title of the album is *The Beatles; Get Back*. And indeed John, Paul, George and Ringo do get back with these recordings—all the way back to the simplicity of their earliest stuff.

Remember the fellows' first Parlophone album *Please, Please Me*, issued in May 1963? Well, the photograph for the new LP cover was taken in exactly the same place by the same photographer, Angus McBean. With the four fellows grouped over the staircase at the offices of EMI Records in London's Manchester Square, just as they had done six years earlier.

The Beatles; Get Back is by far the most informal set of records The Beatles have ever put out. Everything was rehearsed, as you know, down at Twickenham — both those sessions were really to get together the new songs and decide how each one would be treated. Once we moved from Twickenham to Apple all the recording we did was "live" with no "over-dubbing" of extra voices or instruments, no orchestras brought in boost the accompaniments, no special electronic happenings whatsoever. Just three guitars plus

Ringo's drums—with piano and occasional organ contributions from Paul and from Billy Preston who was the only non-Beatle to work with us throughout the series of sessions.

The stereo version of the LP is particularly great—thanks to sound expert Glyn Johns who was the studio engineer for all the recordings.

Gradually since *Please, Please Me* The Beatles have been going for greater and greater studio perfection, using every possible audio and electronic technique to add to and improve the finished productions. This time the policy has been entirely different.

The Beatles; Get Back is The Beatles with their socks off, human Beatles kicking out their jams, getting rid of their inhibitions, facing their problems and working them out with their music. During and in between most of the tracks you will hear lots of studio-floor conversation, each of the fellows chatting, preparing for the next number, shouting comments up to the control room. On other albums all

Looks as though Paul's the only one doing any work during this river crossing.

Evans calls the album the "most informal set of records The Beatles have ever put out." The songs were rehearsed at Twickenham to enable the group to decide on how they were to be treated. Once they moved over to Apple, everything was recorded "live" with no overdubs of "extra voices or instruments, no orchestras brought in to boost the accompaniments, no special electronic happenings whatsoever." Just three guitars and drums with occasional keyboards added by Paul and Billy Preston (the only non-Beatle to play on the recordings). Evans praised the stereo version of the album, complementing engineer Glyn Johns.

Evans described the *Get Back* album as "The Beatles with their socks off, human Beatles kicking out their jams, getting rid of their inhibitions, facing their problems and working them out with their music." Studio banter is heard during and between tracks, left in for fans to hear "just as it happened." The album has nine new songs plus both sides of the single "Get Back" and "Don't Let Me Down," ending with a "brief encore version" of "Get Back." There are also link tracks such as "Save The Last Dance For Me" and "Maggie May." There is only one George song, "For You Blue," with no sitar or other Eastern influences. There is no solo Ringo vocal. Evans indicated that the Beatles had recorded several additional tracks, but were holding them for later release as they didn't want to issue another double disc. There are also enough unused recordings to issue a special rock 'n' roll album with tracks such as "Shake Rattle And Roll" and "Blue Suede Shoes." The group recorded a re-make of their first single "Love Me Do," but it is not on the album.

The disc opens with "One After 909," which is the album's only track from the rooftop concert. The rocker, written by John and Paul ten years earlier, is a "punchy kick-off" to the program, with John and Paul sharing vocals. It features the standard lineup of George on lead guitar, John on rhythm guitar, Paul on bass guitar and Ringo on drums, augmented by Billy Preston on electric piano. This is followed by Paul saying "Thanks Mo" to Ringo's wife Maureen, because she clapped the hardest. After a bit of vamping and guitar stuff, Paul says "Just a minute boys," leading into a brief bit of the Drifters' song "Save The Last Dance For Me," included as a link track to "maintain the fun atmosphere of the whole session." Prior to the start of "Don't Let Me Down," John says "Give me the courage to come screaming in." Evans loves this "slow, bluesy" version of the song, which is a different take than the single.

"Dig A Pony" is mostly John, a blues song "with emphasis on the tune rather than the words." The idea is that "you can do anything you want to do so long as you set your mind to it." Paul and John share vocals on "I've Got A Feeling," which has Paul "coming in with that great screamy style of his" and John replying to Paul and later singing lead on his own part. It features the line "All that I was looking for was somebody who looked like you." Prior to the last track on Side One, Ringo hits a tom tom and asks, "What does that sound like?" The side ends with the title track and Paul singing "Get back to where you once belonged," which is the "main theme not only of this terrific track but of the whole album, The Beatles whole frame of 1969."

The second side opens with George's "For You Blue," with George on acoustic guitar, John on steel guitar, Paul on piano and Ringo on drums. The song is like a "South Sea Beat Ballad with the island effect of John's Fender." The song has "nice words" and a "neat tune," making it one of George's most pleasing recordings. Paul's "Teddy Boy" is a simple story about a mother comforting her son. Its message is "We all need someone to turn to." A later section of the song has square dance calls and an electronic feed-back squeal deliberately left in. John and Paul share vocals in good harmony on "Two Of Us On Our Way Home," a "pleasant medium-paced lazy Sunday afternoon" number. "You and I have memories longer than the road that stretches out ahead. We're on our way home." Once again, we're getting back. George plays the bass lines on his electric guitar. This is followed by Paul saying "So we leave the little town of London, England," leading into the link track "Maggie May." The song is a riot, sung with "much Liverpool gusto." "Dig It" is a "Fast and very rhythmic...great big free-for-all" featuring "Scatty vocal vamping" with John shouting lines like "I can hardly keep my hands still." John is on bass and Paul is on piano. At the end, John says "That was Can You Dig It....Now we'd like to do Hark The Angels Come." This is followed by Evans' favorite track on the album, "Let It Be," with Paul "using his soulful voice, sounding very sincere." Paul is on piano and George plays his guitar through a Leslie speaker, making it sound like an organ. "When all the broken-hearted people living in the world agree, there'll be an answer—Let it be." Paul then sings another slow piano piece, "The Long And Winding Road," about a girl that left him standing there. Then it's back to the beginning with an encore of "Get Back." The LP is a "friendly album that invites you to join in what happens in The Beatles recording studio...Quite unlike the carefully prepared, expertly edited LP productions the fellows have spent so many months on in the past."

As June came to a close, the ongoing saga of the next Beatles LP took an unexpected twist. The June 28 NME reported that the Beatles were "expected to begin work next week [July 1] on completing the second of the two albums they now have awaiting release." The magazine speculated that the second album might be issued first. The other album [*Get Back*] was related to their TV documentary and was to be released by the end of the year.

Two weeks later the confusion continued in the July 12 NME in an article providing "full details" on the Beatles *Get Back* LP and a second album of "old rock classics." The former album was tentatively set for September release to coincide with the TV special. NME noted that the broadcast date for the program had yet to be finalized. If the TV show was delayed until late autumn, an album of rock 'n' roll classics might be released first. The Beatles were hoping to compile a three-hour film for theatrical release which would be edited down to two hours for the television special. The group also planned to publish a book of photographs taken during the sessions. The discussion on the *Get Back* LP contained information similar to that found in Mal Evans' diary report in The Beatles Book. NME reported that although there was no Ringo vocal on the album, the drummer had two songs for a future LP, "Octopus Garden" and "I Should Like To Live Up A Tree." The first song ended up on *Abbey Road*. The second title apparently was a subtitle for "Octopus's Garden." As for the rock 'n' roll LP, possible tracks included "Shake Rattle And Roll" and "Blue Suede Shoes," as well as a new recording of "Love Me Do." Other available tracks for future release included "Polythene Pam," "Maxwell's Silver Hammer," "Not Guilty" and "What's The New Mary Jane." The first two would end up on *Abbey Road*, while the *White Album* outtakes were not released until *Anthology 3* in 1996.

The July 12 Melody Maker reported that the Beatles "long-awaited" new album would be released in late August or early September. The article provided a track list. The next week Melody Maker reported a "Beatles' album switch." Derek Taylor told the magazine that the *Get Back* LP would not be released until December. "Although it is finished and ready to go, the company [Apple] have decided to hold it until the film" which was still in the editing stage. The *Get Back* LP was to be released in August, but another album of new Beatles recordings would be issued instead, most likely towards the end of September. That new album would be *Abbey Road*, which was released in the U.K. on September 26, 1969.

The last-minute postponement of the *Get Back* LP was explained by Mal Evans in the August 1969 issue (No. 73) of The Beatles Book. He revealed that when the Beatles returned from their various trips abroad, they "listened together to the final tapes of all the *Get Back* LP recordings" and "realized that it would be much more appropriate to hold back the whole set of recordings so that they could form an LP which would go out at the same time their TV documentary is shown in Britain and America." Evans said that the group "wanted to get their first 1969 LP out as soon as possible." Some songs were already "in the can," but the group had gone back into the studio at the start of July to record enough new songs for another album. The *Get Back* LP, now planned for a November release, would serve as the TV documentary's soundtrack album and would contain the same recordings as previously reported.

Even though the *Get Back* album was postponed, the magazine ran an in-depth preview of the LP by Tony Barrow under his pseudonym Frederick James. Barrow predicted three of the tracks would become Beatles classics: "One After 909;" "For You Blue;" and "Let It Be." The first, which opens the album, has Paul "letting his voice rip into the fast-moving lines of lyrics with typical McCartney thrust and infectious enthusiasm." With "For You Blue," George is "getting back" to the time before he converted suddenly to Indian music. His composition work is approaching that of Lennon and McCartney. John's guitar has "swirling, curving metallic notes that give us pictures of silver sand, swaying palms and dusky island beauties!" Paul's sentimental "Let It Be" is a "warm song, a charmer put over with friendly persuasion." Its message is simple: "when all the world agrees there'll be a peaceful answer to everything."

Barrow repeats Mal's observation that the group did not aim for technical perfection with the album, instead providing "intriguing glimpses into their unrehearsed studio work, their bits of 'tween-takes conversation, their shouted gag lines yelled up to producer George Martin, engineer Glyn Johns...." The group was also "getting back" to its recording line-up from 1963 and 1964—three guitars and drums—with no electronic tricks or additional musicians except for Paul or Billy Preston adding piano as George Martin did in the early days. The Beatles were back to their "simple, uncomplicated yet commercially musical beginnings," giving the album "tremendous novelty appeal with its intensionally unpolished 'backstage' approach."

With the *Get Back* album postponed, the music magazines and press shifted focus to the Beatles new *Abbey Road* LP. After a few months of silence, NME decided it was time to get back to the *Get Back* album in its November 1 issue with an "In Depth NMExclusive" on the next Beatle album. Oddly, the article was based on "American reports," although most of the information had been previously reported in British publications. In keeping with the American theme, writer Derek Johnson stated that "As usual in America, fewer numbers will be on the LP there than in this country." (Although that was correct from 1964 through 1966, all subsequent U.S. albums were the same as the U.K. discs.) The article went through all of the album's tracks, starting with "Let It Be," described as the group's first religious ballad. It mistakenly attributed "For You Blue" to Paul, leading to the erroneous statement that there were no George or Ringo songs "on the tracks assembled for the American release." Johnson believed that George and Ringo would definitely have their songs on the British version of the album. Disc reported in its November 8 issue that there would be "TWO new 'full-scale' Beatles albums" released in 1970, including the previously reported *Get Back* LP and another "made up of songs John and Paul have stockpiled in recent months." The latter collection never came to be. On December 12, the Beatles song "Across The Universe" made its debut on the charity LP *No One's Gonna Change Our World.* Alan Smith warned in the December 13 NME that the Beatles were "on the brink of splitting." Melody Maker ended the year with its December 27 issue reporting Apple's promise that the *Get Back* LP would be released in early 1970. A single would also soon be issued, although the titles had yet to be selected.

Beatles fans started the New Year with the news that the next Beatles single would be "Let It Be." The January 3 Melody Maker reported that the Paul McCartney ballad from the forthcoming *Get Back* LP would probably be in shops in a few weeks, shortly before the *Get Back* film hit cinemas. The album would be released at the same time as the film and would contain basically the same tracks as previously announced. Disc reported that the Beatles next single would be "Let It Be," with "You Know My Name" as the likely B-side. It would probably be released in February to coincide with the release of the group's 80-minute documentary film and the *Get Back* LP. The January 10 Disc told of a Beatles recording session to add finishing touches to the "Let It Be" single, now set for February 20. The group also recorded a George Harrison song, "I Me Mine," to complete the *Get Back* album. John did not attend. That week NME also reported on "I Me Mine" and stated that the album's title might be changed to *Let It Be.*

Although the "Let It Be" single would not be released until five weeks later, it was reviewed in the January 31 Disc. Ray Coleman, who heard an advance pressing, predicted it should have an impact as big as "Hey Jude." The song was "hymnal in style; loaded with Gospel feeling and the voice of Paul at its most soulful, as on 'Hey Jude.'" It was a beauty that would have you humming it after hearing it once or twice.

The February 7 music magazines reported on and reviewed a new Plastic Ono Band single, "Instant Karma," a John Lennon song produced by Phil Spector and featuring George Harrison, Billy Preston, Klaus Voormann, Alan White, Mal Evans (who claps and plays chimes) and Allen Klein (part of the vocal chorus). The British pressing of the disc was credited on the label as "Lennon/Ono with the Plastic Ono Band." The next week NME reported that Paul would be releasing a solo album of his own songs. This LP was not expected to be issued until after the Beatles next album was released in late March or early April. NME reported that the Beatles disc was being programmed and that it would not follow the format previously reported. Ringo was involved in editing the album, and that the title would most likely be changed to *Let It Be*. It would be a soundtrack LP, not to be considered the follow-up to *Abbey Road*.

The February 21 NME reported that the release of the "Let It Be" single would be pushed back a week from February 27 to March 6 due to "promotional difficulties." The song would be featured in the documentary film which was tentatively set for a spring release. The soundtrack album would be issued the same time as the film, which would be titled either *Get Back* or *Let It Be*. That week Record Mirror also told of the single's delay, as well as reporting that the *Get Back* album might be out by the end of March and that some London shops were already displaying the box the album would be packaged in and were taking orders for the album.

The February 21 Record Mirror further reported that Aretha Franklin's recording of "Let It Be" had been planned as a U.K. single, but was being replaced by another track from her album, "Call Me" (already a hit in the U.S.). In its February 28 issue, Disc also told of the Franklin single switch, explaining that Atlantic Records thought it unwise to put out a version of a Beatles song at the same time the Beatles were releasing the same song. Atlantic claimed that Paul had written the song for Aretha and had sent it to her to record.

The February 28 Disc also featured an article on John & Yoko at Apple. John acknowledged that the group was going through changes, describing it as a "menopause, or something like that." He hadn't seen Paul for two months, noting that McCartney had not been to Apple in ages. John said that they had a "heavy scene last year" on business matters and Paul got fed up. John was hoping that was all it was. He predicted Apple would be bigger than the Beatles.

The "Let It Be" single was reviewed in the February 28 British music magazines. Writing in Disc, Mike Ledgerwood described the song as a beautiful soulful ballad by McCartney that was written a year earlier for the *Get Back* album. Although it had not been considered for release as a single at the time, the song had been receiving airplay in the States along with other pirated recordings from the *Get Back* album. Penny Valentine called the song a "McCartney solo smash!...a song just right for now and has exactly the right commercial hook line to keep everyone singing it forever." She praised Paul's vocal and the "fine throbbing guitar break," pointlessly adding the single would be "hugely huge." NME called the disc an "inspirational ballad with a profoundly philosophic lyric, emotionally delivered by Paul McCartney." The song opened with "clanking piano" and had "swinging organ" on the instrumental break. The heavenly choir behind the lead vocal emphasized the "pseudo-religious nature" of the words and its references to "Mother Mary." Although not as melodically catchy as some of the group's other efforts, it was "stamped with the hallmark of quality," a record to "stop you dead in your tracks and compel you to listen attentively." Peter Jones reviewed the "Let It Be" single in Record Mirror, noting that the song made listeners genuinely wonder "Is this the Beatles?" The track was mostly Paul "on thundering piano...singing with a real touch of plaintives." Dedicated to Paul's mother, Mary, the recording has a gospel feel due to its "wailing choral backing." The single builds in drama and volume, with delicate strings, magnifying the pathos and "philosophic satisfaction." Jones predicted the song would be a smash sing-along, selling to every age group. Chris Welch reviewed the new single for Melody Maker, noting that it seemed a long way from "Love Me Do." The song had a "nostalgic almost somber mood" and a "gospel hymn feel" that made it "one of the best Beatles songs in many a crop of Apples." In that same issue, Trevor Brice of the British pop/rock group Vanity Fare ("Hitchin' A Ride"), in a blind listening test, found it a nice song and loved the bashing piano chords. After failing to identify the artist as the Beatles, when he was told who it was, Brice described the song as "the most un-Beatleish thing they've ever done" and an obvious "gigantic hit."

DISC
and MUSIC ECHO 1s

FEBRUARY 28, 1970   EVERY THURSDAY   USA 25c

Bill Haley, Chuck Berry here soon

SEE PAGE SIX

Paxton and The Band coming!

THE BAND and TOM PAXTON, both stars of Bob Dylan's fantastic Isle Of Wight festival last summer, are set for British trips soon.

The Band, originally Dylan's backing group and today a big name in their own right on the strength of two smash albums and single hits like "The Weight," make their first-ever U.K. solo concert appearance—apart from the Isle Of Wight—in May.

The group is expected on a three-day visit and will play London's Royal Albert Hall on May 7, if plans go through.

TOM PAXTON, the quiet giant of folk music, arrives in London on April 10 for TV and radio dates and opens a three-week tour at London's Royal Albert Hall—to be filmed by BBC-TV for a 50-minute spectacular—on Thursday, April 30.

Full dates for the tour—on which Tom will be accompanied by pianist Dave Horowitz, plus bass and drums, for his two-hour appearances—are: **LEICESTER** De Montfort Hall (May 1), **LEEDS** University (2), **ABERDEEN** Music Hall (7), **EDINBURGH** Usher Hall (8), **NEWCASTLE** City Hall (9), **SHEFFIELD** City Hall (11), **LIVERPOOL** Empire (12), **STOKE** Polytechnic (15), **SOUTHAMPTON** Guildhall (18), **BANGOR** University (19), **MANCHESTER** Free Trade Hall (20), **BIRMINGHAM** Town Hall (21), **BRISTOL** Colston Hall (22), **BOURNEMOUTH** Winter Gardens (23), **HEMEL HEMPSTEAD** Pavilion (27), **CROYDON** Fairfield Halls (28) and **BRIGHTON** Dome (30).

Peter, Paul and Mary jet in

PETER, PAUL and MARY—the world famous folk group with a massive hit, "Leaving On A Jet Plane"—play two concerts at London's Royal Albert Hall in early June.

The trio, who will be in Britain for ten days, will also make TV appearances.

PEOPLE FOR PEACE

Is the Plastic Ono Band the new Beatles?

Has Paul lost interest in Apple?

How is the peace war going?

JOHN LENNON speaks on page 2

"Let It Be" entered the Record Retailer chart at number two on March 14, blocked from the top by "Wand'rin' Star" by Lee Marvin from the film *Paint Your Wagon*. The next week, "Let It Be" dropped to number three behind "Bridge Over Troubled Water" by Simon & Garfunkel, which took over the second spot. "Let It Be" spent nine weeks on the charts, including four in the top ten. The single made its debut in Melody Maker at number 15 on March 14 along with three other Apple songs in the Top 30: "Instant Karma" by Lennon/Ono with the Plastic Ono Band at five; "Temma Harbour" by Mary Hopkin at 12; and "Come And Get It" by Badfinger at 29. The next week the Beatles single moved up to its peak position of three where it remained for two weeks, unable to get past "Wand'rin' Star" or "Bridge Over Troubled Water." The disc charted for eight weeks, including four in the top ten. Its performance was only slightly better than Mary Hopkin's follow-up single, "Knock Knock Who's There," which also charted for eight weeks with four in the top ten and a peak at three. NME also showed a peak at three for "Let It Be." The song's failure to top the U.K. charts was perplexing, but not without precedent. "Strawberry Fields Forever" was blocked from the top by Engelbert Humperdinck's "Release Me." Although the single's performance was somewhat disappointing, it was not a bust. The April 18, 1970, Record Retailer reported that the disc had sold over 250,000 units.

While Beatles fans were waiting for the group's next LP, two solo albums were released. Ringo took his fans on a *Sentimental Journey* of standards his family used to sing on his first solo album issued on March 27, 1970. Three weeks later on April 17 Paul released his *McCartney* album in tandem with an interview in which he stated that he was leaving the Beatles.

The April 25 Record Mirror announced that the Beatles album and film were set for May release. The magazine reported that Phil Spector had remixed some tracks and added orchestration and a choir in certain places. George Martin expressed surprise with Spector's involvement. When asked if he would produce the group again, Martin said "In view of the fact that the Beatles don't exist as the four young men I once knew, I don't want to record them as a split group, but I would like to record them as they were." The article contained a list of the album's songs. The next week Record Mirror announced that the *Let It Be* film would make its U.K. premiere on May 20 at the London Pavilion and the Odeon Liverpool, with the soundtrack album being issued on May 8. The disc was packaged in a presentation box with a book, titled *Get Back*, of interviews and pictures of the Beatles taken during the recording of the album. It was priced at just under three pounds (£2 19s 11d).

The May 9 music magazines all reviewed *Let It Be*. Record Retailer observed that the "Release of this album has had the longest and largest of any in pop history." The magazine stated there was confusion as to whether this would be the last Beatles album and was of the opinion that "If the Beatles were to return to the studio as a group only to fulfill contractual commitments, it is unlikely that the new efforts would compare favorably with those of the past." The packaging was called "flawless in every respect" and "superbly effective and beautifully executed," with the book "overwhelming in its flashy luxury." The magazine observed that the book was in some ways irrelevant as the "excitement of pop-star pin-ups is more attuned to the idolatry of five years ago" and that even with the Beatles, consumers were more into the music than personalities. Spector's work on the album was characterized as being "felt without really being noticed." Four songs were called exceptional: "Let It Be;" "Get Back;" "Across The Universe;" and "The Long And Winding Road." The magazine correctly predicted that although the album's high list price could scare away consumers with only marginal interest in the Beatles, "*Let It Be* cannot fail to be a massive seller."

One of the Beatles earliest and biggest supporters, Alan Smith, wrote a blistering review in NME headlined "New LP Shows They Couldn't Care Less" followed by "Have Beatles sold out?" Smith's ire was primarily directed at the album's packaging and price, although he also called out Phil Spector. Smith stated that if this was to be the Beatles last LP, then it would be a "cheapskate epitaph, a cardboard tombstone, a sad and tatty end to a musical fusion which wiped clean and drew again the face of pop music." He rhetorically asked that, if at nearly 3 pounds, "can this mini-collection of new tracks, narcissistic pin-ups and chocolate dressing really be the last will and testament of the once-respected and most-famous group in the world?" He wondered "What kind of contempt for the intelligence of today's record buyers is it that foists upon them an album at this price with seven new tracks; two bits of dressing in the shape of 'Dig It' and 'Maggie Mae;' and three previously-released numbers 'Let It Be,' 'Get Back' and 'Across The Universe'?" Smith speculated that a pound of the cost is for the book, warning "lump it or leave it, music lovers."

Smith believed that the Beatles had "lost their self-respect." They were always about the music, not "hype in a pretty package." He was pained to see them accept "this load of old flannel and musical castration" and found it tragic that what little remained of the original *Get Back* LP was "some of the best straight rock the Beatles have recorded in years." He lamented that "Almost all of the fun and raw feel has been taken away or polished up by Phil Spector." Smith was fairly complementary of the songs. "Two Of Us" was a nostalgic "honey-soft rocker about going home." John's "Across The Universe" was "ethereal and beautiful." George's "I Me Mine" was "Russian-flavoured" and a "strong ballad with a strong centre." "Dig It" was described as a brief "smile-raising chant." The rockers "I've Got A Feeling" and "One After 909" were "excellent stuff" in which John and Paul worked well together. Smith understood Paul's objections to the choir and strings added to "The Long And Winding Road." In its original form, the ballad had "empty simplicity." Although the track's chorale and strings were acceptable, they were unnecessary. "For You Blue" was a "whispery chunky rocker," another strong song from George. Smith found it tragic that "on the strength of the little new music there is on this LP, the Beatles were never informally better, never more with their feet on the ground." He prayed the Beatles would work together again to "restore the respect of those who admire, appreciate and love them." Smith had "glowed with Merseyside pride" at the group's achievements," but felt that "this glorified EP is a bad and sad mistake."

Richard Williams, writing in the May 9 Melody Maker, saw things differently. Alan Smith viewed the album as a "cheapskate epitaph" and a "cardboard tombstone." Williams also saw an epitaph, but one "packaged in a black box with a lavish black-covered book" with beautiful color and monochrome pictures and conversations between the musicians that were "at least as interesting and revealing...as a dozen interviews." It was a "beautiful thing to own," but the album had the "feeling of finality about it, as if you are holding the last document from that collective personality known as the Beatles."

Williams disagreed with the cover's claim that *Let It Be* was a new phase Beatles album. It had the feel of the pre-*Rubber Soul* era, "when the complexities were still natural and the possibilities of the recording studio comparatively unexplored." He found the differences between *Let It Be* and *Abbey Road* to be enormous. Here they were "singing and playing together, still reveling in it despite the small clashes of interest." The personalities of John and Paul were in each other's songs, whereas on *Abbey Road*, each song was one man's statement. As for Spector reproducing the songs, only "The Long And Winding Road," with its added choir, harp and strings, was noticeably different.

Williams found "Two Of Us" to be poignant, a reminder of times when the Beatles were close. "Dig A Pony" was the only "real" John song on the album, noted for its "funky unison guitar riff...insane words and wandering tune." "Across The Universe" was a different mix than the one on the charity LP. The song has a "floating, disembodied quality" and is "utterly charming." Williams was impressed with "I Me Mine," observing that George put "a lot of strength into this song." He liked the organ and guitar introduction and tempo switches, calling the guitar riffs "one step away from Chuck Berry." "Dig It" was described as "a few seconds of Lennon imitating Jagger." Williams incorrectly described "Let It Be" as a different take from the single (as did all other reviewers), fooled by the different (and harder) guitar solo, mix and edit. "Maggie Mae" was a rough version of the old Liverpool tune. "I've Got A Feeling" was rated the best track on the album, a "knock-out rocker with a bit of Band-style funkiness," "roaring chorus" and "neat background guitar" from Harrison. He found "One After 909" to be interesting because John and Paul wrote it back in their Quarrymen days. The song was described as "Very simple. Jerry Lee [Lewis] lives!" In Paul's "The Long And Winding Road," Spector's strings add a "pleasant fullness in places, but badly intrude near the end and the harps are literally too much." George's "For You Blue" is acoustic country blues, an "amusing trifle." "Get Back" was a "natural born gas." Rarely has the group "swung so hard or with such success."

While Alan Smith complained that the album was a "mini-collection of new tracks, narcissistic pin-ups and chocolate dressing" and was saddened by the prospect of *Let It Be* being the group's last will and testament, Richard Williams felt the album was well worth its near three-pound price, a "packaged deluxe last will and testament." He concluded his review with "The Beatles are dead—long live the Beatles."

Disc presented both sides of the controversy in its review titled "An expensive memento of the Beatles...," noting that the album would be remembered either as the "greatest-ever fan farewell gift, or the biggest disappointment ever!" Some would be disappointed by each side having barely 15 minutes of music, but priced at nearly three pounds due to the special packaging and luxurious book that comes "free of charge." But if you liked looking at pictures of the Beatles as they were a year ago, the book was "unsurpassed." As for the text, the words came across as disjointed without the film to put things in context. One quote from McCartney was singled out as appropriate:

"[The Beatles] haven't been positive. That's why all of us in turn have been sick of the group...The only way for it not to be a drag is for the four of us to think, 'Should we make it positive or should we forget it?'" The book would be viewed as either a priceless treasure or a waste of a pound.

As for the songs, "Two Of Us" was an "intimate charming song, with a hint of sadness." John's "Dig A Pony" had words for sound rather than meaning and a "good harmony chorus." The review incorrectly referred to "Across The Universe" as a one-take song and erroneously assumed that Billy Preston played organ on "I Me Mine," which was actually recorded a year after the *Get Back* sessions. "I've Got A Feeling" had "wailing voices" and was "straight blues." "One After 909" was described as "Chuck Berry stuff," a "typical railroad rocker." The main criticism was directed at Spector for completely ruining "The Long And Winding Road" with orchestration and a female chorus, preventing the song from becoming the "Yesterday" or "Michelle" of the album. The review ended with three questions about the album: "Does it stand up on its own? Will it sound better having seen the film? Is it worth £3?"

David Skan's review in Record Mirror was titled "The Last Beatles LP?" He found it ironic that the album was titled *Let It Be* when that just wasn't done. The album was "tampered with, mucked about, orchestrated, or in the words of the sleeve, 'freshened up.'" Skan then took direct aim at Phil Spector. "Some people will say castrated is a better word" due to the addition of "choirs of falsetto angels" and harps and violin to some of the tracks. "This awful spectre, the very idea that John's or Paul's songs need the prop of slick production techniques, is an impertinence." To Skan, "The whole point of their songs was, eons ago, that they were THEIR songs; songs of innocence and experience. And keep your hands to yourself!"

Skan felt that even with the "intervention of the high priest of processing Phil Spector," the album had a potential standard in "The Long And Winding Road," a sad and beautiful song that he wished he could hear in its original form. He also liked "I Me Mine" and John's jokes between the songs. As expected from Apple, the book and packaging were well produced. Kahn ended his review with a salute of sorts: "So now we say thank you, goodnight and now I know why we don't do it in the road."

The *Let It Be* album entered the Record Retailer LP chart on May 23 and the following week hit its first of two straight weeks at the top before being replaced by Simon and Garfunkel's *Bridge Over Troubled Water*. The disc charted for 59 weeks between 1970 and 1973, including three weeks at number one. The LP entered the Melody Maker chart on May 23 at number three. After one more week at three, *Let It Be* hit its first of eight straight weeks at number one. This was followed by four straight weeks at number two and two weeks at number three. The album charted for 35 weeks, including 19 in the top five. *Let It Be* topped the NME album chart for six non-consecutive weeks.

Writing in the May 8 edition of The Times (of London), William Mann opened his review of *Let It Be* by referencing "Ghoulish rumour-mongers" who were claiming that the record sleeve, accompanying book and outer cover are black-edged because this was the Beatles last LP together. Mann then mocked this view: "Let us attend the funeral when life is pronounced extinct; at the moment the corporate vitality of The Beatles, to judge from *Let It Be*, is pulsating as strongly as ever." After pointing out that the album took its title from the "Let It Be" single and was the name of the upcoming film, he noted that the accompanying book was titled *The Beatles Get Back*, which he found confusing because "Get Back" was the name of a previous single and, for a while, the projected title of the film. He expected this would eventually be sorted out.

Mann viewed the album as a "trailer for the film's music," which explained why "it does not attempt any large-scale musical construction such as distinguished side two of *Abbey Road*." He preferred Side One based on three of its tracks. "Across The Universe" reminded him favorably of "Strawberry Fields Forever" and "Glass Onion." Its "Nothing's gonna change my world" refrain was "haunting" and its instrumentation had "great character." "Dig A Pony" also had a captivating refrain along with "relaxed, imaginative harmony and construction." He immediately took a liking to George's "I Me Mine" with its "easy switches of musical metre." As for the second side, Paul's "The Long And Winding Road" was a good slow ballad, but "not specially distinctive." George's "For You Blue" was a pleasant 12-bar blues with "Hawaiian effect." He properly noted that "One After 909" was an early Lennon-McCartney number, but incorrectly said this was its first recording. (Mark Lewisohn's book on the Beatles recording sessions would not be published until many years later, so Mann had no way of knowing that the Beatles had recorded the song in 1963.)

"I've Got A Feeling" was a song that initially seemed ordinary, but then gradually took "complete possession of the listener's inner ear." Although *Let It Be* was "Not a breakthrough record," it was "definitely a record to give lasting pleasure." As for the Beatles, Mann assured us: "They aren't having to scrape the barrel yet. Strong as ever."

Derek Jewel reviewed the *Let It Be* LP in the May 10 edition of The Sunday Times under the title "Hello, goodbye." He opened his piece with John's "I hope we passed the audition" comment from the end of the album, which he speculated might be the "last to contain a significant quantity of new good songs." Jewel noted that as an epitaph, John's closing words had a "quality of authentic Beatles irony." He observed that "everything else about the album is just right for a last will and testament, from the blackly funereal packaging to the music itself, which sums up so much of what the Beatles as artists have been—unmatchably brilliant at their best, careless and self-indulgent at their least." He found it important that the Beatles were "still working as a group, not as individuals."

As for the music, it was not as sophisticated as the group's albums that followed *Rubber Soul*. "One After 909" was "archetypal rock 'n' roll" and "Get Back" was "hard-swinging and simple." Jewel praised "For You Blue" as the "best and most surprising" track on the album. It mixed "country-style and a jokey bottleneck guitar very excitingly." "Across The Universe" was described as a beautiful song.

Jewel lamented that record "droops most depressingly when the freshness disappears" on songs such as "The Long And Winding Road," which had excessive strings, brass and choir. He assumed this was due the to "re-producing" by Phil Spector, who Jewel described as a "born believer in the over-spectacular." He noted that Paul's ballads needed a "lighter touch."

The album also contained jokes and fragments. And, if the music wasn't enough, it came with a "fat and impeccably produced picture book" with nearly 200 pages of Beatles photographs and conversations. Jewel warned readers that the book pushed the price of the *Let It Be* album package up to nearly three pounds, but noted that "Memorial tablets never were cheap."

Tony Palmer wrote on both the *Let It Be* film and album, as well as the group's place in the world and their break-up, in the May 24 edition of The Observer. He opened with: "The Beatles have a quality of indestructibility that is common to all people of greatness." He then observed that "They have become an integral part of the myth of our time and therefore have neither reality nor truth" being "the crystallization of dreams, hopes, energies, disappointments of a countless host of others who would have been Beatles if they could." Despite his lofty introduction, Palmer found the movie to be a bore: "It's supposed to show how the Beatles work, but it doesn't. Shot without any design, clumsily edited...uninformative, awkward and naive, it would have destroyed a lesser group." Palmer wondered how 200,000 feet of film could have produced "nothing but an extended promotional exercise." The rooftop concert is "outrageously funny," but "shoddily assembled." As for Beatles, they were shown "singing away, charming the pants off the most cynical of pop-music haters." Paul came across as "the No. 1 Beatle fan, trying to organize the rest into some kind of purposeful activity."

While Palmer viewed the film as amateur, he found the music to be "consistently inventive." Rather than run through the songs, he asked "what can one possibly say about the music that has not been said a million times before?" He spoke of "endless Schubert-cynicism" and both complemented and criticized Ringo ("a great talent lurking within that has yet to find its proper outlet"), Spector's arrangements ("nice but niceness was never a characteristic of the Beatles") and Paul's voice ("beautiful but undisciplined"). The only song he named was "I Me Mine," which was simple, yet "gnaws the mind." Overall, Palmer concluded "It's simple music, but that is always the hardest to achieve." He closes with goodbye to the Beatles and "hallo" to John, Paul, George and Ringo, "who together will still be called the Beatles."

Despite some of the negative reviews that found the music lacking and the packaging indulgent and pricey, Beatles fans in the U.K. willingly paid the near three pounds required to take the album and its accompanying book home. No doubt they agreed with EMI's marketing campaign, which touted *Let It Be* as "A Very Special Collection."

The Beatles Let It Be in Canada

by Piers Hemmingsen

Eight months before the *Let It Be* album's official release in May 1970, the Beatles decided to let it be in Canada. Well, actually it was John who set things in motion, and he most likely had no idea what the consequences of his generosity would be. In September 1969, the album that was then called *Get Back* was set for release by the end of the year. But an Australian-born journalist living in Canada let the cat out of the Bag Production, so to say.

In the summer of 1969, Ritchie Yorke was based in Toronto, working as the Canadian rep for Billboard and as the rock editor for The Globe and Mail, a Canadian newspaper. Yorke had met John & Yoko after their arrival in Toronto from the Bahamas on May 25, 1969. He interviewed the couple the next day and followed them to Montreal for the couple's Bed In For Peace at the Queen Elizabeth Hotel.

On September 11, 1969, Yorke paid a visit to Apple's London office, having flown in from Toronto the day before. He was there to coordinate the details of his scheduled September 15 interview with George Harrison for The Globe and Mail. After meeting with Apple press officer Derek Taylor, Yorke stopped by John Lennon's ground floor office to say hello. As fate would have it, John Brower was calling for John at exactly that moment to invite him to the Rock and Roll Revival concert that Brower was promoting in Toronto. When John asked Yorke to vouch for Brower, the journalist obliged, perhaps tipping the scale in favor of a Plastic Ono Band appearance that weekend in Toronto.

Yorke was back at Savile Row on the 15th to conduct his interview with George Harrison, which appeared in The Globe Magazine on October 25, 1969. The back cover of the November 1969 Canadian LP of the Beatles Hamburg recordings, *Very Together*, contained a Harrison quote from the interview: "we got very tight as a band in Hamburg."

Ritchie Yorke interviewing John & Yoko at the Malton Airport in Toronto on May 26, 1969. John later gave Ritchie this acetate of the Beatles "Let It Be" single.

Apple Corpo Ltd. 3. Savile Row London W1

"LET IT BE"

THE BEATLES
STEREO

Custom Recording

On September 16, Yorke returned to Apple for a third visit to interview the beaming, re-energized John & Yoko. The couple was still on a high from the success of their Toronto concert of few days earlier. Yorke's John & Yoko interview would later appear in the October 18, 1969, edition of Rolling Stone. It is likely that on this happy Tuesday afternoon, Lennon provided Yorke with his copy of an early May 1969 acetate of the *Get Back* album, perhaps as a small thank you for his encouraging John to go to the Toronto Rock And Roll Revival. As Ritchie records in his wonderful book, *Christ You Know It Ain't Easy*, "John was extraordinarily grateful to me for the role I personally played in getting him off his backside, across the Atlantic, and as time would prove, out of The Beatles."

The next day, Wednesday, September 17, Yorke arrived back in Toronto with his gift copy of the *Get Back* acetate. It is likely that Yorke quickly made a tape copy of the acetate, but in his haste to get it done, recorded only one of the acetate's two stereo channels. He then visited his "underground radio chums" at CHUM-FM with his tape of the *Get Back* acetate containing performances of fresh Beatles music that only a few Beatles insiders had heard. Immediate negotiations took place for CHUM-FM to obtain the tape, most likely for cash. That evening, just four days after the Plastic Ono Band had performed in Toronto at Varsity Stadium, tracks from the *Get Back* acetate were broadcast by CHUM-FM. The underground FM station chose not to share its *Get Back* tracks with sister station CHUM-AM.

CHUM-FM had been in hot water with Capitol of Canada in November 1968 when it aired several tracks from *The White Album* well before its scheduled release. The station did not want to cross Capitol again, so they proceeded with caution, opting to play the *Get Back* selections late at night without significant promotion. While they wanted to be the first station to air the new Beatles recordings, they knew they were sitting on dynamite. The next day, Thursday, September 18, two "out-of-market" radio stations in southwestern Ontario, CJRN in Niagara Falls and CKLW in Windsor, obtained copies of the *Get Back* tape. These stations most likely paid CHUM-FM a modest sum to enable the Toronto station to recoup what it had paid to Yorke. CHUM-FM trusted these stations not to reveal the tape's source and probably found it safer not to be the only station playing the unreleased Beatles songs. Over the next few days, the stations aired the *Get Back* tracks. Lennon would later recount, "they say it came from an acetate that I gave to someone who then went and broadcast it as being an advanced pressing or something."

A few alert listeners of these stations taped the *Get Back* tracks off the air. On one surviving tape, a CHUM-FM disc jockey states that "this new album was not due to be released until Christmas" and is "music from the future." An enterprising listener of CJRN contacted WKBW-AM in Buffalo, New York, arranging to sell his copy of songs taped off CJRN for about a hundred bucks. The Buffalo station began airing the songs on Saturday, September 20. This prompted a disc jockey at Boston's WBCN to play a different tape of *Get Back* recordings. Some American listeners in turn taped the WKBW and WBCN broadcasts of the songs. Within a few months, bootlegs containing these songs began appearing in stores in the United States and Canada. Things came full circle in early 1970 with the release of a bootleg titled *The Beatles Get Back To Toronto*, which opens with John & Yoko talking about their campaign to make 1970 "Year One of Peace" and the planned Toronto Peace Festival. The track was taped from a January 1, 1970, broadcast of a conversation with John & Yoko recorded at their home by the Canadian Broadcasting Corporation.

As for Canadian radio, the *Get Back* recordings were quickly eclipsed by the release of *Abbey Road* on October 1, 1969, and the "Paul is Dead" controversy that followed later that month. Nonetheless, the airing of the tape of the *Get Back* acetate on CHUM-FM set off a chain of events bringing unreleased Beatles music to the world.

By early 1970, the mainstream press began reporting on the upcoming *Get Back* LP. The January 8 Poppin magazine contained a short article by Ihor Todoruk covering the *Very Together* and *Get Back* albums. In discussing the latter disc, Todoruk commented on the presence of chatter between the songs and the book that comes with the record, all "part of a picture that they paint for you...nothing has been omitted—it's all there for your to hear."

The Canadian News Report in the January 31 Billboard told of the "Beatles' new disk 'Let It Be' getting a world premiere on CKFH almost five weeks before the record gets its national release on Feb. 20." This would mean that the Toronto station aired "Let It Be" on or about January 16, around the same time that British journalist Ray Coleman heard the single. As Ritchie Yorke had received an acetate of the "Let It Be" single from John, it is likely that Yorke allowed his friends at CKFH to tape and broadcast the disc. The song, without its later-added embellishments, had been played on CHUM-FM four months earlier as part of the *Get Back* acetate Yorke had received from John.

After a series of delays, the "Let It Be" single was finally issued in Canada on March 11, 1970, simultaneously with the U.S. release. Many of the copies initially sold were packaged in imported copies of the U.S. picture sleeve (see page 100). The others came in generic "The Beatles on Apple" center die-cut white sleeves. Hudson's Bay stores across Canada sold the single with the picture sleeve for 89 cents. "Let It Be" made its debut in the CHUM-AM survey on March 21 at number 28. The single jumped to the top of the charts the following week and remained there for four weeks before dropping back to number two behind "American Woman" by the Guess Who.

While "Let It Be" was receiving saturation air play, a Beatles-related single by the Inner City Mission was getting enough spins on CHUM-AM to chart for two weeks with a peak of 20 on April 25. "Get Back John" was a bouncy and funky song that included references to John & Yoko's stay with Ronnie Hawkins at his Ontario farm and the couple's War Is Over peace campaign. The song, whose title appears to have been a play on the Beatles "Get Back" single, was recorded at Bay Studios in Toronto.

Shortly before the release of the *Let It Be* LP, Capitol of Canada issued the same single pulled from the album as its U.S. parent company on May 11, 1970. CHUM-AM listed the disc as "The Long And Winding Road"/"For You Blue" during its nine weeks on the charts. The single hit the number one spot on June 13, its fourth week on the charts, and remained there for another week. For Canadians who had heard "The Long And Winding Road" on CHUM-FM the previous September or who purchased a bootleg of *Get Back* songs, the lush strings and choir on the song must have come as quite a shock. Many initial copies of the disc came in imported U.S. picture sleeves (see page 101).

One week after the release of "The Long And Winding Road" single, Capitol of Canada issued the *Let It Be* LP on May 18. This was different than the arrangement south of the border. According to Paul White, "we at Capitol Canada were instructed by legal, Los Angeles about the deal United Artists had for the rights to the soundtrack. Capitol did not have the rights to issue the LP in the States at that time. As EMI had the rest of the world rights, Canada fell into their camp." In the States, United Artists decided to issue the album with a gatefold cover instead of the deluxe box with the 164-page book. Capitol of Canada followed EMI's lead and opted for the deluxe edition of the album.

STEREO

LET
IT BE
(Lennon-
McCartney)

Recorded
in England

THE
BEATLES
Maclen Music,
Inc.-BMI
Intro. :13
Total-3:50

2764
(S45-X47129)
PRODUCED
BY GEORGE
MARTIN

Manufactured by
Apple Records, Inc.

YOU KNOW MY NAME
(LOOK UP MY NUMBER)
(Lennon-McCartney)
Recorded in England

2764
(45-X47130)

MFD. BY APPLE RECORDS, INC.

THE BEATLES
Manufactured by Apple Records, Inc
Maclen Music, Inc.-BMI
Intro. :17 Total-4:20
PRODUCED BY
GEORGE MARTIN

STEREO
THE
LONG
AND
WINDING
ROAD
(Lennon/
McCartney)

THE
BEATLES
Maclen Music
3:40
2832
(S45-X47181)
Reproduced
for disc by
PHIL
SPECTOR
Recorded
in England

Mfgd. by Apple Records

FOR YOU BLUE
(Harrison)
Mfgd. by Apple Records
Recorded in England

2832
(S45-X47182)

MFD. BY APPLE RECORDS, INC.

STEREO

THE BEATLES
Reproduced for disc by
PHIL SPECTOR
Harrison Songs Inc.
2:33

White continues, "The box set was devised by Apple and released in the U.K. and Canada in that format, using our Capitol 6000 series as the release valve. The only thing we did was at our order control meeting we set the initial order and a sales plan. We probably ordered 5,000 copies and ended up selling 12-15,000 in Canada. The States released it as a single album where it charted BIG."

Although Canadian sales were no where near the four million sold in the U.S., the album performed well on the Canadian charts, topping the RPM Music Weekly 100 Albums chart for seven weeks. While Capitol set the deluxe album's list price at $10.98, many retailers sold it at a reduced price. Freimart priced it at $7.98, which was only a dollar more than the list price for *Abbey Road*. RPM's review in its June 6 issue gave stores pragmatic advice: "Don't fight it. Stock heavy. As if disc wasn't enough, Apple includes 164 page beautifully coloured booklet containing shots of famous four in recording studio. Phil Spector touch adds that extra finesse that should bring this fine producer back to where he belongs." The Canadian box set for *Let It Be* would prove to be a fitting finale for the Beatles run of albums in Canada, which began when Paul White released *Beatlemania! With The Beatles* on November 25, 1963.

Unlike the album, the *Let It Be* film was never popular with Beatles fans in Canada, perhaps because the group had already broken up by the time it was released. The May 19 Ottawa Journal newspaper ran a brief review of *Let It Be* by film critic Frank Daley, who observed that unlike his experience with previous Beatles films, there was no line up and there were few people paying to see the film. Before Beatles fans in Ottawa knew it, the film had come and gone. It was the same in other Canadian cities. The Canadian News Report in the June 13 Billboard stated that "The Beatles' Let It Be movie closed after only one week in downtown Toronto because of poor attendance."

I, like many fellow Canadians, didn't see the *Let It Be* film during its initial limited run. I'm not sure why I missed it, but I had to wait until the movie came back at Christmas, this time listed as a second feature to the James Bond film *On Her Majesty's Secret Service*. A few days after Christmas 1970, I went to the Mayfair Theatre in Ottawa to see the double bill of Bond and the Beatles. As strange as that sounds, the first James Bond film, *Dr. No*, and the Beatles first single, "Love Me Do," were both released in the U.K. on October 5, 1962. While I had enjoyed the group's previous up-beat films and loved the music on the *Let It Be* album, I knew going in that the Beatles had officially broken up.

The Bond film screened at 1:15 PM and was absolutely thrilling, living up to the Bond franchise's reputation. I was always a fan of Diana Rigg from The Avengers days. George Lazenby came across as a cool new James Bond. After watching Bond's latest adventure, *Let It Be* was up on the big screen at 3:40 PM. Of course I was excited to see the Beatles, but after 20 or 30 minutes I realized it was NOT THRILLING. Having just seen Bond, James Bond, *Let It Be* was, by comparison, a slow motion drag. I had read in our Ottawa newspapers all about Yoko Ono breaking up the Beatles, and there she was in the studio with them. I was a witness to the breakup all over again. The Beatles were getting divorced in front of my eyes. Earlier I had seen Bond best Blofeld in the Swiss Alps, followed by the tragic death of his new bride. Now I was watching the death of the Beatles. *Let It Be* was so far different from my first visual experience of seeing the Beatles perform on TV in England in 1963. Realizing the perils and bus transfers awaiting me on my upcoming journey home through a winter blizzard, I called it quits like the Beatles and walked out of the theater without ever seeing the rooftop concert! If only I had known about the film's magical ending. As I walked home in the snow, I reflected on seven years of incredible Beatles music. Now it was time to let it be and move on.

1970: The One After 1969
(Beginnings and Endings)

by Al Sussman

December 31, 1969. A decade that had begun in the aftermath of the often-sleepy but subtly-revolutionary 1950s had finally come to an end. The world was a very different place this day from the world of January 1, 1960. Change, both good and bad, had transformed the lives of millions of people in the 1960s and would continue to do so in the coming years. The 1969 Man of the Year awards bestowed by Time magazine and Rolling Stone were indicative of the cultural divide of late sixties. Time named The Middle Americans as Man and Woman of the Year, while Rolling Stone honored John Lennon, seen on the cover with Yoko Ono and doves. In November 1969, President Nixon had asked the "Silent Majority" to support his effort to end the Vietnam War "in a way that we could win the peace." The Woodstock Nation had other ideas for peace, but its innocence fell apart on December 6 with the violence at Altamont. Still, as 1970 began, it was a time to set aside "yesterday's broken dreams" and look "to better times and brighter days," as the Supremes would soon sing in "Up The Ladder To The Roof," their first post-Diana Ross hit. It was time for new beginnings, and some endings as well, as we stood on the threshold of the 1970s.

Of course, the new decade wouldn't begin with a completely clean slate. The turbulence that had dominated the last years of the 1960s and the war responsible for so much of that upheaval both continued apace, but minus the uplifting "miracles" of 1969. The triumph of Apollo 11 and man's first steps on the moon was counterbalanced by the near-disaster of Apollo 13. The good vibes sent out by the aesthetic success of Woodstock, already stunted by the bad trip of Altamont, was nearly snuffed out by the fiasco that was the Powder Ridge rock festival. The baseball world champion New York Mets ran out of miracles and were a mediocre team in 1970. And the Beatles, who had worked as a cohesive unit in the studio in recording *Abbey Road*, almost immediately began drifting further apart in the closing months of 1969, while still giving the public impression of an ongoing unit.

Indeed, on January 3, 1970, Paul McCartney, George Harrison and Ringo Starr gathered at the EMI Studios on the street they had immortalized the previous autumn for the first Beatles recording session since the final *Abbey Road* sessions in August 1969. The nearly-year-old *Get Back* album was being re-purposed, with the TV documentary filmed during the January 1969 rehearsals and recording sessions expanded into a feature film. It included a segment recorded during the Twickenham studio rehearsals of John Lennon and Yoko Ono waltzing to a short Harrison tune called "I Me Mine," which wasn't subsequently recorded during the Apple Studio sessions, so a proper recording was needed. The Lennons were in Denmark on an extended New Year's holiday, but Paul, George and Ringo convened at their longtime recording home, EMI's Studio Two. A rather long session for one song produced a minute and 34-second recording of "I Me Mine" that would be expanded by Phil Spector when he was given the job of putting together an album companion to the *Let It Be* film.

The next day, there was another lengthy session to overdub new backing vocals, a new Harrison guitar solo and brass and cello accompaniment scored by George Martin onto "Let It Be," which would be the next single and the title song of the film and the album. There would be another pass at Glyn Johns' latest version of the *Get Back* album on January 5, a Harrison vocal overdub onto "For You Blue" three days later, and Spector's entrance into the project in March. But it would be 24 years before McCartney, Harrison and Starr would be together in a studio again for what would be called a Beatles recording session. Meanwhile, the January 21 Rolling Stone ran an article titled "Beatles Splitting? Maybe, Says John" that provided the first public hints in America that a Beatles breakup was a possibility.

By mid-January, Apple's Badfinger single of the Paul McCartney-written-and-produced "Come And Get It" had been released and Ringo had resumed sessions for his first solo album, a collection of pop standards called *Sentimental Journey*, with George Martin serving as producer. And, on January 27, Lennon returned to Abbey Road Studios to record a new single, "Instant Karma," with a Plastic Ono Band lineup of George Harrison on lead guitar, Klaus Voormann on bass, Alan White on drums, Billy Preston on keyboards and production by Phil Spector in his first direct work with any of the Beatles. The single was recorded and mixed that day and released in the U.K. on February 6 and on February 20 in the U.S. "Instant Karma" peaked at number five in Britain and number three in America.

While all this was happening in Beatleworld, January 5 saw the debut of a new daily soap opera on ABC-TV called All My Children, which would become one of television's longest-running soaps. A tempestuous soap opera of another kind ended on January 15 with the final performance of Diana Ross with the Supremes at the Frontier In Las Vegas. Ms. Ross would go on to great success in the 1970s while the group, with new lead Jean Terrell, would have several early 1970s hits, but nothing like their 1960s heyday with Ross. And, by the end of January, a group that Ross claimed to have discovered, Gary, Indiana's Jackson 5, had their first of a string of number one singles with "I Want You Back."

The long-running (since September 1969) trial of a group of high-profile radicals who were collectively labeled the Chicago Seven ended on February 18 with the jury finding them not guilty of conspiring to riot during the Democratic Convention in Chicago in August 1968. Although a few of the defendants were convicted of crossing state lines with intent to riot, those convictions were overturned nearly three years later due to the adversarial behavior of Judge Julius Hoffman. Two of the more publicity-hungry of the Chicago Seven, Jerry Rubin and Abbie Hoffman, would latch onto John & Yoko two years later and lead them through the Lennons' radical-chic period in New York.

Less than a month after the Chicago Seven trial ended, three members of the Weather Underground radical group were killed when a bomb they were making in the basement of a Greenwich Village townhouse exploded, destroying the building. Two surviving Weather Underground members escaped and eluded capture until the early 1980s.

A more positive form of social activism, the environmental movement, was an outgrowth of the outrage over the January 1969 Santa Barbara, California oil spill. An Environmental Rights Day was held on January 28, the first anniversary of the Union Oil blowout. The 1969 United Nations Educational, Scientific and Cultural Organization (UNESCO) Conference produced a proclamation creating a day to honor the earth and peace to be celebrated on the first day of spring, March 21. Then, Sen. Gaylord Nelson of Wisconsin proposed an Earth Day to be held on April 22 as a "teach-in." Over 20 million participated in the first Earth Day at educational facilities and in communities all over America. Earth Day has been observed all over the world every year since. By year's end, the U.S. Environmental Protection Agency had been established.

It had been six years since the Surgeon General's 1964 report on the dangers of smoking, which heavily contributed to the reduction of the percentage of adult American smokers from 42% in 1965 to 37% in 1970, where it stabilized. On April 1, Richard Nixon signed the Public Health Cigarette Smoking Act permanently banning cigarette advertising on TV and radio effective January 1, 1971. The ban and subsequent life style changes contributed to the percentage falling to 33% by 1980, 25% by 1990 and 14% by 2017.

By early March, sessions for Ringo's *Sentimental Journey* LP of old favorites of his mum and dad had been completed, along with the initial sessions for "It Don't Come Easy." Paul McCartney, who had recorded much of his first solo album on a four-track machine at his London home, finished the LP under more professional conditions, first at Morgan Studios and then at Abbey Road. On February 25, Apple had released a U.S.-only Beatles LP called *Hey Jude*, a collection of singles that had not appeared on any Capitol/Apple album in America. The main attraction for fans was to hear tracks like "Paperback Writer" and "Hey Jude" in stereo for the first time. The main attraction for the group, according to Allen Klein, was easy money from sales. And, on March 6, "Let It Be" was finally released as the first Beatles single of 1970 in the U.K., with the U.S. release a week later. On March 23, Spector, with Harrison sitting in, began working on a "re-produced" version of the album, now to be a de facto soundtrack of the film. Spector's involvement came at the suggestion of Klein and with the approval of Lennon and Harrison following Spector's production work on "Instant Karma." The climax of this assignment was a tempestuous April 1 session at EMI's Studio One at which Ringo played drums and Spector added orchestration to "I Me Mine," "The Long And Winding Road" and "Across The Universe" and a female chorus to the latter two tracks.

While the accompaniment on "I Me Mine" and "Across The Universe" was understated by Spector standards, the Spectorized "Long And Winding Road" was another matter. What had been a Ray Charles-influenced piano-driven ballad became an extravaganza in Spector's hands, complete with a full orchestra and a female chorus. McCartney, who had written the song, was not consulted regarding Spector's plans for the recording and this just added to the list of perceived offenses that were driving McCartney away from the band. The song was released as a U.S. followup single to "Let It Be" and had the feel of a farewell statement. It was the Beatles 20th and final U.S. No. 1 single.

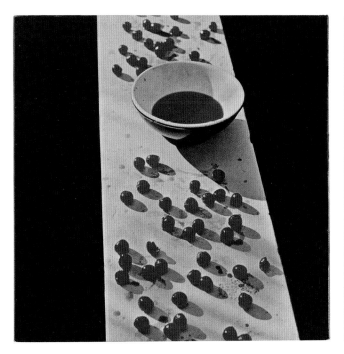
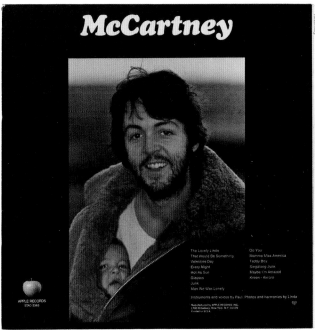

April and May of 1970 would be a momentous time, both in Beatleworld and beyond. In April's first full week, there were renewed rumors of a possible Beatles split, emanating from a McCartney self-interview that was to be included with media copies of his solo debut, *McCartney*. That Friday morning, April 10, the self-interview was officially released. Radio stations reported Paul had left the group. There was no formal announcement, just McCartney's interview, including his statement that he had no plans to work with the Beatles again. This, along with Lennon's previous hints of a possible breakup, convinced fans that the Beatles had indeed broken up.

Paul's album was released in the U.S. on April 20. By May 23, *McCartney* topped the Billboard Top LPs' chart for its first of three straight weeks at number one before being replaced by the Beatles *Let It Be*. Langdon Winner reviewed the album in the May 14 Rolling Stone. Although Winner called the songs on the LP "second rate" when compared to the best of the Beatles work, most were "very tasteful and fun to listen to." His favorites were "Maybe I'm Amazed," "Teddy Boy" and "Junk." While he liked the album, he cautioned that "the people of Troy also liked that wooden horse they wheeled through their gates until they discovered it was hollow inside and full of hostile warriors."

On April 11, the day after news broke that Paul was leaving the Beatles, America's third manned mission to the moon, Apollo 13, was launched from Florida's Kennedy Space Center with a crew of veteran Jim Lovell and space flight rookies Jack Swigert and Fred Haise. Since this was the second mission after Apollo 11's historic voyage the previous July, public interest had waned to the point where none of the three major television networks broadcast the live transmission from the command module and the lunar module on the night of April 13. Shortly after the astronauts signed off, the crew heard "a pretty loud bang" and Swigert and then Lovell told mission control, "Houston, we've had a problem here." There had been an explosion in the service module which caused the loss of all of its oxygen and most of its power. The lunar landing was scrubbed, the command module was shut down to save electricity for re-entry and the astronauts quickly moved into the lunar module Aquarius, using it as a lifeboat. The spacecraft continued traveling to the moon, using a free-return trajectory to swing around the moon and head back to earth, with NASA Mission Control and the crew improvising procedures to keep the lunar module livable and the spacecraft on course until they could re-power the command module for re-entry into Earth's atmosphere. For all involved, failure was not an option.

This crisis in space reawakened the public's interest and the world prayed as one for the safe return of the astronauts during the four days it took for the spacecraft to make the trip back to earth, splashing down in the South Pacific on April 17. Although the mission objective of landing on the moon did not happen, bringing the crew back alive was viewed by many as NASA's finest hour.

In the 1995 Ron Howard-directed film *Apollo 13*, McCartney's exit from the Beatles is used as a plot device, with one of Lovell's daughters being so angry at Paul for breaking up the group that she has to be ordered by her mother to leave her bedroom and go to Mission Control to see her father's live TV broadcast from space on the evening of April 13, 1970. Sharp-eyed Beatles fans noticed that Lovell's daughter is shown in her bedroom carrying a copy of the Beatles *Let It Be* LP, which could not have happened because the album was not released until more than a month later on May 18. While the film accurately depicted the Saturn V rocket, the damaged service module and the interior and exterior of the command and lunar modules, it misfired on its visual representation of the Beatles.

LIFE

JIM LOVELL AND APOLLO 13

FIFTY CENTS

APRIL 27, 1970

THE RETURN

Astronauts Praying After Splashdown

APRIL 27, 1970 50c

Newsweek

The Saga of Apollo 13

Astronauts Swigert, Lovell and Haise

One week after the successful splashdown of Apollo 13, Ringo's *Sentimental Journey* was issued in America on April 24, one month later than its British release. For Beatles fans, solo records by Paul and Ringo brought home the reality that the group might never record together again, although George told the Associated Press on April 29, "Everyone this year is trying to do his individual album, but after that I am ready to go back to work together again." While Ringo's album of big band standards was quaintly charming, its sales were significantly less than those of McCartney's debut. It did, however, peak at seven in the U.K., at 22 in Billboard, 21 in Cash Box and 20 in Record World. The record reportedly sold over 500,000 copies in the U.S. within its first two weeks.

In Rolling Stone, Greil Marcus wrote more of a brief commentary than a review, opening with, "*Sentimental Journey* may be horrendous, but at least it's classy." He then went on to question even that, but admitted "There is a certain charm to hearing Ringo swing immediately and finally fall flat on 'Stardust.'" Marcus completed his piece by running through the heart-warming and heart-breaking plot of the 1945 film *Sentimental Journey* (a favorite of late-night TV) and observing, "Not exactly 'Octopus Garden,' but what the hell." What the hell, indeed.

On April 20, President Nixon addressed the nation on television and radio to give a progress report on his administration's plan to bring a "just peace to Vietnam." Based on the training and equipping of South Vietnamese forces ("Vietnamization") substantially exceeding expectations, Nixon announced plans for the withdrawal of 150,000 American troops by spring of the following year. However, he acknowledged the risks of removing military forces and repeated his position that if increased enemy action jeopardized the remaining American troops in Vietnam, he would not hesitate to take strong and effective measures. On April 23, Secretary of State William Rogers told the House Appropriations Subcommittee that the Nixon administration had no intention of escalating the war with an invasion of Cambodia because a move into Cambodia would defeat the purpose of the Vietnamization program. Additionally, Secretary of Defense Melvin Laird felt that a Cambodian invasion would ignite large-scale domestic protests, comments which National Security Advisor Henry Kissinger branded "bureaucratic foot-dragging."

On April 26, Nixon decided to go ahead with a Cambodian incursion which he and Kissinger felt would strengthen the U.S.'s position at the slow-moving Paris peace talks, reduce allied casualties in South Vietnam and assure the continuation of the Vietnamization program. To the sizable portion of the American populace opposed to the war, this appeared to be simply an extension of the war. Nonetheless, on the evening of April 30, Nixon told a national TV audience "the time has come for action" and announced his decision to send American forces into Cambodia.

Not surprisingly, Laird's fears were confirmed when Nixon's announcement set off a firestorm of protest that weekend, particularly on college campuses. Students believed that Nixon had, like Lyndon Johnson before him, lied about drawing down U.S. involvement in Vietnam and was simply intent on expanding the war. There were student protests all over the U.S. that weekend, with particularly violent ones at Kent State University in Ohio. On Friday night, students leaving neighborhood bars near the campus began throwing beer bottles at police cars. Soon, confrontations between students and police were breaking out while others lit a bonfire in the street. The police used tear gas to disperse the crowd. Kent's mayor, Leroy Satrom, declared a state of emergency and closed all the bars in the vicinity of the campus. The next day, he called Ohio Gov. Jim Rhodes and asked for the deployment of National Guard troops to the university.

By the time the National Guard arrived on Saturday evening, a student demonstration had escalated to the point where one of the protesters' prime targets, the campus ROTC building, was set on fire. The next day, Mayor Satrom declared an 11 pm curfew in hopes of keeping students in their dorms. Before that could happen, another demonstration and a sit-in took place, with Guardsmen using tear gas and, in some cases, bayonets, to restore order. The ultimate confrontation came just after noon on Monday, May 4. About 2,000 demonstrators gathered on the university's Commons. When the Guardsmen tried to break up the demonstration with tear gas, the protesters threw the tear gas canisters back at them along with rocks. Then, 77 Guardsmen lined up and began coming towards the protesters, trying to move them away from the Commons. At about 12:25 pm, a number of the Guardsmen suddenly began firing on the protesters for anywhere from several seconds to a full minute. Two students who had participated in the protest, along with two who were simply walking to class, were shot dead and nine others were wounded. After the demonstration continued for a short time, at the urging of several faculty members, the remaining demonstrators dispersed.

The killings of the four students sent shock waves through the nation. At the White House, presidential press secretary Ron Ziegler gave the administration's reaction: "when dissent turns to violence, it invites tragedy." A Gallup poll taken after the shootings showed 58% of respondents blamed the students. Five days after the Kent State killings, though, over 100,000 demonstrators descended on Washington to protest the expansion of the war and the student killings. A post-Kent State student strike by some four million students led to the closing of over 400 colleges and universities around the U.S., including Kent State, which remained closed for six weeks.

The most high-profile pop culture reaction to what became known as the "Kent State massacre" was a single by the then-hottest group in the rock world, Crosby, Stills, Nash & Young. In the aftermath of the student killings, Neil Young wrote a new song called "Ohio" and the group recorded it, along with Stephen Stills' equally-mournful "Find The Cost Of Freedom," in an emotional May 21 session at the Record Plant in Hollywood. The single hit stores in early June, but only peaked at number 14 because many Top 40 stations wouldn't play it due to the song's opening line, "Tin soldiers and Nixon coming," and the provocative refrain "Four dead in Ohio" ("Why?" "How many more?").

LIFE

TRAGEDY AT KENT

**Cambodia and Dissent:
The Crisis of
Presidential Leadership**

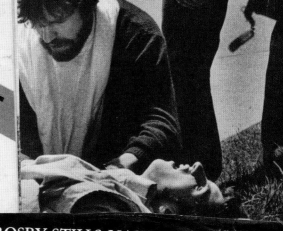

Newsweek

May 18, 1970 / 50 cents

NIXON'S HOME FRONT

CROSBY, STILLS, NASH & YOUNG
Ohio

Atlantic 2740

Tin Soldiers and Nixon Coming
We're Finally On Our Own
This Summer I Hear the Drumming
Four Dead in Ohio
Gotta Get Down To It
Soldiers Are Cutting Us Down
Should Have Been Done Long Ago
What if You Knew Her and Found Her Dead
    on the Ground
How Can You Run When You Know?

Neil Young—©1970 Cotillion/Broken Arrow

Find the
Cost of Freedom

Find the Cost of Freedom
Buried in the Ground
Mother Earth Will Swallow You
Lay Your Body Down

Stephen Stills—©1970 Goldhill Music

On Friday, May 8, four days after the Kent State shootings, a morning anti-war protest by about 1,000 high school and college students was held at the Federal Hall National Memorial in Manhattan. At around 11:45, the rally was crashed by 200 construction workers mobilized by the New York State AFL-CIO and soon-to-be Labor Secretary Peter Brennan. They broke up the rally and began chasing and beating protesters, with little resistance by the police. The construction workers then descended on City Hall, with one raising the American flag that had been lowered to half-staff after the Kent State killings to full-staff. There were further incidents that day in the so-called "Hard Hat Riot." That evening at Madison Square Garden, New York Knicks captain Willis Reed, playing hurt, was the inspirational leader as the Knicks defeated the Los Angeles Lakers for their first National Basketball Association championship, the Big Apple's third sports title in a year and a half, following the previous year's heroics by the Jets and Mets.

Also on May 8, nearly a year and a half after the recording sessions and just short of a month after McCartney's exit from the Beatles, the *Let It Be* album was finally released in the U.K. What would be the last studio album of new material by the Beatles bore scant resemblance to the "Beatles as nature intended" project recorded in January 1969 or any of Glyn Johns' versions of the *Get Back* album, especially with Spector's overdubs on "The Long And Winding Road," "I Me Mine" and "Across The Universe" and his heavy-handed production on the title track. Coming after McCartney's exit from the band and several months of bootleg recordings from the sessions, the *Let It Be* LP had an anti-climatic feel, something never experienced with the release of a new Beatles album. Nonetheless, the album topped the charts of all the British music magazines, including eight straight weeks in Melody Maker. When released in the U.S. on May 18, the album quickly hit number one in the three trade magazines, with four weeks at the top in Billboard, six in Cash Box and five in Record World. The RIAA certified sales of four million units.

On May 13, the *Let It Be* film, which started life as a TV special showing the Beatles at work creating a new album but morphed into a study of a band with major musical and philosophical differences, opened in New York, with a more general American release the following week. The highlight of the film was the band's last public performance on the rooftop of their London headquarters. The movie debuted in London and Liverpool on May 20. Unlike the London premieres of the three previous Beatles films, none of the now-splintered band attended any of the premieres.

By the time of the film's release, the former Beatles had moved on with their lives and careers. Paul and Linda McCartney, with baby Mary and Linda's daughter, Heather, retreated to their farm in Scotland. Little would be heard from Paul for the rest of the year. John & Yoko, after a four-week trial run at primal scream therapy with Arthur Janov in London, were invited by Janov to continue their treatment at his Primal Institute in Los Angeles. The Lennons left for California on April 30 and would be there for four months. A week earlier, George and Patti Harrison and Derek Taylor flew to New York to work on Billy Preston's second Apple album, *Encouraging Words*, do a radio interview with Howard Smith of the Village Voice and visit Apple's New York office (within Klein's ABKCO offices at 1700 Broadway, across the street from the Ed Sullivan Theater, site of the Beatles live U.S. debut just over six years before).

Harrison also got to hang out with Bob Dylan at Dylan's Greenwich Village townhouse and joined him in the Columbia Recording Studios in Manhattan where Dylan was recording his *New Morning* album. Material from the townhouse jam and the studio session has trickled out over the years, first in the underground and then in official releases, principally Dylan's archival *Bootleg Series* releases. *New Morning*'s lead-off track, "If Not For You," and the Harrison-Dylan co-written "I'd Have You Anytime" would soon be recorded by Harrison for his first post-Beatles album, *All Things Must Pass*.

In late May, Harrison recorded 15 songs on acoustic guitar as a preview for co-producer Phil Spector. Sessions for the album began on May 26, with Harrison joined by Eric Clapton on guitar, Bobby Whitlock on Keyboards, Carl Raddle on bass and Jim Gordon on drums. Recording continued through August 12, with sessions at Abbey Road, Trident and Apple. Other musicians included guitarists Dave Mason and Peter Frampton, keyboardists Billy Preston, Gary Wright, Gary Brooker and Tony Ashton, Bobby Keys on saxophone, Jim Price on trumpet, Pete Drake on pedal steel guitar, and Ringo and Alan White on drums. Starr struck up a conversation with Drake, who was based in Nashville. Knowing that Ringo, a country music fan since childhood, wanted to record a country album, Drake invited him to record in Nashville. On June 30 and July 1, Ringo recorded his *Beaucoups Of Blues* album at Music City Recorders with Drake as producer and Elvis Presley's longtime guitarist Scotty Moore as engineer. He was backed by the cream of Nashville's session players of the moment, including guitarist Jerry Reed.

While all this was going on, the Temptations' "Ball Of Confusion," released the week of the Kent State shootings, provided the perfect synopsis: "Segregation, determination, demonstration, integration, aggravation, humiliation, obligation to our nation/Ball of Confusion, that's what the world is today/Fear in the air, tension everywhere/ Unemployment rising fast, the Beatles' new record's a gas/and the only safe place to live is on an Indian reservation/ and the band played on." Bass singer Melvin Franklin's "and the band played on" implied no one was paying attention.

In the wake of Kent State, it did seem as if the United States was part of this "ball of confusion." Ten days after Kent State, Mississippi law enforcement officers killed two students and wounded 12 in a similar attack on demonstrating students at Jackson State University. On June 24, the U.S. Senate repealed the 1964 Tonkin Gulf Resolution, which had given LBJ the ability to escalate American's role in Vietnam. Two months later, protesters bombed Sterling Hall at the University of Wisconsin. On August 26, a Women's Strike for Peace was held on New York's Fifth Avenue. And three days later, a Chicano Moratorium against the war ended in a police riot in which three people were killed.

Conversely, on July 4, a supposedly non-partisan Honor America Day was held in Washington D.C., organized by Rev. Billy Graham (known as the President's preacher), hotel magnate Willard Marriott and comic Bob Hope (known for his USO shows entertaining the troops), with the blessing and, indeed the encouragement, of Richard Nixon. This "Middle America Woodstock" was held on the Mall between the Washington Monument and the Lincoln Memorial, the same ground as the 1963 civil rights March on Washington and several sixties anti-war demonstrations. The crowd was overwhelmingly middle-aged and white, but there were protesters present, upset with U.S. involvement in Vietnam and Cambodia, shouting anti-war slogans. Some waded naked or semi-naked in the reflecting pool and participated in a marijuana "smoke-in" during Graham's morning prayer service. That evening, approximately 350,000 attended a Hope-hosted entertainment program that included Kate Smith, Jack Benny, the New Christy Minstrels and Glen Campbell. To keep the protesters at bay, Capital police used tear gas that blew into the mainstream crowd causing a "mad stampede of weeping hippies and Middle Americans." Newsweek observed that "if the Heartland U.S.A. style of the affair was a far cry from Woodstock, it did generate a sort of soul of its own—a community of belief in God, flag and country." Rennie Davis of the Chicago Seven called the event "a Republican convention-war rally."

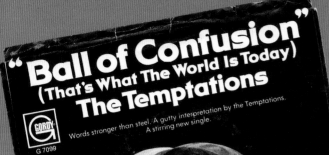

"Ball of Confusion"
(That's What The World Is Today)
The Temptations

GORDY
G 7099

Words stronger than steel. A gutty interpretation by the Temptations.
A stirring new single.

Newsweek

THE PRESIDENT'S PREACHER

Billy Graham and
The Surging
Southern Baptists

Newsweek

The Cambodian Campaign
WAS IT WORTH IT?

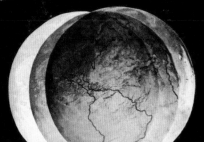

PEACE MAKER

"Ball of Confusion"
(That's What The World Is Today)
The Temptations

People movin' out
People movin' in
Why, because of the color of their skin
Run, run, run, but you sho' can't hide
An eye for an eye
A tooth for a tooth
Vote for me, and I'll set you free
Rap on brother, rap on
Well, the only person talkin'
'Bout love thy brother is the preacher
And it seems,
Nobody is interested in learnin'
But the teacher
Segregation, determination, demonstration,
Integration, aggravation,
Humiliation, obligation to our nation
Ball of Confusion
That's what the world is today

The sale of pills are at an all time high
Young folks walk around with
Their heads in the sky
Cities aflame in the summer time
And, the beat goes on

Air pollution, revolution, gun control,

Sound of soul
Shootin' rockets to the moon
Kids growin' up too soon
Politicians say more taxes will
Solve everything
And the band played on
So round 'n' round 'n' round we go
Where the world's headed, nobody knows
Just a Ball of Confusion
Oh yea, that's what the world is today

Fear in the air, tension everywhere
Unemployment rising fast,
The Beatles' new record's a gas
And the only safe place to live is
On an indian reservation
And the band played on
Eve of destruction, tax deduction,
City inspectors, bill collectors
Mod clothes in demand,
population out of hand
Suicide, too many bills, hippies movin'
To the hills
People all over the world, are shoutin'
End the war
And the band played on.

Copyright 1970 Jobete Music Company, Inc.

With a Woodstock sequel having been effectively outlawed by the elders of New York State's Sullivan County, the East Coast's best chance for a big-time rock festival that summer was the Powder Ridge Rock Festival at the Powder Ridge Ski Area in Middlefield, Connecticut over the weekend of July 31. A shadowy group of promoters promised a festival of 25 major rock acts, many of them Woodstock alumni, and a crowd of around 50,000 paying $20 for weekend tickets. When Middlefield obtained an injunction a few days before the festival, thousands of festival-goers had already arrived at the Powder Ridge grounds. The promoters disappeared and most of the performers failed to show, allegedly because they'd never been paid. Woodstock veteran Melanie and a few local bands performed for the 30,000 attendees. Given how little music there was, many attendees spent their time camping and getting high in an atmosphere that was closer to Altamont than Woodstock, complete with bad drugs and bad vibes. The promoters, who were suspected to have organized crime connections, promised a rescheduled festival, but nothing ever materialized and ticket holders never received any refunds.

The bad trip that was Powder Ridge seemed to be a metaphor for the rock world that summer and early fall. Already, on June 7, the Who became the first rock band to play the Metropolitan Opera House at New York's Lincoln Center, performing their rock opera *Tommy*. Unfortunately, the audience behaved as if they were at the legendary Fillmore rock venue instead of an opera house. The management was appalled. Between August 26-31, the final Isle of Wight Festival was held at Afton Down. The headliner for Sunday night was Jimi Hendrix, whose set was plagued by technical problems, of which there were many at the festival. It turned out to be one of Hendrix's final concert appearances. In the midst of a career transition, Hendrix suddenly died on the morning of September 18 from asphyxia, choking on his own vomit after taking an abnormal number of sleeping pills. He was 27 years old, the same age as Canned Heat's musical leader Al "Blind Owl" Wilson, who had died under similar circumstances on September 3 in Topanga Canyon, California. Then, just sixteen days after Hendrix's death, Janis Joplin, who was in the last stages of recording her second solo album after leaving Big Brother and the Holding Company, was found dead in a Hollywood motel room from an accidental overdose of heroin. Janis, too, was just 27. The deaths of three young, significant figures in the rock world, coupled with the breakups of the Beatles and Simon & Garfunkel and the Powder Ridge fiasco, made 1970 a grim year for rock, leading to renewed speculation about the purported "death of rock."

On the other hand, two of the biggest pop/rock stars of the 1970s had their career breakthroughs that fall. Elton John was an English singer/songwriter whose second album had been released in America early in the year, with its second single, "Your Song," released late in October. This followed a series of sensational performances by Elton late in August at the Troubadour in Los Angeles and just ahead of a great studio performance in New York that was broadcast live on November 17. "Your Song" reached the Top 10 on both sides of the Atlantic, while the *Elton John* LP made the Top Five in the U.S. and U.K. before year's end. This was just the beginning. Within three years, Elton John would be the biggest pop star in the world.

James Taylor was an Apple Records alumnus whose first album received critical acclaim but little commercial success before he and producer Peter Asher left Apple during Klein's purge. They ended up in the midst of the Southern California singer/songwriter scene and Taylor was signed by Warner Brothers. His first WB album, *Sweet Baby James*, was released around the same time as Elton's LP that February. The album and its mournful first single, "Fire And Rain," took their time building momentum. Both became U.S. Top Five successes that fall. By the spring of 1971, JT would be on the cover of Time magazine on his way to becoming the biggest of the decade's singer/songwriters.

A year of beginnings, endings and transitions accelerated as the months rolled by. In England, on June 18, the Conservative Party won the general election, with Edward Heath succeeding Harold Wilson as prime minister. Both had been name-checked in the Beatles 1966 "Taxman." On July 4, Casey Kasem's syndicated radio show American Top 40 debuted on five U.S. stations. At the end of July, newscaster Chet Huntley retired from his nightly TV news show with David Brinkley. John Chancellor would become Brinkley's new partner on the show that became the NBC Nightly News. On September 13, the first New York City Marathon was run, while six days later, the first Glastonbury Music Festival was held in England. In the U.S., the trailblazing Mary Tyler Moore Show debuted that night on CBS-TV.

On September 19, Pro Football, enjoying its first season after the NFL/AFL merger, came to prime time with the debut of Monday Night Football on ABC-TV. Keith Jackson did the play-by-play, while Howard Cosell and Don Meredith began their legendary teaming as analysts. That night, the Cleveland Browns beat the New York Jets, 31-21.

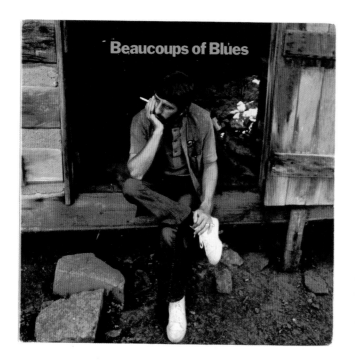

After four months of primal scream therapy, John & Yoko returned to London. On September 26 they began work on separate but connected albums at Abbey Road with Phil Spector co-producing. Lennon had written a number of deeply personal songs during his time with Janov and would record them over the next month, backed mainly by Ringo on drums and Voormann on bass. Spector's production was restrained compared with his work with Harrison. Both John's and George's album projects were wrapped up by the end of October. Meanwhile, Ringo released his second album of year, *Beaucoups Of Blues*, on September 25 in the U.K. and three days later in America. The Country & Western LP failed to chart in the U.K. and peaked at 65 in Billboard, 31 in Cash Box and 38 in Record World.

On October 12, three weeks before the mid-term elections, Nixon announced 40,000 troops would be coming home from Vietnam before Christmas, hoping this would demonstrate Vietnamization was working. On October 26, Garry Trudeau's satiric comic strip Doonesbury debuted in about two dozen U.S. newspapers. On November 3, Democrats swept the mid-terms, including little-known Jimmy Carter being elected governor of Georgia. Republican victories included Ronald Reagan, the new standard-bearer for conservatism, being re-elected governor of California.

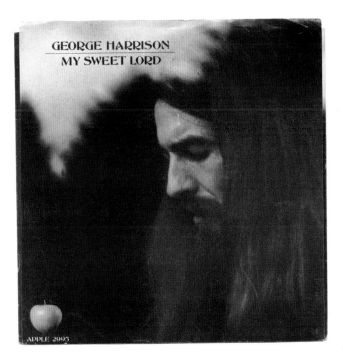

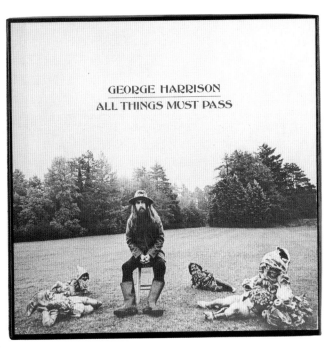

On November 23 came the first release from Harrison's 1970 recording sessions, the U.S. Apple single of "My Sweet Lord"/"Isn't It A Pity," followed four days later by the long-awaited release of Harrison's first post-Beatles album, *All Things Must Pass*. The long-player was a sprawling three-record set that included a disc of studio jams plus George and Ringo's birthday greeting for John, "It's Johnny's Birthday." Most of the tracks were produced in full "wall of sound" style by Spector with input from Harrison. A pleasant exception was "Apple Scruffs," a loving tribute to the female fans who waited outside Apple, Abbey Road and Trident Studios for their heroes. Some of the songs, including the title track "Isn't It A Pity," "Let It Down" and "Hear Me Lord," had originally been auditioned during the *Get Back* sessions nearly two years earlier. So there had to be sweet satisfaction for George when "My Sweet Lord" became the first solo Beatle single to reach number one in the U.S., remaining there for four weeks, and *All Things Must Pass* accomplished a rarity in that era, a Top Five debut on Billboard's album chart in mid-December. Harrison's album outperformed all other 1970 solo Beatles releases, topping the Billboard chart for seven straight weeks. In Rolling Stone, Ben Gerson called *All Things Must Pass* "both an intensely personal statement and a grandiose gesture, a triumph over artistic modesty, even frustration" and dubbed it "the *War and Peace* of rock and roll."

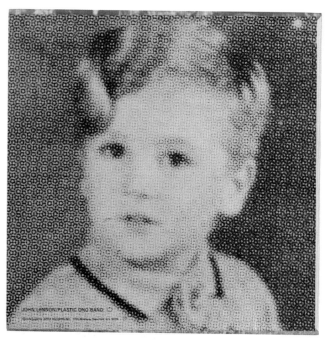

On December 11, John & Yoko's individual post-Janov albums, *John Lennon/Plastic Ono Band* and *Yoko Ono/Plastic Ono Band*, were released simultaneously in the U.S. and the U.K. John's album was a stark, bare wires musical primal scream with little of the commercial appeal of *All Things Must Pass*, though it drew critical raves upon release. In future years the album would be considered a forerunner of 1990s grunge rock. The record peaked at number eight in the U.K. and number six in Billboard, four in Cash Box and two in Record World. Standout tracks included "Mother," "Hold On," "Working Class Hero," "Love" and "Look At Me." The track that hit fans the hardest was "God" in which Lennon laid waste to everything he once believed in, including the Beatles, and declared "The dream is over." Shortly before the album's release, John & Yoko sat down with Jann Wenner of Rolling Stone for what became a no-holds-barred conversation on December 8. The interview would run in two parts in Rolling Stone early in 1971.

On New Year's Eve 1970, Paul McCartney sued his former bandmates, Allen Klein and Apple Records to dissolve the Beatles partnership in London's High Court. It appeared that the dream was indeed...over. We were left with words of wisdom from Paul, "let it be," from John, "you just have to carry on," and from George, "all things must pass."

ALL THINGS MUST PASS

Early 1970: Six Months in Song and Film

by Frank Daniels

Fans of popular music from the years surrounding 1970 will certainly be aware of at least ten of the #1 songs from the first six months of the year — two of which were Beatles songs. These include records released in late 1969 as well as fast-moving singles that leapt up the charts. "Raindrops Keep Fallin' On My Head" by B.J. Thomas topped the Billboard Hot 100 for the first four weeks of 1970. This was followed by one-week appearances at the top by Jackson 5's "I Want You Back" and "Venus" by Shocking Blue, a Dutch rock band. The latter single was number one for three weeks in Cash Box and Record World. "Venus" was the only American hit for Shocking Blue, but it was the song that had people all around the world shouting "She's got it" along with lead singer Mariska Veres. The song was later recorded by several other artists (including Bananarama), none of which touches the original.

By the time we reach 1970, Sly and the Family Stone had been scoring with a string of hits that began with "Dance To The Music" in 1967. The group's first number one had been 1968's "Everyday People," making "Thank You" their second chart-topper (two weeks in Billboard and Record World). The single was also noteworthy as it was marketed as a double A-side, and while "Everybody Is A Star" was not the attention-getting side as far as the pop charts were concerned, it was that side that the soul charts considered the top side of the single — all the way to #1. However, Sly Stone had begun using cocaine and PCP, and he used heavily during 1970. Together with his struggles with other members of the band, Stone's drug use dragged the group's output down to this single alone for the next year. His 1971 album, *There's A Riot Goin' On*, abandons the optimistic, cooperative vibe found on the Family Stone's earlier records for a more pessimistic view of life. Considering that the Family Stone had built their career on good vibes, it is somewhat ironic that the long-awaited *Riot* LP was the band's only #1 album. After the accompanying single, "Family Affair," Sly and the Family Stone never had another top-ten hit on the pop charts.

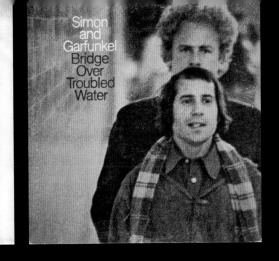

"Bridge Over Troubled Water," which topped the Billboard Hot 100 for six weeks, was the title track and lead single for Simon and Garfunkel's award-winning album. Paul Simon claims that once the song finally came to him, it was revealed via inspiration in a "shocking moment." Simon had written the song in a high register, which his partner, Art Garfunkel, could sing easily. Garfunkel remembers telling Simon that the song was so beautiful that Paul ought to sing it himself. Simon replied, "I wrote it for you," but on the completed recording the two sing together on the last verse. That was appropriate, for Simon was thinking of his wife, Peggy, when he wrote that verse. With the Spector-like construction, the song builds to a pounding crescendo. Its message is a promise of companionship, of care and of true friendship.

Although the album won the Grammy award for Album of the Year, and the single won five Grammys including Record of the Year, *Bridge Over Troubled Water* was Simon and Garfunkel's *Abbey Road*—a combination of magnum opus and last gasp. The highly-acclaimed duo that had begun their career as "Tom and Jerry" simply stopped recording together. They performed together a couple of times in the early 1970s, but they created no new recordings until their 1975 single, "My Little Town." Despite several attempts at reuniting, including a 1982 album of their September 1981 Central Park concert, Simon and Garfunkel have remained apart, and if anything, their personal relationship has soured further. Simon said in 2016 that they would never play together again, and as of this writing, they have not done so — and Paul Simon has stopped touring. Nineteen seventy was the year of their transition.

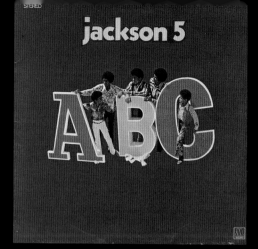

"Bridge Over Troubled Water" was knocked from the top spot in Billboard and Cash Box by the Beatles "Let It Be" single, while in Record World it was first replaced by "The Rapper" by the Jaggerz. The song was written by band member Dominic Ierace, who later recorded as Donnie Iris ("Ah! Leah"). The musical flair was infectious, and the lyrics about a predator who "knows what he's after" struck home with their listeners. It would be their only hit.

The Jackson 5 helped transform Motown from its Sixties sound to its place in the 1970s as the leader in soul music. Their second Motown single, "ABC," was their second chart-topper (two weeks in Billboard), coming on the heels of "Let It Be." Their record earned them a crowd of avid fans. Nearly every record they recorded for Motown made the Top Forty, proving that, for the Jackson 5, recording hits was as "easy as 1-2-3."

In Billboard, "ABC" was followed by "American Woman" by the Guess Who, a group of Canadians who had several hits on both sides of the border. Lenny Kravitz later recorded the song for the 1999 film *Austin Powers: The Spy Who Shagged Me*. Cash Box and Record World also charted the song at number one, but not until first giving top honors to "Spirit In The Sky" for two weeks in early May. Falling perfectly within the "Jesus" movement sweeping across popular music, Norman Greenbaum's record was so memorable that it continues to appear in television programs and movies. One of the song's most distinctive features is the sound that Greenbaum got out of his Fender Telecaster. "Spirit in the Sky" was his only hit. A few years later, the money was gone and he was cooking hamburgers.

Another song with a positive message was Ray Stevens' "Everything Is Beautiful," which topped the Billboard charts for two weeks and Cash Box for one. Stevens was usually associated with the novelty genre, enjoying hits with "Ahab the Arab" (1961) and "Gitarzan" (1969) before recording an album of modern standards that included two songs from *Abbey Road*. "Everything Is Beautiful," one of just two on the LP that Stevens authored, grabbed everyone's attention. Incorporating a verse from a recent devotional song, the lyrics speak against bigotry in all its forms because "there is none so blind as he who will not see." Stevens would have one more number one, the novelty classic "The Streak," which captured a moment in time when running naked through public events was the latest social craze.

While Stevens was telling us "Everything Is Beautiful," Tyrone Davis wanted to "Turn Back The Hands Of Time." His soul classic topped the Record World pop chart and the Billboard R&B Singles chart for two weeks. Also around this time, Simon and Garfunkel topped the Cash Box and Record World charts with "Cecilia," pulled from their *Bridge Over Troubled Water* LP.

The first half of 1970 ended the same on all three charts: two weeks at the top for the Beatles new single, "The Long And Winding Road," replaced by the Jackson 5's "The Love You Save" at number one on June 27. That same week, the Temptations "Ball Of Confusion (That's What The World Is Today)" reached its peak position of number three in Billboard, all the while telling us what we already knew: "The Beatles new record's a gas."

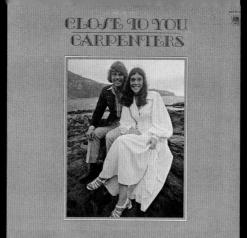

Two selections from women with astounding voices were released during the first half of the year, but did not reach the top until later. Freda Payne's classic "Band Of Gold," written by former Motown writers and producers Holland-Dozier-Holland (under the pseudonym Edythe Wayne) and Ron Dunbar, topped the Record World chart on July 25, 1970. Released on H-D-H's Invictus label, the song captured the magic and groove of sixties Motown and became Payne's signature song. "Close To You" was the first song from the Carpenters mainly associated with the voice of Karen Carpenter. It hit number one in Billboard on July 25 and remained there for four weeks. The song also topped the Cash Box and Record World charts for two weeks. The Carpenters went on to have a dozen Top Ten hits. Their six albums released between 1970 and 1976 earned gold records from the RIAA. Three Dog Night's "Mama Told Me (Not To Come)" was issued in May and worked its way up to number one on all three charts in July. The group's atmospheric version of the Randy Newman song was their second biggest hit behind 1971's "Joy To The World."

Many popular singles from the period never made it to number one, but nonetheless are an important part of the history of rock music. These include: the double A-sided smash, "Travelin' Band" and "Who'll Stop the Rain," from Creedence Clearwater Revival; the positive and inspiring "United We Stand" by Brotherhood of Man; and noteworthy and singable tracks from White Plains ("My Baby Loves Lovin'"), Vanity Fare ("Hitchin' A Ride") and the Chairmen of the Board ("Give Me Just A Little More Time," another H-D-H hit on Invictus). All of these songs were competition for one another in that short time span, with each of them becoming a classic record in its own way.

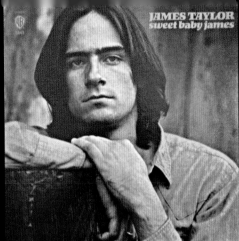

The 1960s brought about the advent of albums that were enjoyed as albums by popular music fans, and by early 1970, artists were recording albums that were intended to be heard as a whole. Irish singer/songwriter Van Morrison's *Moondance* was a critical success with classic songs such as the title track, "Crazy Love," "Caravan," "Into The Mystic" and "Come Running," all of which became staples on FM radio. Having left the Apple label with producer Peter Asher, James Taylor was an immediate success at Warner Brothers where his first album, *Sweet Baby James*, produced two hit singles. Both albums made Rolling Stone's list of greatest albums of all time.

In that same period, you might have walked into a record shop and picked up brand new copies of the Who's great concert album, *Live At Leeds*, which was accompanied by a packet full of inserts as though the record was a souvenir of the performance. *Morrison Hotel* was a return to form and a number four Billboard LP for the Doors. Highlights included "Roadhouse Blues," "Waiting For The Sun" and "Land Ho!" The supergroup Crosby, Stills, Nash & Young released *Déjà Vu* in March. The album yielded three hit singles, but none of them topped the charts, although the album did for one week, its music best enjoyed as a total listening experience.

Déjà Vu was one of only six albums that topped the charts during the first half of 1970. Also holding down the top spot were two 1969 holdovers, *Abbey Road* (three weeks) and *Led Zeppelin II* (six weeks), Simon and Garfunkel's *Bridge Over Troubled Water* (ten weeks), *McCartney* (three weeks) and *Let It Be* (three weeks plus one week in July).

An album of near-instrumentals from Booker T. & the M.G.'s followed up their success in 1969 with the unthinkable: their reimagined version of the Beatles *Abbey Road* album. Just as famous for its cover photo taken outside the Stax Records studio in Memphis, *McLemore Avenue* took the Beatles record that Booker T. described as "courageous" and took it a step further. It is far more than a tribute album. It has its own groove and is dominated by medleys that transition from one sound to another. Beatles fans — and soul-music aficionados — can visit the Stax Museum on McLemore Avenue and have their picture taken crossing the street like the M.G.'s did. You will find this a much simpler task than braving the traffic to cross Abbey Road in London, but, of course, you should do both if you can.

Apple achieved significant success in early 1970 with albums in the Billboard Top LP's charts by the Beatles, John Lennon, Paul McCartney, Ringo Starr and Badfinger. These albums were as different as they could be. Badfinger's *Magic Christian Music* had three songs from the film *The Magic Christian*: the hit single "Come And Get It," "Rock Of All Ages" and "Carry On Till Tomorrow." Paul lent a hand or two on all three. As for the film itself, it was a satirical romp that featured Ringo Starr and starred Peters Sellers. The Plastic Ono Band's *Live Peace In Toronto 1969* is actually the first post-breakup solo-Beatles album, although the public did not know at the time of its release that John had already left the group to chart his own course. Paul's *McCartney* album was essentially 100% Paul, although some of the tracks had harmony vocals from wife Linda. Ringo's *Sentimental Journey* was a sentimental journey through big band standards produced by George Martin. We would hear from Harrison and John (again) by year's end.

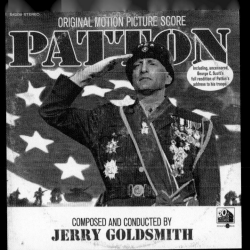

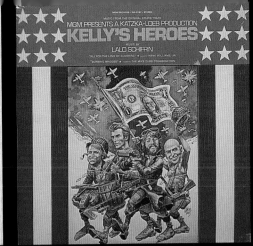

In December 1969, John Lennon was determined to focus on an end to war. It was then that he decided that "Everyone who is into peace and awareness will regard the New Year as Year One A.P. — for After Peace." The new year, 1970, would not be the first year of world peace. It was, however, transitional not only in music but in other areas as well. Several of the movies from early 1970 revolved around a war-and-peace theme. The most serious approach appeared in the saga of General George S. Patton. Premiering in February, *Patton* was immediately noteworthy as an outstanding and almost unprecedented production — being half biopic and half war documentary. It won the Academy Award for the Best Picture of 1970. Another war film, *MASH*, was a poignant farce about the Korean Conflict. The Robert Altman film earned several awards and spawned a long-running TV series. Some well-remembered lines appeared at the end of the movie. Hawkeye Pierce had stolen a jeep on his way to his assignment at the 4077th MASH unit. At the end, as he drives off after being discharged, Col. Blake asks Radar O'Reilly, "Did Hawkeye steal that jeep?" Radar replies, "No, sir. That's the one he came in." Everything evens out, you see.

Another movie from early 1970 that was about war but wasn't really about war was *Kelly's Heroes*. The light comedy features an astonishing ensemble cast who put together a unit in Nazi-occupied France to satisfy their own greed by robbing from the German National Gold Reserves. In the process, they wind up liberating a French town from Nazi oppression, as a general co-opts the line, "History waits for no man." The film was loosely based on the theft of 730 gold bars and other valuables by members of the U.S. armed forces and German civilians in June 1945.

If these varied depictions of armed conflict seem to go in several directions, other movies take an equally serious look at society from different angles. *The Boys In The Band* took a ground-breaking play about gay life to the screen. *A Man Called Horse* adapted a 1950 short story for the big screen, becoming the first American Western to portray Native Americans as protagonists; neither they nor the Europeans are the heroes of the story. Another film, *Beneath The Planet Of The Apes*, first seems to be the same bit of science fiction as the first movie in the franchise. However, this second film focuses more on the conflict between apes and the mutant humans who seem to worship a nuclear warhead. Its message for the viewers appears at the denouement: "In one of the countless billions of galaxies in the universe lies a medium-sized star, and one of its satellites—a green and insignificant planet—is now dead."

Two Mules For Sister Sara stars Shirley MacLaine and Clint Eastwood. The film tells the story of an American Mercenary in Mexico (Eastwood) who winds up helping a woman dressed as a nun (MacLaine). Eastwood won a Laurel award for his performance. Although he was then primarily known for his appearances in Westerns, his Dirty Harry character was just one year away, leading to the films *Dirty Harry* (1971), *Magnum Force* (1973), *The Enforcer* (1976), *Sudden Inpact* (1983) and *The Dead Pool* (1988). Our final movie review looks at the beginning of another lengthy franchise. *Airport* launched the golden age of a genre: the disaster film. The movie's success led not only to several more *Airport* films, but also to disaster plots in other milieu: *The Poseidon Adventure* (1972, a ship capsizes); *The Towering Inferno* (1974, a skyscraper burns); *Earthquake* (1974); *Black Sunday* (1977, a blimp operator becomes a terrorist threatening the Super Bowl); *Avalanche* (1978); and *Hurricane* (1979) – among others.

The comic book genre transitioned in 1970 from its Silver Age of the late fifties and sixties to a new Bronze Age that centered on realistic art coupled with the social relevance of characters that were not previously thought of in that capacity. Leading the way were writer Denny O'Neil and artist Neal Adams, who adapted Batman into a serious crime-solver (Detective Comics #395), moving away from the comedy of the 1950s and 1960s. The dynamic duo of O'Neil and Adams also sent Green Lantern and Green Arrow on a pilgrimage to help address issues like racism in America (Green Lantern #76). Later that year, Superman and Jimmy Olsen received similar modernization, and the following year, both Spider-Man and Green Lantern addressed the urgency of drug addiction.

Like any six months, these six months lasted just—six months. During that short span of time from January 1 to June 30, 1970, transitions took place that shifted the direction of rock music away from the trends of the sixties and toward the singer/songwriters of the early 1970s. As this period came to a close, the Next Big Thing was about to release his first hit single for Uni Records ("Your Song"). His name was Elton John, whose first British album had not been released in the States, but who was about to leave an indelible mark on the 1970s and beyond.

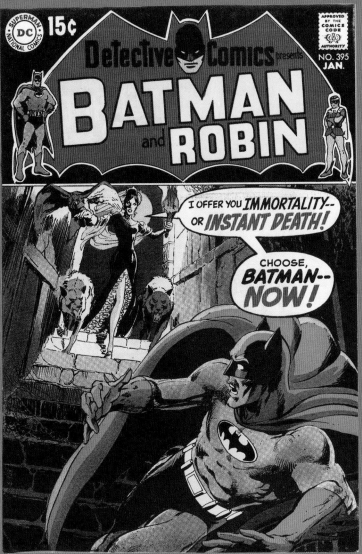

Apple Records

2764

THE BEATLES

Let it be

Apple Records

2832

THE BEATLES

THE LONG AND
WINDING ROAD

From The Beatles' Motion Picture "Let It Be"

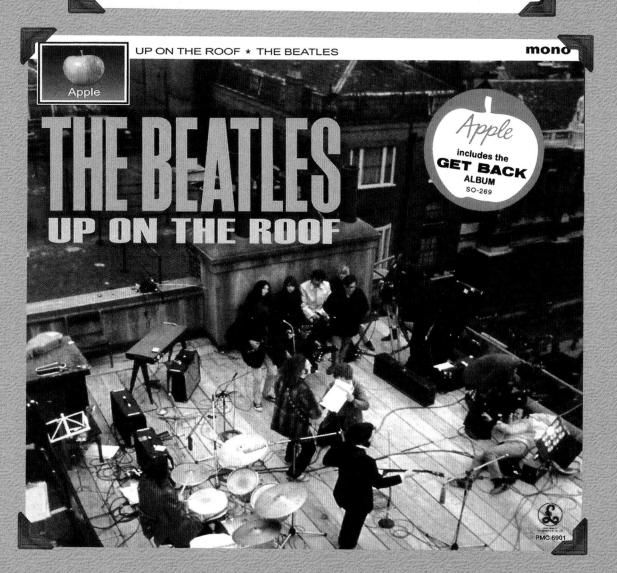

UP ON THE ROOF ★ THE BEATLES

mono

Apple

THE BEATLES
UP ON THE ROOF

Apple
includes the
GET BACK
ALBUM
SO-269

PMC 6901

BOOTLEG CD COVER SHOWING THE BEATLES UP ON THE ROOF
PLUS YOKO ONO, MAUREEN STARKEY, KEN MANSFIELD AND CHRIS O'DELL (SEATED),
MICHAEL LINDSAY-HOGG (STANDING) AND KEVIN HARRINGTON (KNEELING).

You could have hosed me down with ice water and I wouldn't have left the roof that cold winter's day. People look at me in disbelief when I say it was just another day at the office. But I thought going up there was going to be another one of the almost daily crazy and exciting events that could happen at Apple's 3 Savile Row headquarters. Afterwards I realized it was much more than that.

It was very cold and windy up there, especially for an unprepared southern Californian wearing just a white trench coat with a thin lining [shown seated in the photo on previous page]. About half way through that 42-minute concert I did start getting the chills...not the kind that makes you shiver from the cold wind, but a warm fuzzy kind of chill that went through my entire body. Something special was going on before my eyes. I was among about a dozen people in the sweet spot of a small dirty roof on January 30, 1969 ... mere feet away as one of the most historical moments in rock and roll was unfolding before me. The sensation I was experiencing was not in knowing that this would be the last time these four magnificent men would be performing together. It wasn't because I knew they would be breaking up soon after that. It was not any of those things because I didn't know any of that...it was something that was felt.

Yoko Ono, Maureen Starkey, Chris O'Dell and I followed the band down the stairs after the brief concert without saying a word to each other. I flew back to L.A. the next morning still trying to absorb or understand what had happened the day before. I went up there with the Beatles that day without expectations and unknowingly left a piece of myself on that roof forever. The Beatles went up those narrow stairs without a sound check. They came back down with a soul check.

Ken Mansfield
Former U.S. Manager of Apple Records
Author of *The Roof: The Beatles Final Concert*

It was a cold and grey January day in 1969, but the weather wasn't a concern to me. More of a worry was actually getting the Beatles gear up onto the roof for the recording. It proved to be a bit of a struggle. Billy Preston's piano and Paul's speaker were huge and wouldn't go round the turn at the top of the stairs. Mal Evans and I had to haul them through the skylight.

Now set up, the boys started to play and everything seemed to be going all right until John needed a music stand to hold up his lyrics for "Dig A Pony." What to do? No spare music stand. We hadn't needed one in the basement studio and even if we had one, there was no time to get it. The only thing I could do was hold the lyrics for him. As the performance was being filmed, it was tricky to find a place to position the lyrics. I couldn't stand next to John's right in the way of Ringo and I couldn't stay to the left in the way of George, so I had to improvise and make like a music stand and kneel! [shown in the photo on previous page].

Looking at all of the people who had started to appear on the opposite roofs and out of the office windows was amazing. It seemed that half of London had come to see the boys play. But I had the best seat in the house. I was having a great time.

The band played their songs as planned, but then I heard that Jimmy the doorman was keeping the police at bay. Next Mal appeared on the roof talking to a copper and after some discussion Mal came over and switched George's amp off. George cheekily switched it back on, but we were told if the band didn't stop playing they would all be arrested. So that was it, the end of the gig and back to the studio. It was actually pretty good to get off that cold roof.

Kevin Harrington
Beatles Equipment Manager
Author of *Who's The Redhead On The Roof....?*

On the morning of January 30 I was sitting in my office at Apple, despondent and depressed because I, like the other Apple staff members, wasn't allowed on the roof for the Beatles concert. We were told that the structure was too weak to hold all of us. In the days before, I had to endure the pounding and scraping in the hallway outside my office as workmen erected support poles to shore up the roof. With every nail that was hammered in, I was reminded that something huge and monumental was about to happen and I was going to miss it.

All of a sudden, Tony Richmond, the head camera man, stood at the door and asked, "Are you going up?" When I miserably replied that I couldn't, as only essential staff was allowed, Tony smiled and said, "Well, you're coming along as my assistant then." Although concerned that I would be asked to leave, I grabbed my coat and followed him up the rickety steps to the roof. As Tony set up his camera equipment, I sat on a bench next to him by the building's chimney. Ken Mansfield sat next to me and said, "Damn, it's cold up here," his teeth chattering.

Paul was the first Beatle to appear, followed by Ringo and Maureen, who sat next to Ken on the bench. John and Yoko arrived a few minutes later, with Yoko sitting next to Maureen on the far end of the bench [shown in the photo on page 102]. Within minutes, the band started playing. The icy wind kept blowing their hair into their faces. They all blew on their fingers and grumbled about how "bloody cold" it was. After every song, Maureen would clap and softly call out, "Yay!"

Just before the police came onto the roof and ended the concert, I stood up and peeked over the edge of the roof at the crowd below. The look of wonder on their faces was something to behold.

Chris O'Dell
Apple Assistant
Author of *Miss O'Dell*

How could I ever forget that chilly Thursday afternoon in January 1969? As a dedicated Beatles fan growing up in New York City I had vowed to make my pilgrimage to London as soon as I graduated high school. In 1967 this dream became a reality. I continued my education and assimilated into the London scene, Beatling in my spare time.

What started out as a routine walk to exercise my bearded collie, Brian, through Hyde Park and on to Savile Row was anything but routine. There was a buzz and numerous people gathering outside Apple Headquarters despite the frigid temperatures and biting wind. So, as a dedicated Beatle fan, I decided to hang around a bit.

All of a sudden I heard the unmistakable sound of Beatles music coming from above. A total shock – being able to clearly HEAR the Beatles, but not SEE them. After the first few chords, more people started streaming down Savile Row, wanting to catch a glimpse of whatever was happening. Many folks had no idea the music was actually coming from John, Paul, George and Ringo, LIVE, from the rooftop above. Press cameras rolled through the crowd interviewing many proper businessmen who were quite perturbed at the interruption of "their street" during business hours. As cold as it was, the music warmed my soul. New tunes, new words, I had a small notepad with me and I hastily scribbled down a few lines, "I got a feeling" and "don't let me down." I still have this little notepad with the now faded notes.

Looking back, it's almost like a dream to be present at the Beatles last live concert. (Ironically, I was one of the lucky fans at the dress rehearsal of The Ed Sullivan Show on February 9, 1964, their first U.S. performance.) Whenever I see the *Let It Be* film I look really hard at the crowd across the street from the Apple building and look for a lady in a dark red coat with a hairy black and white dog by her side. If only we had cell phone cameras back then.

Leslie Healy, BeatleTripper

Police stop Beatles 'making a din'

RAY CONNOLLY

Police stopped the Beatles from filming on the roof of the Apple offices in Savile Row today after getting dozens of complaints about the noise.

The noise of amplified guitars and reverberating voices infuriated some businessmen.

Company director Mr. Stanley Davis, a next-door neighbour of Apple, said: " I want this bloody noise stopped. It's an absolute disgrace.

"You can't even use your telephones, dictate a letter or have your windows open.

The Beatles were filming a television spectacular, which is being built around a new long-playing record.

But the noise—even of the Beatles' noise—was too much for some people.

A police spokesman said: "We had so many complaints we sent someone round. A tremendous din was being made."

The new-look Paul McCartney,

Hundreds of people thronged Savile Row and adjoining Burlington Gardens and looked up at the roof where about a dozen people could be seen taking part in the recording.

Office girls hung out of windows to listen to the Beatles singing.

"Don't let me down," boomed the voice of Paul McCartney. And "I am to miss the train."

After the police arrived the session came to a halt—despite the groans of hundreds of fans who were enjoying the unexpected show.

"Everyone on the balconies and the roof seemed to be enjoying the session," said Mr. Alan Pulverness, who works in a nearby bank. "Some people just can't appreciate good music."

A spokesman for Apple said: " It was all supposed to be very hush-hush. But when you put the Beatles on top of a building in the middle of London and ask them to sing a song it is rather difficult to keep it a secret."

Raising the roof—The Beatles during their performance for a film sequence on the roof of Apple's Savile Row offices today—before the police called.

With the Beatles here is the film's director Michael Lindsay-Hogg standing next to John Lennon's friend Yoko Ono.

SKULLS FOUND AT SOHO BUILDING SITE

Six human skulls and a

As a teenager, I never met anyone who dreamed of singing with the Beatles, and that includes me, a shy 16-year-old from Rio de Janeiro. I had moved to London in February 1967 with the sole purpose of seeing the boys. My friend Denise and I realized that would be the only way of doing so, since they had stopped touring the year before. We got the trip as a gift for our 15th birthdays, but I had no intention of going back home. I saw all four of them plus Brian leaving EMI Studios after a session for *Sgt. Pepper* THE DAY I arrived, February 14, 1967.

I became a regular outside Paul's house and the studios. A few days shy of one year of my arrival, Sunday, February 4, 1968, my friends and I were at EMI standing inside the building. There were very few of us and the doorman let us stay inside the corridor. We were there, talking, when Paul came out and asked "can any of you girls hold a high note?" I said I could. I had been singing in school choirs since I was very young. A little while later either Paul or Mal Evans came to get me and I asked if I could bring my friend Gayleen. I knew she had also been singing in school choirs.

We walked into the first studio and the four of them were there, plus Mal, Neil, George Martin, the engineer and an assistant. Gayleen and I were quiet, shy girls and we were used to seeing them several times a week, so we remained normal, enjoying their company, laughing at the many funny situations, drinking tea and having the most amazing couple of hours one could possibly imagine.

John asked me to share a microphone with him, and later on Paul asked me to come to his mike. The only line Paul sang was the final "Jay Guru Deva" and I sang it with him, but they didn't use my voice. They also recorded Gayleen and myself on our own. I remember my heart was beating rather fast while on the mike with my beloved John and I kept saying to myself "I love you, I love you" while he was so close to me I couldn't move.

George sat on the floor, lit a stick of incense and played an Indian instrument. At one point, John, Paul and George went to the control room and Ringo stayed with us. They played the song, "Across The Universe," on the speakers for us. I was too young to realize what was really going on: I was recording with the Beatles, the biggest band EVER!!! It was so special to be inside for a change. Watching them, being in that room, it was magical.

I first heard the song on Kenny Everett's radio show. I left London in October 1969, but I didn't hear the song again for a long time until I bought the record and had it sent to Brazil. I wasn't particularly upset about our version not being on the *Let It Be* album. We will always have "our" version and that's the one NASA sent to space.

I remember so many moments from that night, sometimes they play like a little movie inside my head. It still amazes me that all that happened TO ME!

Lizzie Bravo

EMI Summer 1969

Top 40 radio was in full swing in 1969. I remember our local radio station in Hartford, Connecticut, WDRC, doing one of their "exclusives" by playing an advance copy of what was purported to be the *Get Back* album. The Beatles during the *Get Back* period had intended that album to be a back-to-basics, no frills, no overdubs release, warts and all, returning to their roots, essentially playing live as a rock 'n' roll band.

I was excited to hear the raw Beatles bantering back and forth between the songs. However, I was often disappointed with the *Get Back* sessions, which at times lacked the polish and professionalism exhibited at previous Beatles sessions. Paul's material was clearly superior to that of John during this period. The released *Let It Be* album was to produce two McCartney standards with "Let It Be" and "The Long And Winding Road." The closest John came to a standard on *Let it Be* was "Across The Universe," a 1968 leftover that deserved better treatment by the band. The "Wildlife" version of the song was clearly superior to the version on the *Let it Be* album.

The disarray evident in the choice and style of material was only one of the problems. George Martin was not firmly in control at this point and it showed. Glyn Johns made a valiant attempt to salvage the album. Calling in Phil Spector, with his wall-of-sound production, was a controversial move which defeated the original intent of the album.

There are good songs on the *Let It Be* album, but it is evident that the Beatles' time together was winding down. The saving grace was their decision to record one more album, *Abbey Road*, where they truly got back to where they once belonged — at the top of their game! It will be fascinating to see if Peter Jackson's new version of the *Let It Be* movie will significantly alter our perceptions of this phase of the Beatles history.

John Bezzini

I was fourteen years old when *Let it Be* was released. But it all started a year earlier when I first heard that the Beatles *Get Back* album would be released during the spring of 1969, then late summer, then year end (*Abbey Road* was just released) and then in early 1970. The anticipation started after seeing the Beatles singing "Get Back" on the rooftop on the Glen Campbell show in April 1969. Then I heard that the album would be called *Let it Be*. I was able to purchase an early bootleg in March 1970 that had early takes of the album including a stringless "The Long And Winding Road." A couple weeks before the release of the movie and album I won tickets to the *Let it Be* premiere in New Haven, Connecticut. Having the album and attending the first showing was exciting and amazing watching the Beatles in the studio. I still have all my original albums and 45s after all these years. And thanks to Paul for never giving up and releasing *Let it Be... Naked*.

John Schiraj

I was 10 and my brother was 14 when *Let It Be* came out. It was only the second Beatles album we bought on first sight, the first being *Hey Jude* earlier in the year. We ate at an A&W drive-in on the way home from purchasing it, and I remember my thoughts being "more weird Harrisong titles" in the vein of "Love You To" as I read the album details in the car.

When the movie came to town (Lamar, Colorado) a few weeks later, we went to the theater to watch it at least five times. On about the fourth visit, we snuck in a stereo cassette recorder to capture the mono soundtrack for posterity. We were scared to death of getting arrested, but we pulled it off. I still have the tape. Really poor quality with babies crying in the audience and everything. Great 1970 memories.

Kirk D. Carpenter

In 1989 in the USSR me and my brother were beginner, but passionate Beatles fans with only two LPs in our collection. Due to political restrictions it was almost impossible to get any piece of foreign music, except illegally smuggled and expensive items.

Once, my father brought two VHS tapes that his friend left in the office. The first one was a movie featuring Bruce Lee fighting Kareem Abdul-Jabbar. The second one was a treasure, with two Beatles movies in color – *Help!* and *Let It Be*. We were amazed watching John and Yoko dancing, Paul and Ringo jamming and George singing. And a whole new world opened for us unexpectedly by the rooftop concert.

Sadly, we returned the tapes to the owner. Later being invited to his place for a party, we found those tapes. As opposed to Bruce Lee tape, the Beatles one was ignored. Those people, not realizing what treasure they had in possession, kindly presented it to us.

To this day, 31 years later, this tape is one the most memorable items in my collection. If we somehow could count how many times this tape was played during the decades, it could be a Guinness world record.

Yaakov Edisherashvili

I bought *Let It Be* upon its release back in the spring of '70 and remember listening to it for the first time in my bedroom on my mono "suitcase" record player while reading the back cover about "a new phase BEATLES album." I had no idea this "new phase" would sadly be the last phase as well. Then there was the red apple label in place of the normal green apple label. I didn't know the meaning or significance of the red apple, but it had to mean something, since everything the Beatles did back then was important. It wasn't until years later when Bruce explained the label change in his book *The Beatles on Apple Records* that I learned it was a record company executive who simply decided special records should have special labels. So much for hidden meanings!

I still have my original copy of the album, which has the letter "K" stamped sideways in the upper right corner of the back cover. Growing up on the far north side of Chicago, I bought many of my records from the Kenmac Radio Center. To prevent defective records from being returned to the store that were not purchased there, they stamped the "K" on all albums. While immediately rendering all new purchases damaged or non-mint, we never thought twice about it at the time, just happy to be bringing home the latest Beatles releases like *Let it Be*.

Harvey Greenberg

"They are not together any more," my father said when I showed him my 1974/1975 school agenda that contained a wonderful image of the Beatles playing on the Apple headquarters rooftop. I had just discovered the Red and Blue double albums, not realizing as a 12-year- old, that the band I liked the most had split four years ago. I started discovering their albums and began with *Let It Be*. It sounded not as a swan song, but a kick off to embrace their musicality. They never let me down ever since.

Patrick Wouters, The Netherlands

I have very fond memories of purchasing the *Let It Be* album at the Chris-Town Mall in Phoenix, Arizona. Looking at the cover I thought, "When did most of the boys go back and cut their hair since the *Abbey Road* album?" And that beard on Paul sure looks strange! I was only 12 at the time and I had no idea this was an earlier photo session.

I remember noting how sentimental Paul's songwriting had become in penning two of the most emotional songs of his Beatles career with the title track and "The Long And Winding Road." As for the latter, I actually liked all the melodic dripping arrangements Phil Spector added to it in spite of Paul's extreme dislike of the same. Perhaps we embraced it because we heard it that way for so long and it grew on us. While "Get Back" was released prior, it was very nice to have the album's different mix. The remaining tracks are a nice fit to the album as well.

This final album once again proves the Beatles can't even stop themselves from making some of the very best music the world has ever heard even when their personal relationships were on the downside. Indeed, they crafted an album with a sound and style like no other before it which this band did better than any other band in history. How many bands can say that?

There are two different original Apple label issues of *Let It Be*. The first issue Side 1 label credit the song "Maggie Mae" to "P.D." (public domain). Later and scarcer issue labels credit the song to all four members of the band. Check your album to see which one you have! And while you are at it, play it again and enjoy this incredible and final official studio Beatles album. The *Let It Be* album was truly a great bookend to their incredible run of 13 albums. Yes, we were very spoiled to the best from the Beatles and this one did not disappoint.

It's fitting and proper all these years later that the *Let It Be* film will finally officially be re-released soon.

The 42-minute Rooftop concert is priceless and it's so wonderful to see the Beatles smiling and having fun performing together. The music that made us smile through life's issues also made them smile too!

Perry Cox

I became a Beatles fan in 1977 at age 10. I soon learned about all of the Beatles albums and movies. For some reason, the *Let it Be* album was somewhat elusive to me. I didn't realize until years later that the LP was out of print for a few years due to its affiliation with United Artists. I did finally manage to secure a copy and was surprised to find it with a red apple label rather than the traditional green. I was amused by the looseness of the album due to the various audio clips of the Beatles from the feature film. Things like "I dig a pygmy" and "Hark the Angels Come" became ingrained in my memory as will all Beatles lyrics. It was never my favorite Beatles album, but it is still one of the most interesting, and it is the ONLY Beatles album to have three number one singles pulled from it. I actually prefer the *Let it Be… Naked* version from 2003, as it is more tight and polished with the extraneous dialogue removed, and it contains "Don't Let Me Down" which SHOULD have been on the original LP.

I saw the film in 1979 at a local cinema that held midnight movies on weekends. *Let it Be* was paired with *Yellow Submarine*, and the entire audience was smoking pot except for my mom and me. I was 12. Smoking was allowed in movie theaters then, and even though that TYPE of smoking was not, no one got in trouble. So, I got a secondhand high and enjoyed the film along with everyone else. I never found the Beatles in the film depressing, but I did find the film's overall look to be kind of drab, so I'm looking forward to what Peter Jackson will do with the footage when he releases his version of the film.

Mark Arnold

In the Spring of 1969 I bought the "Get Back" single while shopping with my high school friend's family. I had to borrow the money from his mom to get it! I was 16 and thrilled to get another Beatles release. Later, after hearing so much build up on the local Philly FM underground radio station (93.3 WMMR) about the *Let It Be* album coming out as a box set with a colorful book, I couldn't wait to buy it. So while on a break from my part time job at Sears, I walked down to the record department to buy the new LP. Imagine my disappointment when I saw the display and noticed it wasn't in a box with the book. But all was saved when I got home and put it on my record player. The music was incredible. I remember liking "One After 909" and "I've Got A Feeling" the best. It's still one of my favorite Beatles albums.

My high school English teacher was a really cool guy. He went to see *Hair* in New York City and spent a class talking about it and then one day he brought in the bootleg *Kum Back*. To hear all those rare trax in a Catholic high school classroom left an impression on me to this day. My first exposure to a bootleg album. Then he brought in CSNY's *Wooden Nickel*. What a time to be alive.

Charlie Leonard

What makes the *Get Back* project and the *Let It Be* album stand out to me was the advent of bootlegs. I lucked out and found the *Kum Back* and *Silver Album* bootlegs in Louisville at River Music in January 1970. I heard the bare bones of the *Let It Be* album months before it came out. I played the bootlegs for my friends. We were 17. They were only curious. I was thrilled, but a little mystified. I thought the Beatles sounded like any other basement band I'd known. They seemed entirely human. I liked that a lot. To this day, I hear the *Let It Be* album through my sense of those bootlegs.

Allan McGuffey

I remember telling a friend in early 1970 that the Beatles were going to break up. I felt that because they had produced so much amazing music over the last few years that there really wasn't anything else for them to do. In April the break-up sadly came to be.

Later in May, I bought the *Let It Be* album from my favorite record store in Kewanee, Illinois on the day it came out. When I first looked at the cover, I was immediately struck by the idea that this was the "tombstone" that marked the death of the Beatles. The black-bordered cover was sedate and somber compared to most of the preceding Beatles album covers. "Let It Be," "The Long And Winding Road" and even the "You and I have memories" line from "Two Of Us" had a bittersweet finality to them. I felt some of the other songs on the LP, although certainly not bad, were not quite up to the Beatles standards. And of course this was the last Beatles album. This was the period at the end of the sentence.

Michael Rinella

Becoming a teenager in 1970, I spent most of my money buying records. When *Let It Be* was released, I went to the local record store and was given the choice of buying the album with or without the book. I opted for the one with book, although it was a third more expensive. Unbeknownst to me how much its value would rise in future decades, I'm happy now I decided that way.

A few months later the movie *Let It Be* was shown in the cinema of my hometown of Zurich, Switzerland. I am glad I took the chance to watch it with a schoolmate as afterwards there were no official screenings anymore.

While not regarded as one of the best Beatles albums, it's still a fine one – especially for me, as it was only the second Beatles album (after *Abbey Road*) I owned at that time.

Marcel Reichmuth

As a long-time Beatles fan residing in Alberta, Canada, I had started to buy their latest releases with my own money starting with *Yesterday And Today* in 1966. The earlier releases were all traded for or bought from friends. So when the *Let It Be* album came out, I quickly made the trip to our local Woodwards department store. My memory is of seeing a table stacked with copies of the LP and noticing that it was bigger and more expensive than their previous ones. The original Canadian release came in a tray which housed the vinyl plus that amazing book, which unfortunately wasn't well put together. A few of the pages started to separate as I flipped through the book. At that time I didn't think of going back to the store and buying another copy, but I was later able to acquire another copy of the book and keep it from being opened and read.

Some years later in the 70s I bought the U.S. release of the album while on a trip and was surprised to see that it was only a single LP with no accompanying book. It was also on a red apple label whereas the Canadian copy I owned was on the more familiar green label.

The *Let It Be* film was so much fun. I don't recall being aghast at the so-called bad vibes, but rather being in awe of seeing the Fabs live and in person playing in the studio and especially on the rooftop. Unlike the *A Hard Day's Night* and *Help!* viewings there was no screaming as we must have all grown up a bit by then. It had been too long from the *Help!* film to *Let It Be* and in the pre-Internet days it was very hard to find any new footage of the Fabs. All we had were magazines like 16 and Rolling Stone to provide us with the latest news and photos.

Some time in the 70s I was able to acquire a boot of the film's soundtrack and then buy the 1-sheet and 3-sheet of the poster plus the lobby card set while working at the local Theatre Consolidated Services location.

Richard Zahn

The release of the *Let It Be* LP and film came during a colder than normal Australian winter and my feelings towards both releases at the time, as a sixteen year old, were equally gloomy. The Beatles had broken up.

The album was good, but lacked the spark and newness of earlier releases as "Get Back" had been issued as a single 12 months earlier. The highlight was the elegant book, which I poured over and admired the glossy photos.

I first saw the movie on a trip to Sydney with my parents where it was on first release and on continuous play with another film, *The Adventurers*. That meant that I had to watch that movie several times to enable me to watch *Let It Be* a second and third time without leaving the theatre. I did that for the whole day. The film was bleak, elevated only by the ending rooftop concert.

My overriding feeling of gloom around both the *Let it Be* album and movie was driven by the clear reality that the Beatles as a group were no more. For me that meant no more excitement about forthcoming releases, reading about the soon to be released songs in The Beatles Monthly, the exhilaration of hearing that newly released Beatles song for the first time on my newly acquired transistor radio and finally getting the new LP or single home and playing it on my Kreisler stereogram.

While the emerging solo releases somewhat eased the pain, it was simply just not the same. Neither was my taste in popular music which moved from a single focus on the Beatles (and the Stones) to American country rock and other emerging trends. Soon I was in my twenties and married and my life had moved on.

Today *Let It Be* is simply a wonderful memory marking the start of the end of my childhood and the now warm memories associated with that. The initial bleakness and gloom around both releases has long since receded in my memory.

Tim Goodacre

I remember making a copy of the *Let It Be* LP on my reel-to-reel tape player. Unfortunately the entire album would not fit on one side of the tape, so one of the songs had to be left off and it came down to either "Get Back" or "I've Got A Feeling." Oh, what pain! Sitting in my cousin Alexey's living room, surrounded by hand-painted posters of The Fab Four, I had to choose. Alexey, a serious vinyl collector and a foremost jazz expert in the old Soviet Union (he still is, though that country is no more!) was suggesting to leave off "I've Got A Feeling." "It was kind of just dragging along," he explained. His wife Galka, on the other hand, was insisting on dropping the closing number, "Get Back" for being "very repetitive." I hated leaving anything off, even the silly (to my 13-year-old ears) "Dig It," but the space requirements of the reel left me no choice. Alexey was my musical guru, so "I've Got A Feeling" hit the cutting floor and I was left with listening an 11-song Beatles masterpiece for the next 11 years.

I don't regret the decision, but it gives me additional pleasure these days to hear the entire album without anything missing. God bless CDs! Oh, and America!

Alex Pritsker

My fondest memory of *Let It Be* was as a freshman attending the University of Colorado in Boulder starting in August of 1970. As someone taking courses to join the healthcare field, I befriended another freshman who was always in those same classes, my late friend Chuck Davis. Everyone at CU seemed to have the same LPs and one was *Let It Be*. Every Friday after class, Chuck and I would head back to his dorm room and open the window wide. We would then cue up the song "Let It Be," turn up the stereo as loud as it would go, plug in his electric guitar to the amp and play along to celebrate surviving another week not being drafted.

George W. Krieger

The last Beatles album released was actually the first Beatles album I owned, thanks to Mom. In the late 1970s as an 11-year-old, my love of the Beatles blossomed through seeing Beatles cartoon re-runs after school on Chicagoland TV. I remember hearing Beatles music in the house and asked where the records were. Many were misplaced, but the old stereo console produced an original *Let It Be* gatefold album that now belongs to me. I wrote (in pencil) on the inside sleeve the album title, date and who I got it from. I continued that habit for years collecting Beatles records. Upon further examination of the record cover, I thought "They don't look like the cartoons here." I learned that the Beatles were no longer a group and far from the cartoons ABC-TV portrayed them to be. I played the album and some songs were familiar from early childhood. "The Long And Winding Road" was my Grandma's favorite Beatles song, one I heard her singing from the kitchen. Cable TV was new in my house and I was excited to watch the *Let It Be* on Cinemax more than once. *Let It Be* started my record collection, which has grown along with my love for the Beatles forever.

Jennifer Sandi

After the theatrical release of *Let It Be* in 1970, there was no interest from the three broadcast networks to show the film. Pay television, like HBO and Showtime, was years away. In 1978, I was working at Teleprompter Cable TV, the nation's largest cable operator at the time. My team created a low budget pay TV channel called Uptown. In putting the channel together, we determined that we weren't going to program blockbuster movies. We had Blaxploitation films, Kung-Fu, etc. I recommended that we obtain *Let It Be*, knowing that it had not been on any TV outlet to my knowledge. In June 1978, we were probably the first TV outlet for the film.

Cousin Steve Goldmintz

I was 15 when the album and film *Let It Be* were finally released. Of course at the time, nobody realized that all this was recorded and filmed months before the *Abbey Road* album! It was many years before I figured that out! My first impression was visual - Paul with a beard?! (not a fan). The music was a different story — I loved Paul's piano ballads, "Let It Be" and "The Long And Winding Road" and his harmonizing with John on "Two Of Us." Seeing the Beatles play live again on the rooftop was a dream come true! I also loved all the spoken bits between/after songs, John's "I'd like to thank you on behalf of the group and ourselves and I hope we passed the audition" being absolutely brilliant! The only real criticism I had of the movie was that it was too short! Really looking forward to Peter Jackson's new version!

Nancy (Cuebas) Riley

I was so knocked by *Let It Be* that I saw it twice in a row! Through the eyes of a 22 year old, I saw the joy in that film and the love John, Paul, George and Ringo had for each other, especially when they were playing and creating music. Stressful scenes were few and far between. They were brothers and sometimes brothers fight! It was nothing unusual to me (as I have an older brother). The amazing Rooftop Concert was the icing on the cake.

Mark Lapidos

I was a senior in high school during the 1969-1970 school year. I remember going to the Joy Theater in New Orleans with some friends and seeing the *Let It Be* movie poster outside the theater. For some reason I hadn't been paying attention to the Beatles at that time. I wondered aloud "What's this all about?" Some girl chimed in, "Oh, you didn't know? The Beatles broke up." I was stunned. That's how I learned of the breakup and *Let It Be*!

Pat Matthews

The whole back story to the *Get Back* sessions is now well known, having been fully dissected in near-forensic detail over the years since. *Abbey Road* seemed every bit the minor miracle it was on its release in September '69, but by early '70 the rumours of discontent and a possible split of the Beatles seemed harder to dismiss than they had just one year before.

My first hearing of *Let it Be* was courtesy of a local FM radio jock, who played the entire album during the late evening/early hours around its release date in early May '70. I was 15 years old that spring, and on the evening in question just happened to be finding my way through my first 'altered state of consciousness' adventure. (As I recall now, MDA [methylenedioxyamphetamine], had a way of transforming even the most dull, monochromatic event into a full colour synesthetic experience.) With the sound-colour-feel of the music still reverberating in my head, I stepped through the kitchen door of our house and into the dawn light of our sprawling back yard and sat beneath a tree facing the sunrise.

What I still remember now like some time-worn fading photo are the first rays of the sun gleaming off the dew on the spring grass as the lyrics to "Across The Universe" filled my thoughts: "Nothing's gonna change my world, nothing's gonna change my world." Just what was Lennon on about? I really didn't know (hey, cut me some slack — I was only 15), but in my state of mind and in those moments out of time the words seemed prophetic for the new decade we'd all just stumbled into, and a fitting, if all-too-sad, goodbye from the Beatles. "Nothing's gonna change my world?" Actually, it felt more like nothing was gonna be the same after they'd suddenly gone. Thank God then for more minor miracles to come as the year played out: *Plastic Ono Band*, *McCartney* and (especially) *All Things Must Pass*.

Robert Woods

I have mixed feelings about the *Let It Be* album. It's not one of my favorite Beatles albums, although it does have a few great songs. My initial exposure was buying a bootleg of the recording sessions about six months before the official LP was released. It came in a plain white cover with the label that simply stated "KUM BACK, The World's Greatest." Of course the sound quality left a lot to be desired, but it was exciting to hear unreleased material by the Fab Four. I still have that record today.

I saw the film in a neighborhood theater and eventually owned a copy on VHS tape. It was like a peek behind the scenes. Interesting but a bit slow and the lighting was poor in places. Since it has never been available on DVD, I am anxiously awaiting Peter Jackson's new version.

David R. Rauh

In late 1969, months before the release of the *Let It Be* album, I bought a vinyl LP in a plain white sleeve stamped with the words *Kum Back*. It was displayed on a record store counter beside a sign that said "Beatles." The rough mixes on that bootleg – inferior to the official releases – are the *Let It Be* tracks lodged in my memory.

I played *Kum Back* over and over, absorbing every sound: Paul's count-in to "Let It Be," John's laugh on "Dig A Pony" and the clink of a glass before "For You Blue." Rumors of the band's break-up were in the wind and cast a shadow over my listening. "The Long And Winding Road" was wrenching, "Let It Be" was tinged with sadness, and I was sure "Two Of Us" was a salute to John and Paul's friendship. Hearing the band cut loose on "I've Got A Feeling" helped cure my melancholy.

I purchased the official release the following May and years later bought *Let It Be... Naked*. Despite listening to those many times, the version that still plays in my head and resides in my heart is *Kum Back*.

Kathy Urbanic

For me, the arrival of *Let It Be* was anti-climactic when I first saw the film in Langhorne, Pennsylvania. The Beatles had split and the film appeared to be telling us why or how. It was sad, but there was plenty of other great music to listen to during that fantastic period from bands that were staying together!

Later that year, my first in college, a theater owner let me tape the film's soundtrack from the projector's speaker lead. The perfect homework music, I listened to it over and over hoping for an inspiring message.

I later saw a record store display of Elvis' *Worldwide 50 Gold Award Hits,* a massive set of stuff from before my time. And I finally got the good news: the Beatles want us to listen to the old stuff — Elvis, Little Richard, Chuck Berry, Jerry Lee Lewis, Carl Perkins, Buddy Holly, etc. I dove into the sounds that gave us the Beatles. It was a good thing, too, because the seventies brought on a lot of junk. I've been a happy lad ever since.

John Rarig

As a confirmed Anglophile, I made sure to buy the original UK edition of *Let It Be* when it came out, even though it was quite expensive. Needless to say, I tried to keep it as "new" as possible, even though the cardboard cover pack was fragile, and the binding of the book was not the best. Imagine my horror when I came home one day and saw that my roommate had tacked up on the wall several pages from the book. "They just fell out," he said. Uh-uh, yeah.

Stephen M.H. Braitman

I was in junior high in 1970. I skipped school to see the film in Bloomington, Illinois. I would pay to get in at the first showing and remain inside all the way till the last showing. I saw the film 11 times in two days!

Bill Risoli

In April 1970 I was barely 15. My top albums were *American Woman*, *Morrison Hotel* and *The Beatles Again*. My favorite singles were "Instant Karma," "Spirit In The Sky" and "Let It Be," which I thought was issued as a companion, non-album single, to *The Beatles Again*.

Being a Canadian fan of the Fab Four since 1964, I wasn't that worried when I heard that "Paul Quits The Beatles" because it was not the first time I had heard of the band supposedly breaking up. McCartney's solo LP did not add to that speculation for me. I ignored the rumors and just enjoyed Paul's debut album.

The following month I bought the *Let It Be* album with a book so fragile that it sadly had a very short life! The Beatles were still alive with beautiful melodies like "Dig A Pony," "Two Of Us," "I Me Mine" and the mesmerizing but oddly arranged "The Long And Winding Road." I had previously bought *Kum Back* (my first and only bootleg) at Dave Silver's Record Cave in downtown Montreal. I wasn't a fan of the arrangements on *Let It Be*, preferring the raw versions on *Kum Back*. But hey, nothing is perfect.

At some point I had to face it. The Beatles had split up. However, all hope for new music was not lost. In 1970 alone, I got eight albums and six singles from the Beatles, in quartet or solo. John, Paul, George and Ringo would be still creating. In 2003, we got *Let It Be… Naked*, the group stripped-down as it was meant to be. In 2020, with the 50th anniversary of *Get Back/Let It Be*, millennials will have to face the fact that the Beatles are here to stay.

As for the movie, I was sad to see that my heroes could give each other a hard time, even when they knew they were being filmed. And then I thought, "I've got a feeling" that the movie's director emphasized conflicts between the Beatles to the point where it seems they were fighting all the time. Oh well, as I said above, there is no perfection…c'est la vie, let it be!

Normand Tremblay

I remember going to Melody Record Shop in downtown Williamsport, Pennsylvania in early 1970 and asking the manager if she had heard anything about the Beatles *Get Back* album. She pulled out two albums from under the counter. One had a plain white jacket with a rubber stamp of the title "KUM BACK." The other had a plain silver jacket with no writing at all. You can imagine how my eyes lit up! This would be my first bootleg purchase.

Being a poor college kid at the time, I asked her which one she liked best since I only had enough money for one. She told me the sound was better on the silver covered album. She pulled the record out. The label was silver and had the track listings and the title *The Silver Album Of The World's Greatest*. She played a couple excerpts for me and I was sold, buying the $5.77 boot.

When I went back to Penn State in mid-January, I played *The Silver Album*, which I had recorded on my Sony reel-to-reel, for the Beatles buffs back at the dorm. To my surprise, my next-store neighbor had just bought *Kum Back* during Christmas break, so I made a reel-to-reel recording of that album as well. We must have played the tapes of those albums a hundred times!

Rob Foust

I first heard the *Let It Be* songs on a scratchy bootleg in early 1970. I loved them, particularly "Let It Be" with its count-in and "The Long And Winding Road" with its stray piano notes at the end. Very charming. I also thought "I've Got A Feeling" was fab. When the "Let It Be" single came out it was great to hear the song in pristine sound even though it was a different version.

I was looking forward to the *Let It Be* album, but my heart sank when I heard the loud brass on "Let It Be" and the strings and harp on "The Long And Winding Road." The red apple label turned out to be a warning label.

T.H. Spidell

Being born the same year the Beatles landed in America and having a sibling nine years older, I have been a Beatles fan literally my entire life. I remember when my sister brought home the "Hey Jude" single and seeing that green apple label for the first time. I could not wait to see other records with that district green apple. I recall being so excited every time an album or single was released with that cool record label. By the time the *Let It Be* album was released, I was anxious to break open my piggy bank and buy the album. I could not wait to get home from the store and play it on my General Electric Wildcat record player. I will never forget how astonished I was when I took the album out of the jacket and saw the RED apple label as opposed to the green. Like all of the Beatles records, I played it over and over again until I knew every lyric and every note. The end of an era, but not the end of a lifelong admiration for the Beatles and the *Let It Be* album.

Matt Cacossa

I first bought the *Let It Be* box in the late 1970s. It was the first edition with the book and the LP, and on the same day I also bought *Abbey Road* and *The White Album*. I was 14 years old and I had just discovered the Beatles and bought all their singles. That day, as soon as I got home, I opened the box and while listening to the album, I cut out the color pictures of the box and hung them on the wall of my room! A few months later I saw the film in a little cinema and then, God bless that moment, I bought the box again, but I did not cut out this time, and I still jealously keep it in my collection. I have bought many other editions of *Let It Be* since then and eventually wrote an appreciation book, the first in Italy, about the *Get Back* sessions, the rooftop concert and the *Let It Be* film: "Il concerto sul tetto e le sessioni della discordia."

Vincenzo Oliva

The thing I remember most about the *Let It Be* album is the confusion, excitement and disappointment it caused for me at the time. The local Boston FM radio station WBCN had played the *Get Back* album in the fall of 1969. Also, in early February, Ed Sullivan showed clips of the Beatles performing "Two of Us" and "Let It Be." In late February I asked my mother to check the record shop downtown to see if they had the new Beatles album yet. She came home smiling with a bag and said, "They had it." I pulled it out of the bag, saw that great front cover and then total disappointment when I turned it over and saw the song listing. Of course, it was the *Hey Jude* album. I can't describe the disappointment I felt at the time and still have for that album. Finally, the release of *Let It Be* in May did not have the excitement of past Beatles albums. It was almost anti-climatic because we already had two versions of the songs on singles and had been hearing them for a while on FM radio.

Brian Barros

I got back into the Beatles in 1969, first through Hunter Davies' book, then the "Come Together" single and *Abbey Road*. In January 1970, I got *Sgt. Pepper*, *Revolver* and *Rubber Soul* for the first time. I read Circus magazine's review about the *Get Back* album. I couldn't wait to hear it. Then, on that fateful day in April, in junior high, someone told me the Beatles had broken up. I was heartbroken. When the official album came out, I liked it, especially the roof top material, but I didn't like what Phil Spector did to Ringo's drums on the title track. In 1973, a local theatre had a Beatles marathon with *Let It Be*, which I recorded on my cassette player. I played it over and over again. Then came various bootlegs. It was years before I learned the Beatles were not getting along then, but the album and movie are still favorites of mine.

Mark Zutkoff

I was too young to appreciate *Let It Be* when it was first released. We had prayed for the safe return of the crew of Apollo 13 the month before. We held our breaths during the radio blackout that lasted way too long during re-entry. I got into the Beatles by the mid-70s. When I finally got the *Let It Be* album, I loved the gatefold sleeve with all the pictures. And wow, a red apple on the label! Was it symbolic of the end of the Beatles? I was always told you had to hate the *Let It Be* album because of Phil Spector's production. But it had great songs like "One After 909," "I've Got A Feeling," "For You Blue" and "I Me Mine." Maybe not an *Abbey Road*, but still a good album.

Tom Drill

I distinctly remember going to the opening night of *Let it Be* at the Orpheum Theatre in Minneapolis, Minnesota with a couple of friends. As we entered the theater, we encountered an irate fan leaving an earlier showing and yelling "Don't waste your time, it's a ripoff." We went in anyway and loved it. I sat through two show-ings. The film was exciting to see in a theater and better represented the music than the album (I already had a bootleg version). A year or so later I was at a B Dalton bookstore in Minneapolis and saw a stack of the book from the UK pressings for sale. I regret not buying a few.

Greg Helgeson

I saw *Let It Be* upon its initial release in 1970 at the Orson Welles Cinema in Harvard Square. I was in my freshman year at Boston College and remember we were pretty herbed up. I still have the original book of photos from the film that Apple put out in 1969 in pristine condition. It obviously was not an overly flattering portrayal of the band at the time, but I'm really looking forward to Peter Jackson's version...can't wait!!

Louis Yanucci

For me, the year 1969 was the most productive of the Fab Four, starting with the *Get Back* sessions leading to the *Let It Be* album and film the following year. It all started with the release of the single "Let It Be." It was shocking to listen to that majestic ballad for the first time and then flip the disc and instantly hear "You Know My Name (Look Up The Number)." Thanks to Mal Evans, I was able to find out about the *Get Back* project, but it was more exciting for me to hear (thanks to a friend) the bootleg *Kum Back*, where most of the songs that were released on the album *Let It Be* first appeared.

The premiere of the film was close to the release of the album. In Argentina, as with many countries of the world, the album was issued in a box with the *Get Back* book included. The first time I saw the book was through the window of a business, and I was paralyzed. I will never forget the day of the premiere of the film. For me, the strongest moment was seeing John sing "Don't Let Me Down." I went back to see the film many times, including once when I brought a camera and managed to take several pictures, although only two can be seen more or less well. This movie and album will always be in my heart, for one simple reason: the Beatles are magical, and magic is eternal like the Beatles themselves.

Horacio Dubini

The title of Bruce's book, *The Beatles Finally Let It Be*, made me think back and realize just how true it was, the "finally" bit that is. I was just 15 when I first read about something that would become *Let It Be*. The October 1968 Beatles Monthly Book said that a Beatles concert would be televised to the world. After learning in NME that the concert would be filmed at the Roundhouse, I wondered how I could go. Then the December 1968 Beatles Book announced that 100 FREE Beatles show tickets could be won in a "Lucky Dip." All I had to do was fill in a form and return it by December 31. The magazine reported that the TV show wouldn't be seen until February or March. If I didn't win tickets I would have to wait months, so I sent in my form for that Lucky Dip.

I was disappointed when I didn't win any tickets, but then I read in NME that the January 18 concert was canceled. So I hadn't missed it after all. In the February issue of Beatles Book I learned that the group had written eight new songs for the show. Wow! Another album so soon. That was great news.

Then I read about the Apple Rooftop performance on January 30th, which left me devastated. Being from the Midlands, from Stoke on Trent, I might as well have been a million miles away.

In the March issue of Beatles Book, Mal Evans wrote that there were 12 new songs and that a new album would be released in April or May. He promised that the next issue would have full details of the tracks. I couldn't wait! It didn't happen! Then out of the blue a new single! "Get Back" and "Don't Let Me Down." April 18 the Beatles perform "Get Back." That must have been footage from the rooftop. The April 19 NME reports on two TV specials on successive nights to go with the release of the new LP. And a paperback book! In the next NME, I learn the Beatles have another single coming out: "The Ballad Of John And Yoko" with only John and Paul on it!

In an interview in the May 3 NME, John says that the next album's music is straightforward with nothing weird! It'll be like "Get Back." It will be out in eight weeks! The June 7 NME says the LP is titled *Get Back, Don't Let Me Down and 12 Other Tracks*. The Beatles Book runs Mal's report on the *Get Back* LP. It will be out in August, along with a special book and a film on TV.

NME then says the LP is set for September and that another album of old rock classics may be issued later. The August Beatles Book prints an preview of the songs on the *Get Back* album. I had never known so much about Beatles songs without actually hearing them! Very frustrating. Then the *Get Back* album is pushed back to November. There will be a different album out first! It's called *Abbey Road* and now the *Get Back* LP is postponed until the end of the year! It will be the perfect Christmas present if it ever comes out! The September 20 NME tells me that the *Get Back* film will be out early in the New Year and will tie in with the release of the *Get Back* LP.

Bad news! The Beatles Book ceases publication! How am I going to know what was happening with the *Get Back* LP? Fantastic news! A new Beatles song, "Across the Universe," is being released on a charity album. Then Christmas comes, but no new Beatles LP in my stocking.

Then NME reports that there is going to be a single from the album called "Let It Be" out on February 20th, and the album will follow soon, I hope. Then I learn that the *Get Back* LP will be called *Let it Be* after the single.

Sometime in February 1970 I see an ad in the back of NME for an album called *Kum Bak*. I buy it for around £2. It's a bootleg of *Get Back* songs! I love it!

On March 7 I buy the "Let It Be" single, but have to wait two more months for the *Let It Be* album to finally come out. It cost an extra pound due to the book, though it was well worth it, as was the wait.

Garry Marsh

The Beatles had always made me happy. I mean, after all, they literally "guaranteed to raise a smile." But after days of twisting my parents' arms (and shouting) to drive me to New Orleans to see the Beatles newly-released film, *Let It Be*, I discovered something disconcerting: the boys weren't handing out free grins anymore.

In fact, as I entered the NOLA theater — proudly wearing my John Lennon sweatshirt and every single one of my prized Lennon and Beatles buttons — I was stopped dead in my tracks, discovering fewer than 20 people in the darkened room. "Number 18!" someone shouted in a voice as frustrated as I felt. "She's number 18!" And, as Number 18, I took a seat in the middle back of the vastly empty theater. "Ugh," I thought, already a bit down, the Beatles had failed to fill the house!

Of course, in May of 1970, the boys had everything going against them. They had disbanded. Their latest hit, "The Long And Winding Road," hadn't been a tea-cup-rattler like "She Loves You" or an edgy, innovative experiment such as "Tomorrow Never Knows" or a mad rocker like "Helter Skelter." Furthermore, the Beatles had other interests: John had become enthralled with Performance Art and the peace movement. Ringo was knee-deep in films. George had firmly established his own career, releasing *Wonderwall Music* in November 1968, and Paul had released his *McCartney* LP, featuring "Maybe I'm Amazed." The Beatles had moved on. And from one glance at the number of film-goers, so had the world. The Beatles seemed so, um, "yesterday."

But I was still a die-hard fan, no matter what. And on that spring afternoon in New Orleans I wanted one more chance to fall in love with the lads again.

Admittedly, the film had a slow start, and about a half-hour into the reel — despite a lively piano duet between Ringo and Paul — three of the twenty viewers got up and left the theater! "Come back Numbers 9, 10, and 11!" the

Official Counter shouted. We all chuckled, but it really wasn't funny. People were walking out — on the Beatles!!!

The film was a bit hard to take: the Beatles weren't happy or funny or quirky (well, except for John's waltzing) or anything we'd come to expect. Ringo looked cold and bored. John looked only at Yoko. On the whole, *Let It Be* looked to be a rather bleak production.

But then, George Martin joined George and Ringo for a run-through of "Octopus's Garden," and the old EMI vibe was instantly back. It felt like "the old days" again. Who knew Ringo could play such a mean piano? And who knew that the boys still had the Cavern charisma hiding inside? I found myself grinning to "Shake, Rattle And Roll" and tapping my toe to "Lawdy Miss Clawdy." I felt as happy as Billy Preston looked.

And then they were on the roof of their Apple Savile Row headquarters getting back to where they once belonged. It was clearly cold up there, with John and George wearing fur coats and Ringo in a red mac. After Paul sang about Jo Jo and Sweet Loretta, John belted out a great version of "Don't Let Me Down" before the boys when into "I've Got A Feeling" and "One After 909." For "Dig A Pony," John's grin was almost as big as mine. And in the end, John had the last word, saying he hoped they had passed the audition! After a brief reprise of "Get Back," the boys and I were "on our way home."

Let it Be didn't "send me" the way that *Help!* and *A Hard Day's Night* did. It wasn't a joyous reunion of the group. But that afternoon I left the theater uplifted, nevertheless, because for another hour or so of my life, I had been privileged to hang out with John, Paul, George and Ringo. I had been invited up on the roof. I had been given the chance to forget the world and remember the Beatles. And always, always… "you know that can't be bad."

Jude Southerland Kessler
Author, The John Lennon Series

A Fan's Notes:
April 7, 1970, I Read The News Today

by Bill King (originally published in Beatlefan #93, March 1995)

It was an unforgettable I-remember-where-I-was moment. Tuesday morning, April 7, 1970. I'd just come up from my downstairs bedroom for breakfast when my mom, who'd been listening to the radio, broke the news. "Paul has left the Beatles," she said.

That didn't sound right. "Are you sure it was Paul?" I asked. I mean, I wouldn't have been all that surprised if she'd said John had left. After all, he'd been venturing away from the group more and more the past couple of years, with his peace campaign, his bed-ins with Yoko and his Plastic Ono Band recordings. He even had a hit on the radio at the moment in "Instant Karma!" But Paul leave The Beatles? "That's what they said on the radio," Mom confirmed.

I couldn't wait to get to school and discuss this with Charles, my homeroom buddy, and Mike, an ROTC classmate with whom we'd spent countless hours the past few months skipping out on study hall to listen to the Beatles on the 8-track tape player in Charles' car.

True, it had been only six years since that first Ed Sullivan show, but those had been six of the most impressionable years in our lives. No Beatles? We could not imagine such a thing. They were such an integral part of our lives.

Their importance was more to me during my final year in high school than any other since 6th grade. For some reason, I was more fascinated than ever with the Fab Four, probably because I'd found some guys to hang out with who also were heavily into the Beatles.

In the fall of my senior year I learned that Charles and Mike were major fans of the Beatles. As seniors, with all our tough courses behind us, we basically were cruising through the semester, just marking time at Athens High School until next year, when we'd go across town to the University of Georgia.

Frankly, we didn't have that much studying to do. We worked a scam where the teacher in charge of study hall thought we were going to the ROTC department to "work on records." We were all less-than-gung-ho officers in the cadet corps who'd signed up basically to avoid P.E. Instead, we'd head out to Charles' car to play his growing collection of Beatles 8-track tapes.

Remember 8-tracks? Was there ever a worse format for listening to music? And yet, they were all the rage that 1969-70 school year, with car units the big thing — probably the birth of the sort of "portable" music phenomenon that later would see music lovers embrace Walkmen, iPods and smartphones.

There even were stores devoted entirely to 8-track tape cartridges. In fact, it was at an 8-track place called Tape Town a few weeks earlier that Charles had found our favorite tape of the moment — a bootleg called *Kum Back* consisting of songs from the Beatles unreleased *Get Back* album.

Bootlegs were a new and exciting thing, and Tape Town had some from other big groups of the time, such as Creedence Clearwater Revival and Crosby, Stills, Nash & Young.

Being a college town of about 50,000 at the time, Athens didn't have a progressive rock radio station, so we hadn't heard the *Get Back* tapes when they'd first hit radio in larger U.S. markets the previous September. But the two local Top 40 stations recently had started Saturday night progressive programs—"Electric Circles" on WDOL and "96 Dimensions" on WRFC. We started calling the stations to request our unreleased favorites, particularly "Two Of Us" and "Let It Be," which we soon would see the Beatles play in advance clips from the *Let It Be* movie on Ed Sullivan's "Beatles Songbook" special.

In early January, Apple had released a song Paul had written for Badfinger, "Come and Get It." The tune was featured in the film *The Magic Christian*, co-starring Ringo Starr. Charles and I went to go see the movie, oblivious to its sexual and drug references.

Then came John's single "Instant Karma!" which pounded its way into my heart during a week I spent in bed with the flu, listening to the radio blast out Simon & Garfunkel's "Bridge Over Troubled Water," Brook Benton's "Rainy Night In Georgia," Tee Set's "Ma Belle Amie," the Chairmen of the Board's "Give Me Just A Little More Time" and that ubiquitous Hollies hit that got played each hour, "He Ain't Heavy, He's My Brother."

We didn't take "Instant Karma!" as a sign that the Beatles might be in their last days. The British music weeklies had covered the disintegration of the Beatles, but we didn't see those papers, nor Rolling Stone, which wouldn't be sold in Athens until June, when I bought my first issue, the one focusing on *Let It Be*.

So we weren't aware of how close the band was to breaking up. After all, John had put out a couple of other singles ("Give Peace A Chance" and "Cold Turkey") plus those avant-garde albums. Those were just sidelines, we figured. Besides, there was that surprise Beatles LP that suddenly had shown up in stores!

It wasn't the *Get Back* album we'd been expecting. We weren't even sure if it was titled *Hey Jude* or *The Beatles Again*. The songs ranged from "Can't Buy Me Love" to "Paperback Writer" to "Ballad of John & Yoko."

Two weeks later the official "Let It Be" single was released. We sneaked off-campus and bought it.

Then came the word about Paul leaving the band. At school, no one knew any details. When I got home, though, that afternoon's Atlanta Journal had the dread headline over its Newsmakers column: "McCartney on Own Dooms Beatles?" Saturday brought news of Paul's interview from the previous day, making it "official."

His debut solo album hit stores the following Friday, April 17. I had a mixed reaction to the album — I liked the songs with vocals, particularly "Maybe I'm Amazed," but the instrumentals seemed like filler.

Looking back, I realize what a tumultuous spring that was. The same day Paul's album came out, the crippled Apollo 13 safely returned from space. I was with hundreds of folks at a giant hot dog joint with TV viewing rooms and will never forget the cheers and tears when that chute finally appeared in the sky.

From there, it got really crazy. President Nixon announced U.S. troops were going into Cambodia, and the nation's college campuses erupted in protest. Four kids were killed by National Guardsmen at Kent State and, even in Athens, the university closed for a day.

Shortly after that, a race riot at our school, where bomb scares had become almost routine, spread to the town at large, and our own National Guard came in to keep order. What a way to finish your senior year.

But that wasn't our main concern. The weekend we finished classes, *Let It Be* opened. We watched with a mix of elation and sadness, the same way we felt at graduation a few nights later. It was time for us to move on, just like our friends John, Paul, George and Ringo.

The Beatles Again: The *Hey Jude* Album

In September 1969, Allen Klein negotiated lucrative new contracts for the Beatles with EMI and Capitol Records. *Abbey Road* was the first album covered by the new arrangement, which gave the group a higher royalty rate. When Klein recommended that the Beatles *Get Back* TV special be converted into a feature-length film, the release of the *Get Back* album was delayed until 1970 to coincide with the release of the movie. According to Allan Steckler, who worked for Allen Klein at Abkco (Klein's management and music publishing company), Klein was anxious to have another Beatles album delivered to Capitol under the terms of the favorable new contract. In late November 1969, Klein asked Steckler, who had been assigned to manage Apple, if there was any material available to put into a "new" Beatles album for the American market.

Steckler reviewed the Capitol catalog to determine what songs had yet to appear on an American album. He selected ten songs covering the Beatles entire career and programmed the running order. This information was forwarded to EMI with instructions to compile a stereo master tape for the LP. Four of the pre-1969 songs had never appeared on a British album and needed to be mixed for stereo. Existing stereo mixes were used for the other selections.

With the exception of "Don't Let Me Down," the album was programmed in chronological order. Side One rocks from start to finish, opening with "Can't Buy Me Love" and closing with "Revolution." Side Two, which contains only four songs, opens with "Hey Jude" and closes with "The Ballad Of John And Yoko."

The album's opening tracks, "Can't Buy Me Love" and "I Should Have Known Better," were featured in the film *A Hard Day's Night* and were on the United Artists soundtrack LP, but had not been issued on a Capitol Beatles album. The former was issued as Capitol's second Beatles single on March 16, 1964. It topped the charts and sold well over a million copies. The song appeared on Capitol's 1964 compilation album *Big Hits From England And The U.S.A.* "I Should Have Known Better" was the B-side to the Capitol single "A Hard Day's Night," which was released on July 13, 1964. Billboard charted the flip side separately at number 53.

When "Paperback Writer" and "Rain" were issued on a Capitol single on May 23, 1966, the disc quickly shot to the top of the charts and sold over a million copies. The B-side "Rain" charted at 23.

"Lady Madonna" was the A-side of the Beatles first single of 1968, issued on March 18. Although the song sold over a million copies and received heavy air play, it stalled at number four in the Billboard Hot 100.

"Revolution" was the B-side of the Beatles first Apple single issued on August 26, 1968. Billboard separately charted the song at number 12. This rocking version was recorded specifically for the singles market. The original version of the song, titled "Revolution 1," is on *The White Album*.

The second side opens with the A-side to Apple's first single, "Hey Jude." It topped the Billboard Hot 100 for nine straight weeks in the fall of 1968 and sold nearly five million copies in the United States. With a running time of over seven minutes, "Hey Jude" is one of the longest songs released by the Beatles, eclipsed only by the sound collage "Revolution 9" and "I Want You (She's So Heavy)."

George's "Old Brown Shoe" was the B-side to "The Ballad Of John And Yoko," which was released on June 4, 1969. It is the only song on the album that did not make the Billboard Hot 100.

"Don't Let Me Down" was the flip side to "Get Back," which began appearing in stores on April 25, 1969. The song charted at number 35 in the Billboard Hot 100. Although a different version of the song was slated to appear on the *Get Back* album, the song is not on the revised *Let It Be* LP.

The album closes with "The Ballad Of John And Yoko," which only reached number eight in the Billboard Hot 100. The song's relatively poor performance was due to its limited air play resulting from the song's controversial lyrics. While radio programmers were reluctant to play the single, Beatles fans were not offended and purchased over one million copies of the disc.

While the *Hey Jude* LP contains ten songs making their Capitol album debut, it was not intended to fill all the gaps. At the time the record was programmed in November 1969, the following additional songs had yet to appear on a Capitol Beatles album: "Misery" and "There's A Place" (both were on Vee-Jay's *Introducing The Beatles* LP); "From Me To You;" "Sie Liebt Dich" (the German-lyric version of "She Loves You;") "A Hard Day's Night" (on the United Artists soundtrack LP); "I'm Down" (the hard-rocking flip side to "Help!"); and "The Inner Light," the lovely B-side to "Lady Madonna."

Americans first learned of the new Beatles collection in early 1970. The January 21 Rolling Stone reported that the *Get Back* album had been pushed back again, with an "album of rare Beatle oldies" to take its place. The new album, titled *The Beatles Again*, was tentatively scheduled for release around the first of the year. The article mentioned that the *Get Back* LP was being held up to time its release with the Beatles movie of the same name. The oldies album was described as an "Allen Klein money-making brainstorm."

The magazine also reported that Klein would love to get the Beatles on tour and that the name of their film was now *Let It Be*. There was also an article on the possibility of the Beatles splitting up.

Having lost the distribution rights for the *Get Back* album to United Artists (which would distribute both the *Let It Be* film and its soundtrack LP), Capitol was anxious to get another Beatles album out. The company printed Apple labels for the disc with the title as "The Beatles Again" and the catalog number as SO-385, signifying a Stereo disc with a list price of $6.98. Although *Abbey Road* had a then-high list price of $6.98, the "new" album had only ten songs, all of which had been previously released. After receiving negative feedback from retailers, Capitol lowered the list price to the standard $5.98 and changed the catalog number to SW-385.

Capitol used photographs taken at John's Tittenhurst estate on August 22, 1969, for the album cover. An initial design features a photo of the group on the lawn of John's estate with his white house and a brick wall in the background. "BEATLES AGAIN" appears in black letters curved above a potted plant. This was to be the front cover. The back cover has the group standing in front of the wooden front door to the estate's Victorian assembly hall. A black and white picture of the group standing in a wooded area of John's estate is superimposed above the door. The song titles appear in black letters on the marble slab in front of the door. This back cover design, minus the song titles, was used for the final front cover design (shown on the previous page). A second early design has the same front cover as the released album. Its back cover featured the lawn photo on the back, but with a large pink border with the song titles in white at the bottom and "BEATLES AGAIN" in curved pink letters.

Perhaps due to *The Beatles Again* being a non-descriptive title, the album's name was changed to that of the biggest hit in the collection, "Hey Jude." This necessitated a change of the back cover. One of the designs under consideration had a blue/gray background and an ornate white patterned design surrounding the lawn photo. The album's new title, "HEY JUDE," appears above the photo in white. The song titles surround the other sides of the picture.

The back cover selected for the album is similar to the earlier cover that featured the lawn photo surrounded by a large pink border, but with a black border and no album title above the plant.

Neither the group's name nor album title appears on the front cover. Some covers came with a white background sticker with "HEY JUDE" in either red or purple ink. The group's name and album title are on the cover's spine. Later copies of the album have labels with the new title (HEY JUDE) and record number (SW-385).

The *Hey Jude* LP was released on February 26, 1970. Billboard noted that "Those four rich kids with a reputation for Gulliver-sized hits at the drop of a phonograph record have another ticket to ride... via some past hits....music you can bank on." Billboard charted the album for 33 weeks, including four at number two. Cash Box also showed a peak at two, while Record World reported the album at number one. By June 1970, it had sold 3.3 million units.

This "Allen Klein money-making brainstorm" clearly served its purpose. Although not a greatest hits collection, the disc was full of great Beatles songs making their Capitol album debut. It was a convenient collection and a great listening experience. For fans, it was a new Beatles album to play while waiting for the release of *Let It Be*.

The Beatles: In The Beginning (Circa 1960)

Let It Be was not the only Beatles album issued in the U.S. in May 1970. On May 4, Polydor Records released *In The Beginning (Circa 1960)*. Both discs contained songs that had been recorded prior to the group's previous album, *Abbey Road*, and both featured another musician playing with the group on most of its tracks. But while most of the songs on the Apple album were recorded 15 months earlier and featured the Beatles augmented by American keyboardist Billy Preston, the Polydor collection reached back nearly a decade for songs that, for the most part, had the Beatles serving as the backing band for British singer/guitarist Tony Sheridan.

In the early sixties, the Beatles made several trips to Hamburg, Germany, for extended club appearances. On April 1, 1961, the group, then consisting of John Lennon, Paul McCartney and George Harrison on guitars, Stuart Sutcliffe on bass and Pete Best on drums, began a three-month stay at the Top Ten Club. Also on the bill was Tony Sheridan, who was often backed by the Beatles.

On the recommendation of popular German singer Tommy Kent, producer Bert Kaempfert dropped by the club to check out Sheridan and the Beatles. He was impressed with their performances and signed both to his production company. By the time contracts were signed, Stu had quit the band, forcing Paul to move to bass.

The Beatles first professional recording session took place on June 22 (and possibly 23), 1961, at Friedrich-Ebert-Halle in Harburg, a suburb of Hamburg. The session was produced by Kaempfert, with Karl Hinze serving as engineer. A total of seven songs were recorded. Five feature Tony Sheridan backed by the Beatles. The other two were exclusively Beatles recordings. The group later recorded an additional backing track for another song, "Sweet Georgia Brown," on May 24, 1962. Sheridan later added his vocals.

The first Hamburg recordings to be released in America were "My Bonnie" and "The Saints (When The Saints Go Marching In)," on Decca 31382 on April 11, 1962. The single, credited to Tony Sheridan and the Beat Brothers, did not chart.

After Beatlemania exploded in the U.S., MGM Records issued the same single on January 27, 1964, this time credited to "The Beatles with Tony Sheridan." Even though Sheridan was the lead vocalist, "My Bonnie" still got to 26 in Billboard, 29 in Cash Box and 31 in Music Vendor (which would soon become Record World).

On March 27, MGM issued a follow-up single, pairing two more Hamburg tracks, "Why" and "Cry For A Shadow." The latter was actually a pure Beatles recording, an instrumental written by and credited to John Lennon and George Harrison. Billboard charted "Why" for one week at 88. The disc failed to crack the top 100 of the other trades, stalling at 129 in Cash Box and 138 in Music Vendor.

The remaining four Hamburg recordings were released by Atco Records on a pair of summer singles. The first featured "Sweet Georgia Brown" and "Take Out Some Insurance On Me Baby." The A-Side had a re-recorded Sheridan vocal with the line "In Liverpool she even dared to criticize the Beatles hair with their whole fan club standing there." Even with its Beatles reference, "Sweet Georgia Brown" sold poorly, charting at 120 in Record World.

Atco's second single, "Ain't She Sweet" b/w "Nobody's Child," was issued on July 6, 1964. This disc did much better as the A-side featured a John Lennon lead vocal. The song peaked at 19 in Billboard, 14 in Cash Box and 13 in Record World.

The Polydor collection of the Beatles Hamburg recordings contains all eight of the previously issued songs plus four Sheridan recordings that had no Beatles involvement. The same album was released in Canada six months earlier under the title *Very Together*. Its cover, featuring a candelabra with one of four candles extinguished, was a tasteless reference to the 1969 "Paul is dead" rumor.

In contrast, the U.S. cover is first class. It features a striking Joel Brodsky photo of a stack of old Mersey Beat magazines on a cobblestone sidewalk, tied in a bundle as if they had just been left there by an early morning delivery truck. The back cover has a long George Harrison quote that includes "we got very tight as a band in Hamburg." This is preceded by a small print consumer warning: "The release of this album is justified by the enormous influence the Beatles have had on contemporary pop music. Many record collectors will be curious about their earliest recording dates, others will find this album a bummer. In any event, here is an album that takes its place alongside the large body of Beatles recordings."

Billboard reviewed the album in its May 9 issue, describing the "pre-Beatlemania album" as "another chapter in the history of the rock movement which the Beatles helped to form in 1964." The LP peaked at 117 in Billboard, 94 in Cash Box and 138 in Record World.

Boxes, Books and Gatefolds: The Packaging of *Let It Be*

The Beatles initial concept for the cover of their *Get Back* album was to match the "get back to their roots" approach of the recordings with a jacket mimicking the cover to their first LP, *Please Please Me* (below left). On May 13, 1969, the group was photographed by the same photographer (Angus McBean) in the same location (the interior stairwell at EMI's Manchester Square headquarters) in the same pose (looking down over the rail) in the same order (Ringo, Paul, George and John). The idea was to duplicate the cover's graphics with the group's name in tall yellow letters, the album's title in red and the reference to the other featured track and number of other songs in blue.

Printer's proofs were made for the second version of the *Get Back* LP (see page 185). The resulting front cover (below right) was clever and effective. The back cover had the same layout as the group's first album with liner notes by Tony Barrow that incorporated some of his notes from the first album augmented by new text such as: "Here we are 19 singles, 16 tours, 11 albums, 7 years, a few beards and some children later and, at last, you're invited into a Beatles recording session." A comparison of the 1963 *Please Please Me* photo with the *Get Back* picture from 1969 shows how much the group changed in six years time. This cover was not used because it had nothing to do with the film.

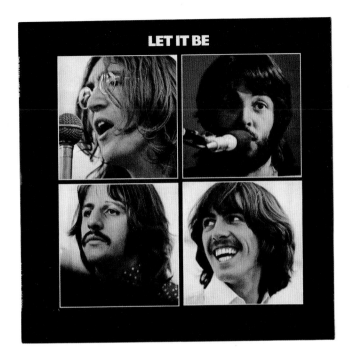

The cover for the *Let It Be* album features the same color photographs of the faces of John, Paul, George and Ringo used to promote the film (from the *Get Back* book and "Let It Be" picture sleeve). The only text on the black background cover is the album's title in white. The back cover also has a black background. The top has text about the album in white followed by the song titles. The center of the cover has four black and white photos of each Beatle. The text below thanks George Martin, Glyn Johns, Billy Preston, Mal Evans, Peter Brown, Richard Hewson and Brian Rogers and credits "Design by John Kosh" and "Photographs by Ethan Russell." There is a red Apple logo below the text. The lower part of the back cover varies among countries, with each providing its own manufacturing information.

The *Get Back* album was initially slated to be the follow-up to the double-disc *White Album*. That album's elaborate packaging included four portraits and a poster.

The *Get Back* LP's packaging would be even more intricate. The album came with a 164-page book full of photographs by Ethan Russell (most in color) and extensive text by Johnathan Cott and David Dalton, which consisted primarily of edited transcriptions of studio discussions taped during the filming of the Beatles rehearsals at Twickenham Film Studios and the subsequent recording sessions held in the basement at Apple. This was mixed with words from the authors.

The LP's elaborate packaging necessitated a higher list price (by about a pound) than a normal single disc release. In the U.K., the album would sell for just under three pounds (two pounds, 19 shillings, 11 pence at a time when there were 20 shillings to the pound and 12 pence to a shilling). Had the *Get Back* LP been released by Capitol Records in the U.S. as originally planned, its list price would have been $10.98 (an increase of $4.00) to cover the added costs of the deluxe packaging.

John Kosh's packaging design called for an outer slipcase to house the contents. The case was made of thin cardboard and features the same four color photos of the Beatles as on the album's jacket against a black background, but without any text. The case contains a cardboard inner tray custom fit to hold the 164-page softcover book. The vinyl disc was placed inside a standard size LP jacket, which fit inside the slipcase on top of the book. The entire package is shown on the next page.

The book cover has the same four photos, but are rectangular rather than square. Because the book was designed several months before the name of the film and album was changed to *Let It Be*, the spine to the book reads "THE BEATLES GET BACK." The books were printed in the U.K. by Garrod & Lofthouse, Ltd. EMI shipped the books to other markets. Unfortunately, the glue binding of the books was problematic, often leading to pages separating from the spine.

In the United States, the *Let It Be* album was distributed by United Artists as part of its film deal with the Beatles. The company was afraid that a $10.98 list price would negatively impact sales and refused to issue the LP with the book. A compromise was reached under which the album would come with a gatefold cover and list for $6.98. Although fans in the U.S. who knew about the deluxe packaging in other countries may have felt deprived, most Americans were unaware of the book. If the album had been packaged with the book and listed for $10.98, sales most likely would have been significantly lower. The open gatefold is shown below.

The labels to the U.S. album feature the same distinctive full and sliced apples as earlier releases, except that the apples are red rather than the usual green (see page 14). Abkco's Allan Steckler made the decision, believing that special albums should have special labels.

Capitol Records of Canada and Discos Capital de México issued the *Let It Be* LP with the full packaging.

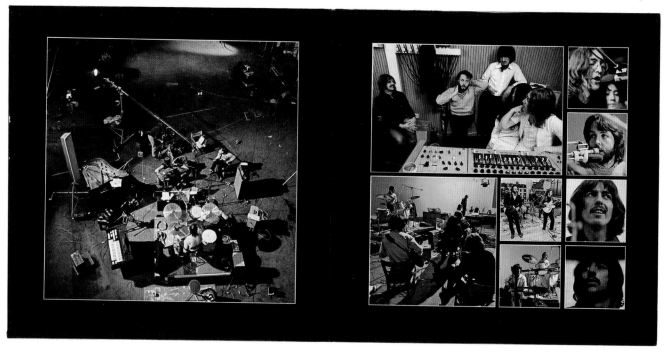

> This is a new phase **BEATLES** album...
> essential to the content of the film, **LET IT BE** was that they performed live for many of the tracks; in comes the warmth and the freshness of a live performance; as reproduced for disc by **PHIL SPECTOR**

Had the above liner notes appearing on the back cover of the *Let It Be* LP been subjected to truth-in-advertising law, they might have read something like this:

This is a new phase **BEATLES** album....well, actually it's the last **BEATLES** album as Paul recently announced he's quitting the band and John actually left over a half year ago, and we don't think that this is just a phase they're going through, they really mean it, the **BEATLES** are over, kaput...and as for new, well, to tell the truth, most of these recordings are over 15 months old...

essential to the content of the film, **LET IT BE** was that they performed live for many of the tracks...well, actually, they performed live for all of the tracks in the film...we didn't tinker with the film's soundtrack, but as for this LP, let's just say that the "new phase" approach allowed the group to abandon its original concept of making an honest live-in-the-studio album without any overdubs...

in comes the warmth and freshness of a live performance; as reproduced for disc by **PHIL SPECTOR** ...well, actually, some of you will think "in comes **PHIL SPECTOR**, out goes the warmth and freshness of a live performance; as overproduced for the disc by **PHIL SPECTOR**;" but if you can forgive him for his fruity arrangement of "Let It Be" and the excessive strings and choir on "The Long And Winding Road," you will marvel at the warmth and freshness of "Two Of Us," "For You Blue" and the unaltered rooftop performances.

Had liner notes similar to the above been prepared for the *Get Back* album in the summer of 1969, they might have read something like this:

This is a new phase **BEATLES** album...essential to the content of their TV special, **GET BACK** was that they performed live for all of the tracks joined on keyboards by **BILLY PRESTON**; in comes the warmth and freshness of a live-in-the-studio performance; as produced for disc by **GEORGE MARTIN** and engineered by **GLYN JOHNS**

As originally planned, the *Get Back* album would have indeed been a new phase Beatles album. After the studio wizardry of *Revolver*, *Sgt. Pepper's Lonely Hearts Club Band*, *Magical Mystery Tour* and, to a lesser extent, *The White Album*, the Beatles were truly getting back to their roots. When the Beatles recorded their first two albums, *Please Please Me* and *With The Beatles*, they were limited to a two-track recorder. Nearly all of their songs were recorded live in the studio, with the band playing their instruments and singing at the same time until they captured the best take. There were only minimal overdubs and edits. On some songs, the group was joined on piano by George Martin.

Get Back would be recorded the same way, with the band playing live in the studio and joined on most tracks by Billy Preston on keyboards. The goal was to record the songs without any overdubs or edits. They would keep playing the songs again and again until they got it right. And they often did.

The Recording Sessions

The January 1969 session from which the *Let It Be* album eventually evolved grew out of a totally different concept. The initial plan, conceived by Paul McCartney in September 1968, was to have the group give a concert in a small venue such as the Roundhouse in London. The show, which was later tentatively scheduled for January 18, 1969, would be the group's first public performance in over two years and would be filmed for a one-hour television special.

In late November 1968, Apple announced that the concert would not take place at the Roundhouse, but did not name a replacement venue. The group would perform three separate shows for invited audiences, with each set recorded in color on video tape. The television program would consist of the best performances from these shows. Most of the songs would be from the Beatles recently released double album, with a few oldies thrown in.

The driving force behind the show was Paul, who wanted the group to return to live performances. Many of his ideas for the project can be traced back to the band's promotional clips for "Hey Jude" and "Revolution." These performance videos were directed by Michael Lindsay-Hogg and were shot before an audience of invited fans on September 4, 1968, at Twickenham Film Studios. McCartney was pleased with the dynamic promotional films and reenlisted Lindsay-Hogg to serve as director for the television program.

Although the initial plan was to have the TV show revolve around and plug *The White Album*, the group later decided they should learn about eight new songs for the concert. This would require a week or two of rehearsals, which could also be filmed in a manner similar to the filming of the Beatles July 30, 1968, "Hey Jude" session. According to Mal Evans, the plan was to make a "Beatles At Work" documentary separate from the TV special that could be viewed at a later date to show what goes on as the Beatles build up a new set of songs.

Denis O'Dell, president of Apple Films, decided that the proceedings should be shot using 16 mm film rather than video tape, and booked Twickenham for rehearsals commencing on January 2, 1969. That fit in well with his schedule as O'Dell was serving as producer for *The Magic Christian* (starring Peter Sellers and Ringo Starr), which was set to begin filming at Twickenham on February 3. During the month-long Beatles project, cameramen shot approximately 475 rolls of film. Most of the proceedings were filmed by two cameras, although four cameras were used for the rooftop segment.

The sound crew used two Nagra mono reel-to-reel tape recorders each paired with a camera. The reels of tape were run at a high speed resulting in a recording time of only 16 minutes per tape. Although each recorder would have down time to change reels, most of the proceedings were captured because while one machine was having its tape replaced, the other was still recording. Approximately 530 reels of tape were used, yielding about 141 hours of music and dialog. While some of this is duplicated between reels from the two recorders, there are probably over 100 hours of unique recordings. A significant portion of the Nagra tapes has been bootlegged.

Glyn Johns also recorded some of the band's performances on January 7, 8, 9, 10 and 13 so that the group could listen to playbacks of the songs. These tapes were most likely recorded over or lost. Johns was recruited by McCartney to serve as balance engineer for the sessions. Johns' experience included work as either an engineer or producer for several high profile acts including the Rolling Stones, Small Faces, the Steve Miller Band, the Move and Traffic. George Martin attended only a few of the Twickenham rehearsals, but took a more active role when the group relocated to their new Apple basement studio. Johns was there from the start and was present throughout the entire proceedings, serving as unofficial producer when Martin was absent.

Although none of the Twickenham rehearsals were properly recorded on multi-track equipment, over ten hours of performances from the later January 21-31 sessions held at Apple's Savile Row headquarters were recorded on the new studio's eight-track recorder. When the Beatles felt they were ready for a serious take of a song, they instructed Glyn Johns to roll the tape. Some of these performances were given rough mixes by Johns and then transferred to acetates so that the Beatles could evaluate their new songs. The original unreleased *Get Back* album was compiled solely from recordings made at Apple.

On the morning of January 2, 1969, the Beatles arrived at Twickenham to begin rehearsing songs for the show. On this first day they worked primarily on "Don't Let Me Down," "I've Got A Feeling" and "Two Of Us," although other songs were introduced, including "Dig A Pony" and George's "All Things Must Pass." During discussions about the planned concert, Paul suggested it take place at Twickenham, but also expressed an interest in holding it outdoors.

The next day the Beatles worked on "Don't Let Me Down," "All Things Must Pass," "One After 909" and "Maxwell's Silver Hammer." George sang some Dylan songs and the group ran through bits and pieces of several oldies such as Little Richard's "Lucille," Larry Williams' "Short Fat Fanny" and the Coasters' "Three Cool Cats."

During the *Get Back* sessions, the Beatles often resorted to playing songs from their old stage show. Sometimes they would turn in fairly complete and competent versions, but more often it was a case of no one really remembering the words. Many of these performances broke down after a verse or two. At one time there was talk of releasing an entire album of oldies performed during the sessions, but this idea was abandoned when the group realized that while some of these recordings were interesting and entertaining, the musicianship and singing sounded amateurish and was not up to their usual high standards.

The group also played a few contemporary songs such as Canned Heat's "Going Up The Country" and Janis Joplin's "Piece Of My Heart." George showed his fondness for Bob Dylan and the Band by leading the group through songs such as "I Shall Be Released," "The Mighty Quinn (Quinn The Eskimo)," "Positively 4th Street" and "To Kingdom Come." At times, the group engaged in extended jams.

After taking the weekend off, the Beatles returned to Twickenham on Monday, January 6. It was during these weekday sessions that things really deteriorated. The group went through tedious rehearsals, but didn't seem satisfied with their performances of the new songs. They had numerous discussions about the live show, but could not agree on a location. (Lindsay-Hogg suggested that the show be filmed at an ancient outdoor Roman amphitheater on the shores of North Africa. Although this idea was abandoned, it was given serious consideration, with plans for Mal Evans to fly to Tripoli on January 13 to inspect the theater.)

John, who was often strung out on heroin, was going through a phase where he preferred nonverbal communication to talking. His lack of participation in serious discussions frustrated both Paul and George. At times, Yoko would speak for John, and her constant presence at the rehearsals added to the tense atmosphere. George was becoming increasingly frustrated with the group's indifference towards his songs, his role in the band and John's failure to communicate. Ringo showed up to play drums, but did not participate in most of the discussions about the upcoming concert or the band's future. By default, Paul was forced into the role of running the sessions, often leading to resentment from the others.

The *Let It Be* film contains a segment from January 6 showing Paul criticizing George's guitar playing on "Two Of Us." Paul tells George his riffs are complicated and need to be made simpler. When George disagrees with Paul's assessment, McCartney says "I'm trying to help you, but I always hear as though I'm annoying you." He later adds "I'm not trying to get ya. What I am really trying to just say is 'Look lads...should we try it like this?'" To emphasize his point, McCartney says "This one is like 'Should we play guitar all through "Hey Jude"?' Well I don't think we should." This reference to Paul's previous ordering of George not to play lead guitar fills on "Hey Jude" causes Harrison to replay "Yeah, OK, well I don't mind. I'll play, you know, whatever you want me to play, or I won't play at all if you don't want me to play. Whatever it is that will please you, I'll do it."

That evening, the Beatles held a business meeting and discussed the planned live concert. The next morning, Paul expressed his continuing desire to do the show, but the others were less enthusiastic. John observed that even if they didn't do the show, they would still have a film about making an album. Paul discussed how pessimistic the group had become since the death of their manager, Brian Epstein. After Paul stated that they could either work to improve things or call it quits, George agreed and gave his opinion that the Beatles were coming to an end. Further discussions indicate that John and George not only had little enthusiasm for the concert, but also were losing their desire to put their creative energies into any group project. When George later suggested that the band break up, John asked who would get possession of the children. After Paul reminded them how stupid it would be to break up the group and unsuccessfully tried to engage in a serious discussion with John, the band returned to rehearsing new songs. During part of these discussions, George symbolically sang a few verses of "I Shall Be Released."

By the end of the week, George had enough. He felt stifled by Paul telling him what to play and was feeling negative vibes from John and Yoko. He had no interest in the concert. On January 10, after the group's lunch break, he quit the Beatles. Although the exact incident triggering this decision remains unknown (the press reported it was a fight between him and John), the actual moment of George's departure was captured by one of the Nagra tapes.

APPLE
An abkco managed company
presents

THE BEATLES "Let it be"

TECHNICOLOR® **United Artists**
Entertainment from
Transamerica Corporation

70/169

While John plays the opening riff to Chuck Berry's "I'm Talking About You," Harrison calmly tells him "I'm leaving the band now." Lennon asks "When?" and George replies "Now." The sound of Harrison's footsteps is accompanied by his advising the others to "Get a replacement and write the NME and get a few people."

After George's departure, the remaining Beatles resumed rehearsals, but these were not very productive. On January 12, the group met at Ringo's house for a previously scheduled meeting. Although George attended, he left the meeting early after becoming fed up with John's lack of input and Yoko's habit of speaking for John.

The following morning both George and John were no-shows at Twickenham. While no music was played, the tape machines recorded a series of frank conversations involving, at different times, Paul, Neil Aspinall, Linda Eastman (Paul's future wife), Mal Evans and Michael Lindsey-Hogg. While Paul went out of his way not to condemn Yoko, he recognized her effect on John's behavior. By devoting himself to Yoko, John was no longer fulfilling his responsibilities to the group. Paul was concerned that if he confronted John on this matter and suggested that Yoko's involvement with the Beatles be curtailed, John would quit the group. But Paul also acknowledged that George was no longer willing to put up with the situation.

When Mal later reached John on the phone, the call was put through to Paul, who talked John into returning to Twickenham. After Lennon's arrival, he and Paul discussed George's departure, with John believing that George was no longer satisfied with his role in the group. While John had previously been reluctant to talk about the band's current problems, he was much more open during this discussion. Lennon expressed his belief that Paul directed George and him on what to play because McCartney was concerned that he wouldn't like their playing if he left it up to them. After John discussed his and Paul's different approaches to recording sessions (Paul in charge versus John wanting suggestions which he can take or leave), Paul wondered how he could avoid hurting George's ego when he tells Harrison how to play. The brief rehearsal session held that afternoon featured the three remaining Beatles working on "Get Back," with emphasis on completing the lyrics.

The January 14 session was extremely unproductive as George did not attend, and John did not arrive until after lunch and spent his initial time being interviewed by Canadian journalists. After a bit of jamming, the group decided that continuing without George was a waste of time. At the end of the day, Mal packed up the group's instruments, bringing an end to the tumultuous Twickenham sessions.

Although memories differ as to exactly when, how and where things got patched up, George's recollection in the *Anthology* book was that he was called to a meeting at Ringo's house where it was decided that the group should get back together and finish the record. "Twickenham Studios were very cold and not a very nice atmosphere, so we decided to abandon that and go to Savile Row into the recording studio."

The group had entrusted the job of turning Apple's basement into a state-of-the-art studio to Alexis Mardas, a friend of John's who supposedly was an electronic genius. "Magic Alex," who was appointed head of Apple Electronics, boasted that he would build a studio vastly superior to EMI's facilities. It would have 72 tracks instead of EMI's measly eight. And rather than placing baffles (soundproof walls) around the drums to prevent leakage to microphones, Magic Alex would invent and install a sonic beam force field device that would magically stop the drum sounds from reaching the mikes. When the Beatles arrived at the basement studio on January 20, they were confronted with a total disaster. Magic Alex had put in 16 speakers for his 16-track recorder, but, as Harrison pointed out, "You only need two speakers for stereo sound." The speakers were quickly removed. Engineer Dave Harries described the mixing console as being made of "bits of wood and an old oscilloscope" and looking like the "control panel of a B-52 bomber."

When the Beatles tested the system, the playback tape was full of hums and hisses. George Martin had EMI send over two four-track consoles to pair with Apple's eight-track recorder. Because Magic Alex had neglected to put holes in the wall between the studio and control room, the cables had to be run through the door. The building's heating and air conditioning system, which was located in the basement, provided additional problems. It had not been soundproofed, so the system had to be turned off when the tapes were rolling.

Despite its flaws, the makeshift basement studio provided a vastly superior atmosphere to Twickenham's soundstage. Rehearsals resumed on January 21, with the group running through a mix of oldies and new songs. Some takes were recorded that afternoon, although most were recorded over. An early version of "She Came In Through The Bathroom Window" survives and is on *Anthology 3*.

The switch from Twickenham to Apple was not the only change in the project. The prospect for doing a live concert was looking grim, so the focus shifted from learning eight new songs for the TV show to recording 14 tracks for an album.

APPLE
An **abkco** managed company
presents

THE BEATLES "Let it be"

TECHNICOLOR® **United Artists**
Entertainment from
Transamerica Corporation

The other significant development was the addition of Billy Preston, who sat in on keyboards. On January 19, 1969, George went with Eric Clapton to see Ray Charles' concert at the Festival Hall. Prior to Ray coming on stage, Billy Preston warmed up the crowd by singing, dancing and playing organ. After Charles introduced Preston to the crowd, George remembered meeting him in Hamburg in 1962 when Preston was in Little Richard's band. Harrison had Billy tracked down and invited to Apple. When George was informed of Preston's arrival during the January 22 session, he met him at reception and asked him to come down to the basement studio and play keyboards. Billy's presence caused everyone to behave better leading to a "100% improvement in the vibe in the room." According to Harrison, "Having this fifth person was just enough to cut the ice that we'd created among ourselves." George Martin agreed that Preston was a very good keyboard player who "helped lubricate the friction that had been there."

A portion of the January 22 session with Billy Preston was recorded by Glyn Johns. Paul's handwritten comments on the back of the EMI tape box indicate that he was not impressed. Although McCartney wrote "Only good for conversation (if anything)," Johns placed the entire "Rocker & Conversation, Save the last Dance into Don't Let me Down" and the entire "Dig a Pony into I've Got a feeling" segments on the *Get Back* album. Johns also recorded Paul leading the group through Canned Heat's "Going Up The Country."

Much of the January 23 session was spent rehearsing "Get Back," which had become the top contender for the band's next single. The next day, prior to Billy Preston's arrival, John suggested that Preston be made a permanent member of the group. Although Paul wanted Preston to play during the sessions and on the television concert, he was against expanding the group's membership. Other songs rehearsed that day included "Two Of Us," "Teddy Boy" and "Dig It."

The Beatles decided that they needed to work through the weekend, so sessions were held on January 25 and 26. Highlights of the first day included the recording of the finished master for "For You Blue," as well as recorded rehearsals of "Two Of Us" and "Let It Be." John and Paul also sneaked in a bit of the Everly Brothers' "Bye Bye Love." The Sunday session included extensive work on "Let It Be" and "The Long And Winding Road," although the group found time to run through several oldies, including a medley of "Rip It Up" and "Shake Rattle And Roll," a medley of "Miss Ann," "Kansas City" and "Lawdy Miss Clawdy," Carl Perkins' "Blue Suede Shoes" and two

songs by the Miracles, "You Really Got A Hold On Me" and "Tracks Of My Tears." George also performed a largely solo version of "Isn't It A Pity." Glyn Johns prepared an acetate containing some of the day's recordings and titled it "Beatles Sunday."

The idea of performing an unannounced concert on the roof of Apple's Savile Row headquarters reportedly evolved on this day. According to Johns, the Beatles had expressed their desire to play to the whole of London. During the lunch break, the conversation turned to Apple's building, with Ringo commenting that the group was thinking of putting a garden on the roof. Johns suggested that they go up to the roof and told them his idea of having the band play up there, thus enabling the Beatles to play to a part of London.

Johns also takes credit for the concept of releasing an album containing loose performances and studio banter. "One night I took a couple of reels of the eight-tracks away with me to Olympic Studios and mixed two days of rehearsals with a lot of chat and humor and so on. I thought it would make the most incredible Beatles album ever, because it was so real." He gave copies of his rough mixes to each of the Beatles. The following day he was told that his concept for the album was a terrible idea, so he thought no more about it.

On January 27, the group worked primarily on "Get Back," although Johns also taped performances of "I've Got A Feeling," "Oh! Darling" and the tail end of a fun rendition of Jimmy McCracklin's "The Walk." The January 28 session was highly productive, with solid performances of "Get Back" and "Don't Let Me Down" being recorded. The group's first single for 1969 was pulled from these recordings. Johns also recorded the group working on "Dig A Pony," "I've Got A Feeling," "One After 909" and "Teddy Boy," as well as two Billy Preston songs and a rough version of their first single, "Love Me Do."

On January 29, the group rehearsed songs intended for the rooftop concert, which was scheduled for the next day. The band also ran through songs that would later appear on George's first album ("All Things Must Pass" and "Let It Down") as well as several oldies. The tapes rolled for "One After 909," "Teddy Boy" and "I Want You," as well as Buddy Holly's "Mailman Bring Me No More Blues" and a medley consisting of "Cannonball," "Not Fade Away," "Hey Little Girl" and "Bo Diddley." Johns also recorded the group having fun with the Latin standard "Besame Mucho" (recorded by the Coasters), which the Beatles had previously performed at their Decca audition on January 1, 1962, and at their EMI commercial test session at Abbey Road held on June 6, 1962.

APPLE

An abkco managed company

presents

THE BEATLES "Let it be"

TECHNICOLOR® G   United Artists
Entertainment from
Transamerica Corporation

Taped conversations from the day's session reveal that the group thought they could not finish 14 songs for an album before Ringo began filming *The Magic Christian* in a few days. Only "Get Back" and "For You Blue" were considered good enough for release, with producer George Martin believing that the others were not beyond the rehearsal stage. Paul recognized that the project had shifted from the planned television concert to a documentary about the Beatles making an album, and was worried that without the live concert, there was no payoff. Fortunately for all concerned, the following day's rooftop concert would provide the payoff needed to end what would later become the *Let It Be* film.

During lunchtime on January 30, 1969, the Beatles, with Billy Preston, climbed to the roof of their Savile Row headquarters to give what would be their last public performance. On this cold and windy day, the group gave a 42-minute show to both the delight and frustration of London's busy business district. The band played, in order, "Get Back" (two performances), "Don't Let Me Down," "I've Got A Feeling," "One After 909," "Dig A Pony," "God Save The Queen," "I've Got A Feeling," "Don't Let Me Down" and "Get Back."

Towards the end of show, the police arrived on the roof to put an end to the concert. During the final performance of "Get Back," Mal Evans became concerned that the group would be arrested if they didn't immediately stop, so he turned off the power to John and George's Fender Twin Reverb amps. While the others kept playing, George let Mal know the group would finish the song and flipped his amp back on. Mal then flipped the switch to John's amp and the band was full strength again. During the song's coda, Paul made fun of the incident by singing, "Oh, get back, you been out too long, Loretta. You been playing on the roofs again and that's no good 'cause you know your mommy doesn't like that. Oh she gets angry, she gonna have you arrested, get back." At the end of the song and concert, John stepped up to the mike and made his classic remark, "I'd like to say 'thank you' on behalf of the group and ourselves. I hope we passed the audition."

The next day the Beatles returned to the basement studio to record and film three songs that were inappropriate for their rooftop concert: "Two Of Us," "The Long And Winding Road" and "Let It Be." Complete performances of all three songs are shown in the film. This final session is well documented on bootleg collections.

Prior to recording "Two Of Us," the group warms up with a bunch of oldies with John and Paul on acoustic guitars, George on his Telecaster and Ringo on drums. The fun starts with Paul singing what sounds like an old folk song leading into Hank William's "Hey Good Looking." Next is a medley lasting nearly nine minutes and consisting of two Lonnie Donnegan songs ("Take This Hammer" and "Lost John"), Johnny Cash's "Five Feet High And Rising," Rufus Thomas' "Bear Cat," Blind Blake's "Black Dog Blues," Dr. Feelgood's "Right String But The Wrong Yo-Yo" and the group's own "Run For Your Life." After two unsuccessful attempts at recording an acceptable take of "Two Of Us," John realizes his guitar is out of tune and sings about it to the tune of "Turkey In The Straw."

Paul then returns to "Step Inside Love," but sung with Spanish-sounding lyrics. John and Paul follow that with a quick stab at Cole Porter's "Friendship" (with an off-color line by John) that leads into "Tales Of Frankie Rabbit," a song by Drew and Dy, who were signed briefly to Apple. After a perfect, upbeat take of "Two Of Us," the group performs an improvised medley of the jazz standard "Deed I Do" (written by Fred Rose and Walter Hirsch), "In The Middle Of An Island" (written by Nick Acquaviva and Ted Varnick and a top ten hit for Tony Bennett in 1957) and the middle eight of "All Together Now" with John trashing the lyrics. The group then records one more take of "Two Of Us," taken at a slower pace. The song and acoustic guitar session comes to an end with John and Paul strumming their guitars and singing "Oh, yeah" followed by Ringo's drum thud.

The piano session opens with over a dozen takes of "The Long And Winding Road," interrupted only by the group messing around with "Lady Madonna" for about four minutes, including an improvised verse by Paul: "Lord and Lady Dacca in your private yacht/All the people wonder why you got such a lot." After a pair of satisfactory takes (designated 18 and 19), John says he is satisfied.

Paul sings lead on John's "I Want You" before leading the band through a rehearsal and then a series of performances of "Let It Be." In between takes there are a few diversions, including Paul playing a bit of the jazz tune "Twelfth Street Rag." The group performs two takes of "Oh! Darling," with John singing along in spots, the Foundations recent hit "Build Me Up Buttercup" and a bit of Wanda Jackson's "Let's Have A Party." Everything comes together for the last two takes of "Let It Be," which are nearly flawless. Take 27A is close to perfection, marred only by George hitting a few off notes in his guitar solo. This take, with various modifications, was used as the master take for the *Get Back* album, the single and the *Let It Be* album versions of the song. Take 27B appears in the film. This brought an end to the Apple sessions and, except for a few later tweaks, the *Get Back/Let It Be* recording sessions.

APPLE

An **abkco** managed company

presents

THE BEATLES "Let it be"

TECHNICOLOR® **United Artists**

Entertainment from
Transamerica Corporation

LIB-10

THE BEATLES "LET IT BE"
AN APPLE FILMS LIMITED PRODUCTION
Produced by NEIL ASPINALL   Directed by MICHAEL LINDSAY-HOGG
COLOR by Technicolor (R)   UNITED ARTISTS, Entertainment from Transamerica Corporation

Two Of Us

Recorded: January 24, 25 and 31, 1969 (Apple basement)
Mixed: March 25, 1970 (Phil Spector)

Producer: George Martin (January 31 and maybe January 24 & 25)
Engineers: Glyn Johns; Neil Richmond (January 24); Alan Parsons (January 25 and 31)

Paul: Lead vocal; acoustic guitar (Martin D-28)
John: Harmony vocal; acoustic guitar (Gibson J-200); whistling
George: Lead guitar (Telecaster) (playing bass part)
Ringo: Drums

"Two Of Us," originally titled "On Our Way Home," was written by Paul for Linda. He introduced the song to the group on January 2, playing acoustic guitar, teaching the chords to John and George and vocalizing drum parts for Ringo. At this stage the song's lyrics were essentially complete, although the arrangement had not been finalized. The next day Paul continued with stop and start rehearsals, this time playing bass. John began singing with Paul during the verses. Although John and Glyn Johns suggested an acoustic arrangement, the band initially rejected this idea and played the song with electric guitars, probably to facilitate its inclusion in the planned TV concert.

The Beatles returned to "Two Of Us" on January 6, with Paul playing a galloping bass riff to open the song and to lead into the bridge. During these tedious rehearsals, Paul and George got into a lengthy argument over how songs should be developed. Part of this discussion appears in the film (and is quoted on page 134).

The group turned in an entertaining up-tempo performance of the song on January 8 with John and Paul sharing a microphone. During the middle eight, Paul resorted to an Elvis impersonation, and John ended the song singing "We're goin' home" in a deep bass voice. An edited version of this performance appears in the film.

The following day, the Beatles continued with rehearsals of the song. The arrangement retained the galloping bass and guitar riff and added vocal harmonies by George on the bridge and part of the verses and chorus. On January 10, the band experimented with the middle eight, trying a bossa nova beat with Ringo's drumming patterned after Buddy Holly's "Peggy Sue" and a shuffle beat.

Although snippets of "Two Of Us" were performed on January 23, rehearsals of the song did not resume until January 24. The initial runthroughs were horrendous, with the group taking the song at too slow a pace. After John suggested they play the song with acoustic guitars, the lineup was revised to feature Paul on his Martin D-28 acoustic guitar, John on a Gibson J-200 acoustic guitar, George on his Telecaster (playing a bass part on the top strings) and Ringo on drums. The first performance with acoustic guitars featured a solo John vocal on the first verse and, while a bit ragged, showed that the "unplugged" approach was the way to go.

As the group continued with a series of runthroughs, the song's now-familiar features began to emerge, including Paul's bending notes used to open the song and lead into the verses. Paul began singing solo on the middle eight. George worked out a bass pattern on his Telecaster guitar and Ringo perfected his drum part. The new arrangement with John and Paul sharing vocals and acoustic guitars reminded McCartney of the Everly Brothers (Phil and Don), whose vocal harmony style influenced the Beatles. *Anthology 3* contains a charming performance in which Paul acknowledges the duo by saying "Take it Phil" after the first middle eight. On later takes John began whistling over the song's ending. Paul also ended one of the performances by singing a bit of the "Maori finale" from "Hello Goodbye." The Nagra tapes captured John jokingly offering a variant for the lyric "spending someone's hard-earned pay" with "smoking someone's hard earned grass." Glyn Johns selected a January 24 take of the song (without Lennon's whistling) for the *Get Back* album.

The following day the group continued with a series of "Two Of Us" rehearsals, concentrating on the middle eight, with John working out a harmony part to sing on its second line. The band also performed a few complete runthroughs. Paul led the band through additional rehearsals on January 28 and 29. The final runthrough of the song on January 29, with goofy vocals from John and Paul, marked the end of the sessions leading up to the rooftop concert.

On January 31, the Beatles returned to the Apple basement studio for filming of their acoustic and piano songs. They recorded three performances of "Two Of Us," designated Takes 10, 11 and 12. The first take came to a quick halt when the group realized they were playing too slow. After a brief pause, the band completed a mediocre performance that plodded along with out-of-tune guitars. For Take 11, Paul and Ringo picked up the tempo. This made all the difference in the world, inspiring the group to give their best performance of the song. Although Glyn Johns passed over this version in favor of an inferior recording from January 24, Phil Spector wisely chose this upbeat performance, which appears in the movie, for the *Let It Be* album. Take 12, which is played at a slightly slower pace, is almost as good. Spector thought highly of the song, selecting "Two Of Us" to open the *Let It Be* album.

143

Dig A Pony

Recorded: January 21, 22, 24 & 28 (basement); Jan 30 (rooftop)
Mixed: March 23, 1970 (Phil Spector)

Producer: George Martin (Jan 28 & 30; maybe Jan 21, 22 & 24)
Engineers: Glyn Johns; Neil Richmond (January 24); Alan Parsons (January 23, 28 and 30)

John: Lead vocal; electric guitar (Casino)
Paul: Backing vocal; bass guitar (Hofner)
George: Lead guitar (Telecaster); intro vocals (not in final mix)
Ringo: Drums
Billy Preston: Electric piano (Fender Rhodes)

"Dig A Pony" (which was sometimes referred to as "All I Want Is You" during the sessions) was written by John, who later dismissed the song as a "piece of garbage." Shortly after performing "Don't Let Me Down" for George at the start of the initial Twickenham session on January 2, Lennon performed a runthrough of the song on electric guitar. This was essentially a solo performance, although George added some lead guitar towards the end. While John had yet to complete the chorus, many of the lyrics to the verses were in place.

The group returned to the song on January 7 with a rough uninspired rehearsal that ended abruptly when John lost interest and asked "Has anybody got a fast one?" A portion of this performance is shown in the movie. Although John played bits of the song on January 13, no serious attempt to develop the song was made until the sessions moved to Apple's basement studio.

The initial January 21 rehearsals of the song were marred by sloppy playing and John's inability to remember the lyrics. From this point forward, the song begins and ends with "All I want is you" background vocals. Later rehearsals from the day showed progress as Paul experimented with his falsetto harmony and George worked out his guitar solo. This encouraged Lennon to have Glyn Johns record two takes of the song, which are flawed but played with spirit. *Anthology 3* contains one of these takes. After listening to a playback of Take 1, the band returned to the song, but only managed a few false starts before moving on.

The Beatles continued rehearsing the song on January 22, with Johns recording some of the performances. Other runthroughs from this part of the session have Lennon goofing around with his vocals and even singing one verse in a staccato style. John also spent time instructing Ringo on where he should emphasize his cymbals.

Shortly after Billy Preston was brought to Apple's basement studio for the first time, the Beatles showcased the song for him. After running through other songs, the band returned to "Dig A Pony" with Preston, whose electric piano added musical depth.

Glyn Johns pulled an entire sequence of songs from the January 22 session for the *Get Back* album. After "Don't Let Me Down," John says "Well ladies and gentlemen, I'd like to change the [begins quickly strumming his guitar] tempo a little." Upon completing his rhythm guitar improvisation, Lennon adds "OK, let's do the next song then." After George asks "Is he [Glyn Johns] tapin' then?," John replies "Yeah, we'll do 'Dig A Pony' straight into 'I've Got A Fever' [meaning "I've Got A Feeling"]." While George is practicing riffs from the song, John says "OK... You never changed drumming now. Yeah, that's OK. OK. Alright Glynis, we're off again." In the background Paul is practicing his bass and George is singing the song's "All I want is you" introduction over matching guitar notes. After John's count-in, a deliberate three-note false start and John's second count-in, the group launches into an acceptable but somewhat ragged performance of the song that ended up on the *Get Back* LP.

The Beatles returned to the song on January 28. Of the eight takes recorded by Glyn Johns that day, only two were complete. At the end of Take 8, John sings "I think the other one was much better, let's do 'Get Back.'"

The group ran through "Dig A Pony" as part of its January 29 rehearsal for the rooftop concert. John's vocals were laid back because he did not want to strain his vocal chords.

"Dig A Pony" was performed by the Beatles as part of their January 30 rooftop concert. Because John had a tendency to muff the words, he asks for them to be provided. Apple equipment manager Kevin Harrington complies by kneeling in front of John with a lyric sheet attached to a clipboard. Just as the song is about to begin, Ringo calls out "Hold it," so he can blow his nose. This is followed by Lennon's count leading into the instrumental start of the song. Paul and George add "All I want is..." vocals prior to John entering with his lead vocal. Rehearsals have paid off, as the group delivers a tight performance of the song. The song ends with the "All I want is you" vocals. John then says, "Thank you brothers...me hands gettin' too cold to play the chords."

Phil Spector selected this rooftop performance for the *Let It Be* album, leaving in Ringo's pre-song banter and John's count-in, as well as John's remarks at the song's conclusion. Spector mixed out the opening and closing "All I want is you" vocals from the song.

APPLE
An **abkco** managed company
presents

THE BEATLES "Let it be"

TECHNICOLOR® United Artists
Entertainment from
Transamerica Corporation

LITHO. IN U.S.A.

4

70/169

Across The Universe

Recorded: February 4 and 8, 1968 (Abbey Road Studios 3 & 2)
Overdub Session: April 1, 1970 (Abbey Road Studio 1)
Mixed: April 2, 1970 (Phil Spector)

Producer: George Martin (Feb 4 & 8); Phil Spector (April 1)
Engineers: Martin Benge and Phil McDonald (Feb 4); Ken Scott and Richard Lush (Feb 8); Peter Brown and Richard Lush (April 1)

John: Lead vocal; acoustic guitar (Martin D-28); organ
Paul: Backing vocal; piano; bass guitar; acoustic guitar (Take 2)
George: Tamboura; wah-wah guitar
Ringo: Tom-toms; svaramandal (Take 2); drums (April 1)
George Martin: Organ

Outside Musicians: 18 violins, 4 violas, 4 cellos, 1 harp, 3 trumpets, 3 trombones and 2 guitars; 14 person choir (April 1)

Although the Beatles had recorded "Across The Universe" in February 1968, John was not satisfied with the results and felt the performance could be improved. So John resurrected the song when they got together at Twickenham in January 1969. Because the group was shown rehearsing the song in the *Let It Be* film, the decision was made to include it on the "soundtrack" album.

John considered "Across The Universe" one of his best lyrics. According to Lennon, the song wrote itself. One evening his wife Cynthia had been "going on and on about something and she'd gone to sleep." John "kept hearing these words over and over, flowing like an endless stream." Knowing that he couldn't get to sleep until he put it on paper, Lennon got out of bed and went downstairs to write. The song's verses contain beautiful and somewhat trippy imagery. The chorus mixes the Sanskrit words "Jai Guru Deva" (victory to the Guru-God) and "Om" (Hindu's most sacred mantra or holy sound) with the phrase "Nothing's gonna change my world."

The Beatles recorded six takes of the song on February 4, 1968. The first take was an instrumental track consisting of John on his Martin D-28 acoustic guitar, George on tamboura and Ringo on tom-toms. Take 2 features a beautiful Lennon vocal, John and Paul on Martin D-28 acoustic guitars, George on tamboura and Ringo on svaramandal. This pure unadulterated recording is on *Anthology 2*.

The Beatles experimented with different arrangements for Takes 4 through 7 (there was no Take 3). The deluxe *White Album* anniversary edition contains Take 6, which is a live recording of John on vocal and acoustic guitar accompanied by Ringo on tom-toms. Take 7 has the same basic arrangement as 6, but adds George on

tamboura. All instruments were run through a Leslie speaker and subjected to artificial double tracking. John's lead vocal was then recorded with the tape running at a slower than normal speed to give it a sped-up effect upon playback.

John and Paul wanted to add falsetto vocals, but realized that the desired high harmonies were out of their range. Rather than attempt to round up professional singers on a Sunday evening, Paul asked if any of the female fans hanging out in Abbey Road's corridor could hold a high note. After 16-year-old Lizzie Bravo said she could, she and 17-year-old Gayleen Pease were brought to Studio 3 to sing "Nothing's gonna change my world" over the song's backing track.

After the girls completed their parts, Take 7 was given a reduction mix (designated Take 8) to allow for additional overdubs. One of the newly vacated tracks was filled with backwards recordings of Paul's bass and Ringo's drums. The Beatles then recorded three takes of sound effects, which included multi-layered humming, guitar and a drone-like sound. The tapes of these embellishments were played backwards and added to Take 8. A mono mix was made and transferred to an acetate for John. This unique mix of the song is known among collectors as the "Hums Wild" version.

On February 8, all the backwards additions from October 4 were removed from Take 8 to allow for new overdubs, including a new lead vocal from John, organ by Lennon and George Martin, maracas and wah-wah guitar by Harrison, piano by McCartney at the end and backing vocals from John and Paul. Although everyone thought the song was great, John did not want it issued as the single.

Comedian Spike Milligan happened to be at Abbey Road when the sessions took place and visited George Martin and the boys in the control room to Studio No. 2. At that time he was organizing a benefit album for the World Wildlife Fund. When he learned of the group's decision not to issue the song, he boldly asked the Beatles if they would be willing to contribute "Across The Universe" to the project. Much to his delight, the group agreed to do so. When the song was mixed for mono at the end of the session, bird sound effects were added to the beginning and end of the track. This may have been done at the suggestion of Milligan or Martin.

John's unhappiness with the 1968 recording of "Across The Universe" prompted him to resurrect the song during the *Get Back* sessions. The first attempts at the song took place on January 6, 1969, with John on his Epiphone Casino, George on his Telecaster and wah-wah pedal, Paul on his Hofner bass and Ringo on drums. John sings whatever words he can remember and Paul joins him on the choruses. These performances are miserable, suffering from a slow tempo and uninspired playing and singing. On one runthrough, George improvises a guitar solo over the third verse when John fails to sing. Things don't get any better after John switches to organ. When George asks him about the earlier recording, John insists it can be bettered. Later attempts prove him wrong.

The January 7 performances are not much better, although John is able to sing the words when Apple's Eric Brown brings him the lyrics. After John once again expresses his dissatisfaction over the 1968 recording, George says how much he likes it. Although the earlier recording was donated to the charity album, John is concerned the album won't be issued and wants to include the song in the current project. After experimenting with different tempos and sounds (including one pass with George on organ), the group tries a heavier approach with Paul singing along with John. Portions of these performances appear in the film. The Beatles attempted the song a few more times on January 9 with mixed results.

On January 23, after the Beatles moved the sessions to Apple, George asked John if they were going to rerecord "Across The Universe." Lennon replied that they were not since the song was coming out on an EP. The extended play disc John was referring to was to include "Across The Universe" as a bonus track along with the four new songs recorded for the *Yellow Submarine* film. The group had received some negative feedback for the just-released *Yellow Submarine* LP because it only had four new Beatles tracks. The EP would give fans a lesser-priced option to obtain the film songs. A tape for the EP was later compiled and banded on March 13, 1969; however, the idea was dropped and the disc was never issued. The mono mixes of the five songs made for the EP were later released in 2009 on the *Mono Masters* CD.

By the fall of 1969, the World Wildlife Fund album was finally taking shape. The inclusion of an unreleased Beatles recording was a real coup. A line from "Across The Universe" was modified to form the album's title, *No One's Gonna Change Our World*.

On October 2, George Martin, with engineers Jeff Jarratt and Alan Parsons, mixed the song for the stereo LP. Martin sped up the tape of Take 8, shifting the song up a half step from D major to E flat. This shortened the song by ten seconds (not counting the opening second effects) and raised the pitch of John's voice.

The following day, George Martin compiled and banded the album, which was released as Regal Starline SRS 5013. Although the LP was not issued in the U.S., copies were imported. The Wildlife version of "Across The Universe" made its official American debut in 1980 on Rarities. It also appears on *Past Masters Volume Two*.

By the time Glyn Johns was told to add "Across The Universe" to the *Get Back* album, the charity album had already been released. Thus, he needed to make the recording sound different than the Wildlife album track and make it fit into the *Get Back* concept. On January 5, 1970, Johns went back to Take 8 (without the added sound effects) and made a fresh stereo mix with the tape running at its proper speed. He mixed out the Beatles backing vocals but kept the voices of Lizzie Bravo and Gayleen Pease because their vocals were part of the reduction mix of Take 7 and could not be mixed out of Take 8. To give the song its *Get Back* flavor, Johns left in a brief bit of studio chat that precedes the start of the song on the master tape (Lennon's "Are you alright, Ritchie?"). Johns then added the song to the revised *Get Back* LP.

Phil Spector also included "Across The Universe" on his version of album. Like George Martin and Glyn Johns before him, Spector started with Take 8. But while Martin sped up the song and Johns left its speed alone, Spector slowed it down so that the song dropped from D to D flat and ran nine seconds longer. On April 1, he made a reduction mix of Take 8 (designated Take 9) onto three tracks of eight-track tape, leaving him five open tracks for overdubs. Later that day, Spector recorded Richard Hewson's score of 18 violins, four violas, four cellos, one harp, three trumpets, three trombones, two acoustic guitars, a 14-person choir and Ringo on drums. The orchestra was conducted by Hewson.

Spector mixed "Across The Universe" the following day. The song opens with John's acoustic guitar, which is heard as part of the reduction mix of Take 7. His guitar, along with George's tamboura, disappears during the chorus and other parts of the song where the Take 7 reduction mix is faded out. By using John's February 8 vocal from Take 8 and acoustic guitars recorded on April 1, Spector was able to fade out the reduction mix of Take 7 during the chorus, thus eliminating the backing vocals of Lizzie Bravo and Gayleen Pease. He mixed in maracas and Harrison's wah-wah guitar from Take 8 during the chorus. McCartney's bass piano notes appear towards the end of the song. With the exception of John's acoustic guitar intro, the mix is dominated by Spector's trademark wall of sound, though Lennon's lead vocal is prominently featured.

Let It Be... Naked also uses Take 7, but prior to embellishments. This mix has John's vocal and acoustic guitar, George's tamboura and Ringo's drums, with reverb progressively added towards the end.

THE BEATLES "LET IT BE"
AN APPLE FILMS LIMITED PRODUCTION
Produced by NEIL ASPINALL   Directed by MICHAEL LINDSAY-HOGG
COLOR by Technicolor (R)   UNITED ARTISTS, Entertainment from Transamerica Corporation

LIB-12

I Me Mine

Recorded: January 3, 1970 (Abbey Road Studio 2)
Overdub Session: April 1, 1970 (Abbey Road Studio 1)
Mixed and edited: April 2, 1970 (Phil Spector)

Producer: George Martin (January 3); Phil Spector (April 1)
Engineers: Phil McDonald and Richard Langham (January 3);
Peter Brown and Richard Lush (April 1)

George: Lead vocal; acoustic guitar (Gibson J-200); electric
guitars (Les Paul)
Paul: Backing vocal; bass guitar (Rickenbacker); organ
Ringo: Drums

Outside Musicians: 18 violins, 4 violas, 4 cellos, 1 harp,
3 trumpets, 3 trombones and 2 guitars

"I Me Mine" is George's statement "about the ego: the eternal problem." Harrison wrote the song on the evening of January 7, 1969, and introduced it to the group the following morning. Prior to the arrival of Paul and John, he sang and played the song for Ringo on John's unplugged Casino electric guitar. A portion of this initial performance appears in the film.

The Beatles rehearsed "I Me Mine" several times during the day. The tune's waltz tempo and flamenco guitar break led John to joke that the Beatles play rock 'n' roll and have no place in their playlist for a Spanish waltz. The band stayed in their standard lineup of two guitars, bass and drums for the song, although John took a break from a few of the runthroughs to dance with Yoko. During the afternoon session, Paul and George worked out harmony vocals for the chorus. Paul's suggestion that the song be made heavier by rocking out on the instrumental break was initially rejected by George. Part of the group's final runthrough of the song was used in the film. For reasons unknown, the group did not return to George's composition during the Apple recording sessions.

Nearly one year later, on January 3, 1970, George, Paul and Ringo got together with George Martin at Abbey Road to record "I Me Mine" for the soundtrack LP because the song was in the film. John was on a month-long vacation in Denmark and did not attend. Even if John had been in London, he still may have missed the session. By that time he had told the others he was quitting the group.

Before Take 15, George announced to those present in Studio Two, "You all will have read that Dave Dee is no longer with us. But Micky and Tich and I would just like to carry on the good work that's always gone down in number two." George's remark referred to reports in the press that Dave Dee was splitting from the British pop rock group Dave Dee, Dozy, Beaky, Mick & Tich, which had eight top ten British hits, including the number one "The Legend Of Xanadu." George's reference to "number two" was Abbey Road's Studio Two. Harrison's comment was full of irony as John had quit the Beatles, leaving George, Paul and Ringo to carry on.

The trio recorded 16 backing tracks of "I Me Mine" with George on his Gibson J-200 acoustic guitar and guide vocal, Paul on his Rickenbacker bass and Ringo on drums. Take 16 was then overdubbed with fresh lead vocals from George, backing vocals from George and Paul, organ, lead acoustic guitar and two distorted Les Paul guitars. The arrangement dropped the flamenco guitar instrumental break featured in the Twickenham performances. In its place is the hard-rocking "I I me me mine" middle eight first suggested by McCartney nearly one year earlier.

The finished master, which runs a mere 1:34, was mixed for stereo by Glyn Johns at Olympic Studios on January 5, 1970. In keeping with the spirit of the other tracks on the *Get Back* album, Johns edited in Paul fooling around on bass along with some studio chatter before the start of the song:

George: Alright. Are you ready, Ringo?
Ringo: Ready, George.

Anthology 3 contains an unedited mix of Take 16 preceded by George's Dave Dee announcement.

While compiling his version of the *Let It Be* album, Phil Spector decided the song needed orchestral embellishments for its waltz section. On March 23, Spector made his initial mix of the song from Take 16. He eliminated one of George's two lead vocals to free up a track for later overdubs and extended the song by 51 seconds with a clever edit. At the 1:21 mark, just after the line "flowing more freely than wine," the song jumps back to the :31 mark to the line "all through the day." This leads back into the hard-rocking "I I me me mine" segment and continues past "flowing more freely than wine" until the end of the song.

On April 1, Richard Hewson's orchestral score was superimposed over the extended edit of the song. Spector recorded the same musicians that played on "Across The Universe," including Ringo on drums, but thankfully did not use the choir. His April 2 mix of "I Me Mine" keeps the orchestra in the background and allows the Beatles rocking performance to shine through.

THE BEATLES "LET IT BE"
AN APPLE FILMS LIMITED PRODUCTION
Produced by NEIL ASPINALL   Directed by MICHAEL LINDSAY-HOGG
COLOR by Technicolor (R)   UNITED ARTISTS, Entertainment from Transamerica Corporation

LIB-9

Dig It

Recorded: January 24 & 26 (Apple basement)
Mixed: March 27, 1970 (Phil Spector)

Producer: George Martin
Engineers: Glyn Johns; Neil Richmond

John: Lead vocal, guitar (Casino on Jan 24; Fender Bass VI (Jan 26)
Paul: Backing vocal; bass guitar (on Jan 24); piano (Jan 26)
George: Lead guitar (Telecaster)
Ringo: Drums
Billy Preston: Organ
George Martin: Shaker

"Dig It" is more of a jam than a structured song. Although it started life as one of John's creations, the improvised participation by the band led to the song being credited to all four Beatles.

The group's first pass at the song on January 24 was little more than John repeatedly singing "Can you dig it?" over some delta blues-style guitar. Paul later joined in on the vocals with the pair exchanging variations of "dig it" lines such as "I can dig it" and "everybody dig it." John's guitar playing on the song is similar to his playing on an earlier delightful runthrough of "Singing The Blues."

After a couple of brief stabs at the song, the group turned in a four-minute romp in which John expanded his rudimentary lyrics to include references to insurance and the need for a guarantee. Paul added some levity to the song by pretending to be a remote location DJ with his announcement "Coming to you from the heart of Chicago's blues land, Blind Lame Lennon." He also sang "I think you're out of tune, boy" to John towards the end of the song.

The next take lasted nearly five minutes and featured Billy Preston on organ. At the end, John announced "That was 'Can You Dig It' by Georgie Wood. And now we'd like to do 'Hark, The Angels Come.'" Lennon's remark was used to link a different version of "Dig It" to "Let It Be" on both the *Get Back* and *Let It Be* albums.

On January 26, after working on "Let It Be," John improvised a bossa nova-style riff that led into the chorus of Bob Dylan's "Like A Rolling Stone." The band kept playing behind John as he began singing the words to "Twist And Shout" at the 1:44 mark. Paul's daughter Heather was then handed a microphone. Her wailing, reminiscent of Yoko's vocal style, continued until the ten minute mark, often drowning out John. At 3:17 into the jam, John sang "Well can you dig it?" and moved the performance into an extended version of "Dig It." Just as the song began to wind down after ten minutes, Paul

began singing his own "dig it" lyrical improvisations as a counterpoint to John's singing. At the 11:35 mark, John sang "Like a rolling stone" three times, followed by "Like the FBI, and the CIA, and the BBC, B.B. King, and Doris Day, Matt Busby, dig it...." Paul then dominated the vocals for a minute or so before the group moved into an instrumental jam leading to John and Paul improvising vocals to the end of the song. The entire performance run for over 15 minutes.

Lennon's calling out of names is reminiscent of a January 9 blues jam (known as "Get Off!") during which Paul and (occasionally) John tossed out 46 names, including James Brown, Judy Garland, Wilson Pickett, Malcolm Evans, members of the Quarrymen (their first group), Dusty Springfield, Richard Nixon, David Frost, Betty Grable, Clark Kent (Superman's secret identity), Sean O'Mahony (publisher of The Beatles Book), Bill Harry (founder of the Liverpool pop newspaper Mersey Beat), Tony Sheridan and Winston Churchill. For "Dig It," John limited his list to the Federal Bureau of Investigation, the Central Intelligence Agency, the British Broadcasting Corporation, blues guitarist B.B. King, American actress Doris Day and Matt Busby (manager of the Manchester United soccer team).

Glyn Johns placed a four-minute edit from the end of the January 26 performance of "Dig It" on the *Get Back* album. He then tagged on the end of the final January 24 take of the song, including John's "Hark, The Angels Come" comment to lead into "Let It Be." The film contains a 3:25 edit from this part of "Dig It." Phil Spector made a 51-second edit of the Glen Johns edit for the *Let It Be* album, fading in for "Like a rolling stone" and fading out after "...Doris Day, Matt Busby, dig it...."

The reason the January 26 version of "Dig It" sounds so different from the earlier performances is that the group was playing different instruments. For the later performance the lineup was the same as that used on *Let It Be*, which featured Paul on piano, John on the Fender Bass VI (played like a guitar for "Dig It"), George on his Telecaster, Ringo on drums and Billy Preston on organ.

The Beatles, without Paul, turned in a brief performance of the song on January 28. The following day John led the group through an up-tempo performance of the song, propelled by Ringo's steady drumming, that lasted for nearly seven minutes. While John sang his basic "dig it" lyrics, Paul provided a scat vocal in the background. About half way through the song John began singing out the titles to the Beatles songs recorded during the sessions. The final minute of the song is at a slower pace and is exclusively instrumental after John belts out a few German phrases.

Let It Be

Recorded: January 25, 26 & 31, 1969 (Apple basement);
April 30, 1969 (guitar solo overdub)
Overdub Session: January 4, 1970 (Abbey Road Studio 2)
Mixed (single version): January 4, 1970
Mixed and edited (album version): March 26, 1970 (Phil Spector)

Producers: George Martin (January 26 & 31, 1969; Jan 4, 1970);
Chris Thomas (April 30, 1969)
Engineers: Glyn Johns and Alan Parsons (January 25, 26 & 31,
1969); Jeff Jarratt and Nick Webb (April 30, 1969); Phil McDonald
and Richard Langham (January 4, 1970)

Paul: Lead and backing vocal; piano (Blüthner grand); maracas
John: Backing vocal; bass guitar (Fender VI)
George: Backing vocal; lead guitar (Telecaster)
Ringo: Drums
Billy Preston: Organ (Hammond B-3)

Outside musicians: 2 trumpets; 2 trombones; 1 tenor saxophone;
cellos

"Let It Be" was written by Paul during a difficult time in his life. John had become obsessed with Yoko, putting a strain on his relationship with Paul. The drugs, the stress and the tiredness were taking their toll on John and Paul. In Miles' *Many Years From Now*, Paul tells of the genesis of the song:

"One night during this tense time I had a dream I saw my mum, who'd been dead ten years or so. It was so wonderful for me and she was very reassuring. In the dream she said, 'It'll be all right.' I'm not sure if she used the words 'Let it be' but that was the gist of her advice, it was 'Don't worry too much, it will turn out okay.' It was such a sweet dream I woke up thinking, Oh, it was really great to visit her again. I felt very blessed to have that dream. So that got me writing the song 'Let It Be.' I literally started off 'Mother Mary,' which was her name, 'When I find myself in times of trouble,' which I certainly found myself in. The song was based on that dream."

Although the reference to Mother Mary was to Paul's mother rather than the Virgin Mary, many people took it as a religious statement. This interpretation doesn't bother Paul. "Mother Mary makes it a quasi-religious thing, so you can take it that way. I don't mind. I'm quite happy if people want to use it to shore up their faith." Paul also acknowledged that the song helped get him through some tough times. "I was really passing through my 'hour of darkness' and writing the song was my way of exorcising the ghosts."

Paul began writing "Let It Be" towards the end of *The White Album* sessions. Although he decided against recording the song

for the album, the group rehearsed "Let It Be" during a September 1968 session. Taped rehearsals were typically recorded over; however, a part of a "Let It Be" rehearsal survived and was included on the deluxe edition of *The White Album*. This performance features Paul's vocal backed by organ and piano.

On the morning of January 3, 1969, while waiting for the other Beatles to arrive at Twickenham, Paul played the first verse and part of the chorus of "Let It Be" on piano. Five days later on January 8, he again played the song on piano, accompanied at times by a disinterested John on guitar and Ringo on drums. John was not initially impressed with the song, kidding Paul that he should change Mother Mary to Brother Malcolm (a reference to the group's loyal assistant Mal Evans). Although Paul did not replace his mother with the Beatles roadie in the song's lyrics, he did at times resort to singing "Brother Malcolm" when he found himself in times of trouble during a botched performance of the song. After a break for lunch and runthroughs of several other songs, Paul returned to "Let It Be," calling out the chords for George. Ringo worked on his drum part and John occasionally sang on the choruses.

During rehearsals held on January 9, the song began to take shape. The most accomplished performance starts with Paul on piano and vocal for the first verse, with John and George supplying backing vocals on the chorus. During the second verse, Ringo falls into place, starting with his bass drum and tambourine kit before going to a tom-tom fill leading into the chorus and moving to his high-hat. John adds his Fender Bass VI during the second chorus, which is followed by an instrumental break featuring a George Harrison guitar solo and backing vocals by John, George and Paul. At this stage Paul had not completed the lyrics, so some of the performances contained ad-libs and lines such as "read the Record Mirror, let it be." The following morning Paul played the song on piano for music publisher Dick James, who dropped by the Twickenham rehearsals.

By the time Paul returned to "Let It Be" on January 23, the sessions had moved to Apple's basement studio and Billy Preston had been invited to sit in on keyboards. While no group rehearsals of the song took place that day, Paul sneaked in two solo performances on piano, thus providing an opportunity for Preston to hear the ballad.

Even though Billy Preston was not present on January 25, Paul wanted to rehearse the song, reasoning that Preston would pick up on it quickly. The initial rehearsals were dreadful, marred by John's poor bass playing and other issues. Ringo hadn't perfected his drum part and the backing vocals were erratic.

APPLE
An abkco managed company
presents

THE BEATLES "*Let it be*"

TECHNICOLOR® United Artists
 G Entertainment from
Transamerica Corporation

COPYRIGHT © 1970 UNITED ARTISTS CORPORATION   LITHO. IN U.S.A.   2   70/169

In an attempt to rally the troops, Paul says: "OK, you watch us, we're gonna do this now. OK, boys now, come on. Pull yourselves together." After John replies with "You talkin' to me?," George kick-starts the band into an impromptu performance of Chuck Berry's "I'm Talking About You." Paul, wanting to carry on with "Let It Be," brings things to a halt with "Come on now, back to the drudgery." When John angrily reacts with "It's you that's bloody making it like this," Paul sarcastically replies "The real meaning of Christmas" and calms things down with the soothing opening chords to "Let It Be." This is followed by a few mediocre rehearsals of the song.

Despite the sinking mood of the session, Paul is confident the band can pull it together and instructs Glyn Johns to record the next take. *Anthology 3* contains this performance, which is introduced by Paul's assurance that "this is gonna knock you out." Although Paul had yet to complete the lyrics, he turns in an excellent performance, highlighted by graceful piano playing and soulful vocals, backed by John and George on the choruses. During the second verse, the others join in with Ringo starting on his high-hat, John playing rudimentary bass on the Fender VI and George playing his Telecaster through a Leslie speaker. George's guitar solo is simple but effective. Although the band played a few more takes before abandoning the day's session, these were unproductive as the group's energy level and interest were all but fully depleted.

On January 26, Billy Preston rejoined the sessions, playing Hammond organ on the numerous rehearsals and recorded takes. The song's structure was settled, but Paul was still working on the last verse. This sometimes led to bizarre ad-libs, including one take where Paul sings "Now somewhere out in Weybridge is a cat whose name is Banagy." After Paul sings the usual "And in my darkest hour, she is...," George adds "sitting on the lavatory," causing John to repeat the phrase in a chuckling voice. On another take, Paul mumbles his way through the first line of the final verse before coming up with "You will be a good girl, let it be." While most of these performances were substandard, Glyn Johns mixed one of the takes in January 1969 and included it on an acetate of songs from the *Get Back* sessions.

Paul led the group through more rehearsals on January 27. At times, John added inappropriate vocal ad-libs, perhaps out of boredom. On some performances, George and John played guitar and bass riffs during the early part of the song. Preston experimented with different organ parts and George worked out his lead solo over the song's final chorus. Paul sometimes sang scat vocals during the

still unwritten third verse. The group did not rehearse the song the next day and turned in a pathetic performance on the 29th.

On January 31, the Beatles and Preston returned to Apple's basement studio to record (with cameras rolling) proper takes of songs not suitable for the previous day's rooftop concert. The group went through numerous takes of "Let It Be" (designated Takes 20 through 27 to coincide with take numbers from the film's clapper board). Some of the clapper board takes actually consisted of more than one performance as there were some false starts and break-downs. Take 27 contains two complete performances of the song.

Take 20 is a fine performance that is called off towards the end of the first chorus by Glyn Johns. After Johns explains that the vocals were popping, Paul responds "This isn't very loud, Glyn," and John adds "Poppin's in, man." A false start is followed by a fairly decent performance, although John muffs his bass part before the instrumental break and spews out an expletive. As the song concludes, John admiringly asks, "Let it be, eh?" After Paul says "Yeah," John adds "I know what you mean."

Take 21 breaks down shortly after the instrumental break, leading Paul to sing a few words in the voice of a drunkard. Although Take 22 was showing promise, Paul apparently realized it wasn't going to be the final take. Thus, for the last verse, he sings, "When I find myself in times of heartache, Brother Malcolm comes to me."

Prior to the start of Take 23, John asks "Are we supposed to giggle in the solo?" to which Paul replies "Yeah," followed by John's "OK." This bit of dialog was edited in before the start of "The Long And Winding Road" on both versions of the *Get Back* album and also before the start of "Let It Be" on *Anthology 3*. Although John doesn't giggle during the solo of this spirited take, at the end of the performance he admits "I lost a bass note somewhere."

Take 24 gets into trouble during George's guitar solo, although Paul encourages him on by singing "Let it be, yeah, whoah." After Paul hits a sour chord going into the final verse, he sings "When I find myself in whoah," which prompts Billy Preston to play some soulful swirling organ. After a few gospel tinted lines, John calls the song off with an "OK, OK." Without missing a beat, Paul sings "OK, she stands right in" before admitting defeat by stopping the song.

When Take 25 unravels at the start of the chorus, John lets out a few expletives and engages with Paul in brief pseudo-German banter, including a unique count-in to a fresh start for Take 25. At the conclusion of the second Take 25, which is another "Brother Malcolm" version, the following conversation takes place:

John (sarcastically): I think that was rather grand. I'd take one home with me.

Glyn: No, that was fine.

John (in a voice mimicking the computer HAL 9000 from *2001: a space odyssey*): Don't kid us, Glyn. Give it to us straight.

Glyn: That was straight.

Paul: Ah, what do you think, Glyn?

Glyn: I don't think it's yet.

Paul: C'mon.

John: OK, let's track it. [Sharply intakes breath creating a "Huh!" sound.] You bounder, you cheat!"

John's last remark mocks the group's normal practice of overdubbing or tracking additional parts to their recordings, a definite "no no" for the *Get Back* project, which was originally intended to present the group live without any studio enhancements. The first and last of John's above comments were edited on to the end of "Let It Be" on *Anthology 3*.

Take 26 begins with Paul quickly abandoning the song and hitting the first few notes to "Twelfth Street Rag." The next attempt at the song lasts longer, but falls apart at the start of the final verse.

After a film crew member announces "Take 27, sync to second clap," Paul follows with "Sync to second clap, please" before starting the performance that would be used as the basic master for the single and album versions of the song. The take is near perfect, flawed only by a few sour notes during George's guitar solo.

Although Paul thought the take was "very fair," he still wanted to go "one more time." As Paul begins his piano introduction to the song, George asks Paul to hold briefly to allow him to tune a guitar string. After Harrison gives him the "OK," Paul remarks "Second clap," which causes George to break out in laughter during the start of the song. This excellent performance brought an end to the *Get Back* sessions and was featured in the film after being edited with a portion of the chorus from an earlier take.

After sifting through numerous recordings of "Let It Be," Glyn Johns ultimately determined that the first Take 27 was the best version of the song and made a stereo mix of the tune on March 10, 1969. Although it was an excellent performance, George's guitar solo was substandard. To correct this problem, an exception was made to the "no overdubs" policy of the *Get Back* project. At the start of a session held on April 30, with Chris Thomas serving as producer, George overdubbed a new guitar solo onto the eight track tape of Take 27. The augmented tape was later mixed for stereo on May 28. This mix was selected for both versions of the unreleased *Get Back* album.

Additional overdubs were added to Take 27 during a George Martin session held on January 4, 1970, which was attended only by Paul, George and Ringo. John was on vacation in Denmark. McCartney and Harrison (and possibly Linda McCartney) added backing vocals to Take 27. George Martin prepared a score for brass instruments (two trumpets, two trombones and a tenor saxophone), which was overdubbed live during three separate tape reductions designated Takes 28, 29 and 30. Take 30 was marked "best" and given further enhancements: a slightly raunchy lead guitar solo by George, additional drums by Ringo and maracas by Paul. Martin also scored a part for a few cellos, which was added towards the end of the song. Two stereo mixes were then made. On remix 2, which was used for the single, George's January 4 raunchy guitar solo was mixed out and the brass was kept in the background.

Phil Spector drastically altered the feel of the song included on the *Let It Be* album. He added echo to Ringo's hi-hat, featured George's raunchy solo and brought the brass up in the mix.

Maggie Mae [spelling changed from "May"]

Recorded: January 24 (Apple basement)
Mixed: March 26, 1970 (Phil Spector)

Producer: George Martin (maybe)
Engineers: Glyn Johns; Neil Richmond

John: Lead vocal; acoustic guitar (Gibson J-200)
Paul: Lead vocal; acoustic guitar (Martin D-28)
George: Lead guitar (Telecaster) (playing bass part)
Ringo: Drums

The Beatles returned to their Quarrymen skiffle origins with a brief recording of "Maggie May." The song, about a Liverpool prostitute, was recorded by the Vipers Skiffle Group in 1957. The British version of the tune is based upon an American minstrel song from 1856, "Darling Nellie Gray," credited to Benjamin Russell Hanby.

The group fooled around with "Maggie May" on January 24 in between performances of "Two Of Us." The song has the same lineup of John and Paul on acoustic guitars and vocals, George on his Telecaster and Ringo on drums. The first attempt at the song lasted about a minute, but the second fell apart after ten seconds. Glyn Johns recorded the third performance and included it on the *Get Back* LP. This 38-second track also appears on the *Let It Be* album.

LIB-16

THE BEATLES "LET IT BE"
AN APPLE FILMS LIMITED PRODUCTION
Produced by NEIL ASPINALL   Directed by MICHAEL LINDSAY-HOGG
COLOR by Technicolor (R)   UNITED ARTISTS, Entertainment from Transamerica Corporation

I Got A Feeling

Recorded: Jan 22, 24, 27 & 28 (Apple basement); Jan 30 (rooftop)
Mixed: March 23, 1970 (Phil Spector)

Producer: George Martin (Jan 27, 28 & 30; maybe Jan 22 & 24)
Engineers: Glyn Johns; Neil Richmond (January 24); Alan Parsons (January 27, 28 and 30)

Paul: Lead vocal; bass guitar (Hofner)
John: Lead vocal; electric guitar (Casino)
George: Lead guitar (Telecaster)
Ringo: Drums
Billy Preston: Electric piano (Fender Rhodes)

"I've Got A Feeling" is a merger of two songs started separately by John and Paul. John's "Everybody Had A Hard Year" was written in late 1968. During a visit by Lennon to McCartney's Cavendish Avenue home, the pair realized that John's song had the same tempo as Paul's "I've Got A Feeling." The two unfinished songs were linked together and completed by the duo as an equal collaboration. The final arrangement of the song features John and Paul singing their separate contributions over each other during the last verse.

Prior to Paul's arrival on January 2, John played his contribution to the song for George, who unsuccessfully attempted to add lead guitar lines over Lennon's strumming guitar. After singing a bit of the "Everybody Had A Hard Year" section, John kept the same rhythm and sang "Well I've got a feeling, deep inside." This unique performance has a folk feeling reminiscent of Bob Dylan and shows how the song might have evolved had McCartney not been involved.

After Paul arrived, he led the group through several run-throughs of the song, sometimes calling out the chords for John and George. He often stopped the song to explain the arrangement and at one point switched to acoustic guitar to show the changes.

The Beatles resumed rehearsals of the song on January 3 with a mix of runthroughs and work on selected segments. On January 6 they managed only one complete pass at the song. Rehearsals continued in earnest the following day with emphasis on the vocals. Paul also spent time working with Ringo to perfect his drum part.

The group turned in a respectable take of the song on January 8, highlighted by Paul's scorching vocal. The *Let It Be* film contains an edit of this performance, including McCartney's enthusiastic shout of "Good morning" after the middle eight, mixed with bits of the January 9 rehearsals of the song. During this later performance, John messes with the lyrics and sings "Everybody got a face-lift."

The movie also shows Paul explaining to John and George that the descending guitar riff after the middle eight is coming down too fast and should have no recognizable jumps.

On January 10, Paul played the song on piano while waiting for the others to arrive. The group later performed a more familiar arrangement. After George quit the group during the day's session, the remaining Beatles turned in a horrendous attempt of the song.

The Beatles returned to "I've Got A Feeling" on January 21. The day's only known surviving take has the descending guitar riff replaced by a series of vibrato notes and John shouting "Can you dig it?" towards the end. The first performance on January 22 is fairly solid, but breaks down in the final verse. During later rehearsals the group tried a softer country & western swing approach to "get more feeling." After the late morning arrival of Billy Preston, the group worked through a couple of extended rehearsals of the song.

Glyn Johns selected one of the January 22 performances for the *Get Back* album. Although a spirited take, the song breaks down at the 2:40 mark (just before the final verse) when Lennon realizes he's playing too loud. As the music stops, John admits "I cocked it up tryin' to get loud." After Paul says "Yeah," John retorts with "Nothin' bad though." Johns included the above dialog on the *Get Back* LP. This spirited but aborted take of the song is on *Anthology 3*.

On the morning of January 23, the group jammed on riffs from "I've Got A Feeling," but did not rehearse the song. Towards the end of the day's session, the group briefly played the start of the song, the first eight seconds of which are on the March 10 acetate.

The group continued work on the song on January 27. One of these takes was mixed by Glyn Johns and included on the March 13 acetate. Shortly after the song begins, John's guitar begins to feed back through his amplifier, bringing the performance to an end. He quickly starts over, singing "I'm so ashamed, I goofed again."

Additional rehearsals were held the next day. One of these performances was taken a slower pace and contained extra vocal interplay between John and Paul. After McCartney left the session to attend a meeting, John led the group through a couple of passes at the song, singing Paul's vocal part as well as his own. These versions make for interesting listening due to Lennon's different singing style and phrasing. More work was done on the song after Paul's return.

The Beatles, without Billy Preston, performed the song as part of their rooftop rehearsal on January 29.

"I've Got A Feeling" was performed twice during the rooftop concert. The first take is in the movie and on the *Let It Be album*.

One After 909

Recorded: January 28 & 29 (Apple basement); Jan 30 (rooftop)
Mixed: March 23, 1970 (Phil Spector)

Producer: George Martin
Engineers: Glyn Johns; Alan Parsons

John: Lead vocal; electric guitar (Casino)
Paul: Backing vocal; bass guitar (Hofner)
George: Lead guitar (Telecaster)
Ringo: Drums
Billy Preston: Electric piano (Fender Rhodes)

"One After 909" is literally a blast from the past. It was one of the first songs written by John, dating back to 1957. The song's railroad theme and rhythm suggest that John may have been influenced by Lonnie Donegan's skiffle recording of Huddie "Leadbelly" Ledbetter's "Rock Island Line," which charted in 1956 at number eight in England and at number ten in the U.S. In Miles' *Many Years From Now*, Paul recalls he and John "trying to write a bluesy freight-train song." Rehearsal tapes from 1960 and 1962 demonstrate that "One After 909" was a part of the band's early repertoire.

In the *Let It Be* film, Paul is asked about the tune and states that "One After 909" was from the days he and John used to "sag off every school day" and go to the McCartney house on Forthlin Road to write songs. After explaining that during this period they wrote about a hundred unsophisticated songs, Paul confesses "We always hated the words of 'One After 909'" and recites its opening lines: "Baby said she's travelin' on the one after 909. I said move over honey, I'm travelin' on that line. I said move over once, move over twice, come on baby don't be cold as ice."

Although they may have hated the words, the Beatles recorded "One After 909" at one of their first EMI sessions. On March 5, 1963, after completing the songs for their third single ("From Me To You" and "Thank You Girl"), the band ran through five rough takes of the song. George's lead guitar was so mediocre that at the end of the second take, John asked "What kind of solo was that?" A comparison of that clunker with the rooftop performance shows how much Harrison improved over the years. Because none of the 1963 takes proved satisfactory, the song was passed over and forgotten until resurrected by the group in 1969. *Anthology 1* contains bits of Takes 3, 4 and 5 followed by a 1995 edit of Takes 4 and 5 of the 1963 recording.

"One After 909" was introduced to the *Get Back* sessions on January 3. In his Playboy interview, John admitted that the song was probably resurrected for lack of material. The early performances of the song feature John on rhythm guitar and vocals, Paul on bass and vocals, George on lead guitar through a wah-wah pedal and Ringo on drums. At this stage, the song retained a bit of a skiffle beat that would soon be replaced as the song evolved into an all-out rocker.

While the initial pair of January 6 performances were taken at a slow tempo, the group picked up the pace for its third and final runthrough of the day. The January 7 and 8 performances show that the song's transformation to rocker was complete, with Paul and Ringo providing a solid backing. The *Let It Be* film contains an edited version of the January 9 rehearsals.

By the time the Beatles returned to the song on January 28, Billy Preston had joined the sessions. The addition of Preston on electric piano and George's decision not to use his wah-wah pedal improved the song. During one of the day's spirited performances, Paul encourages George during his solo by shouting "yeah, rock 'n' roll." When John muffs his vocal, he gamely carries on after singing "Oh I did it again, oh yeah."

The group's first January 29 rehearsal of the song took place prior to the arrival of Billy Preston. For this performance, George's guitar is more prominently featured. The band ran through the song two more times later that day.

While the Beatles were bored with many of the songs they rehearsed during the sessions, there is no doubt that they truly enjoyed playing "One After 909."

The Beatles performed "One After 909" as part of their January 30 rooftop concert. The song is preceded by sounds of the band getting ready, including a chord from Billy Preston's electric piano and a few stray guitar notes. This is followed by a member of the film crew shouting "All cameras four" (indicating Take 4), the sound of the clapperboard and John's count-in to the song. The Beatles then play an inspired performance with John and Paul sharing lead vocals. George's lead guitar and Billy Preston's piano riffs highlight the tight musical backing. This performance, along with the pre-song sounds, was used as the opening track for the *Get Back* album compiled by Glyn Johns. Phil Spector also selected the rooftop recording for the *Let It Be* album, but without the pre-song chatter. He left in John's brief rendition of "Danny Boy" following the song.

THE BEATLES   "LET IT BE"
AN APPLE FILMS LIMITED PRODUCTION
Produced by NEIL ASPINALL   Directed by MICHAEL LINDSAY-HOGG
COLOR by Technicolor (R)   UNITED ARTISTS, Entertainment from Transamerica Corporation

The Long And Winding Road

Recorded: Jan 26 & 31, 1969 (Apple basement)
Overdub Session: April 1, 1970 (Abbey Road Studio 1)
Mixed: April 2, 1970 (Phil Spector)

Producer: George Martin (Jan 26 & 31); Phil Spector (April 1)
Engineers: Glyn Johns and Alan Parsons (January 26 & 31);
Peter Brown and Richard Lush (April 1)

Paul: Lead vocal; piano (Blüthner grand)
John: Backing vocal; bass guitar (Fender VI)
George: Lead guitar (Telecaster)
Ringo: Drums
Billy Preston: Organ (Hammond B-3)

Outside Musicians: 18 violins, 4 violas, 4 cellos, 1 harp,
3 trumpets, 3 trombones and 2 guitars; 14 person choir (April 1)

As was the case with "Let It Be," Paul began writing "The Long And Winding Road" during the sessions for *The White Album*. After Alistair Taylor told Paul of his fondness for the melody, McCartney recorded the unfinished tune and gave the tape to Alistair as a present for his wife Lesley. According to Paul, he wrote the tune with Ray Charles in mind, thus explaining the song's "slightly jazzy" chord structure. In Miles' *Many Years From Now*, McCartney recalled: "I was a bit flipped out and tripped out at that time. It's a sad song because it's all about the unattainable; the door you never quite reach. This is the road that you never get to the end of."

Paul played a brief segment of "The Long And Winding Road" on January 3, 1969, while waiting for the others to arrive at Twickenham. He returned to the song on January 7 under similar circumstances, this time spending nearly five minutes working through the tune. Although the chords and melody for the verses and bridge were in place, the lyrics had yet to be completed, with Paul only having one verse and a part of the bridge. After Ringo and George arrived, Paul played part of the song again, but made no effort to teach it to the others. He also slipped in a bit of the tune later in the day between rehearsals of other songs.

On January 8, Paul made his first efforts to teach the song to the band. John showed some interest in learning the chords when Paul briefly played the song during a break in rehearsals for George's "I Me Mine;" however, he did not participate when Paul returned to the song later that day.

The next two mornings, Paul included the ballad as part of his piano warm up while waiting for the others to arrive at Twickenham.

He also played instrumental versions of the song on the afternoons of January 10 and 22. Paul slipped in two additional performances of the ballad on January 23.

By the time Paul finally got the band to rehearse the song seriously on January 26, he had completed the lyrics. The Beatles, joined by Billy Preston on organ, went through about a dozen performances of the song with Paul on piano, George on his Telecaster played through a Leslie speaker, John on the Fender Bass VI and Ringo on drums. After Paul taught the others the chords, the band plowed through a few dreadful performances before getting a feel for the song. John's initial bass playing was obtrusive and awkward. To add a touch of levity to the session, the group performed a cha-cha Latin-influenced version until Paul called it off with "All right lads, that's enough" after a minute and a half. Part of this segment appears in the *Let It Be* film. On one of the later performances, George experimented with playing a lead guitar melody line throughout the tune.

After a few stop and start runthroughs during which Paul instructed Ringo on how he wanted the cymbals played, McCartney asked Glyn Johns to record the song. Although this take began with two false starts, the completed performance was quite good and was selected by Johns for inclusion on the *Get Back* album. It also served as the basic track for the version of the song released on the *Let It Be* album and as the group's last American single on Apple.

After the band listened to a playback of the performance at the end of the day's session, the group and George Martin discussed the possibility of adding brass and strings. Over 14 months later, Phil Spector would add brass, strings and a choir to the track. Details regarding Spector's overdubs are discussed below. The unaltered take is on *Anthology 3*. This performance is somewhat unique in that it features Paul singing the words to the bridge over what is normally the instrumental break in the song.

Apparently Paul was not satisfied with the January 26 performances of the song, so he ran the group through additional rehearsals the following day. The band turned in a few deliberately off-the-wall performances, including one in which John did most of the singing and Paul mimicked Al Jolson. Although one serious complete take was recorded, it was not as good as the best from the day before.

On January 28, Billy Preston, on electric piano, led the band through a blues jam reminiscent of T-Bone Walker's "Call It Stormy Monday." The song is referred to as "The River Rhine" because

Preston repeatedly sings that he's "moving along by the River Rhine." Shortly before the two-minute mark, Paul, who is on bass, sings about a minute of lyrics from "The Long And Winding Road" in a bluesy voice. This performance is interesting in that it shows how the song might have sounded if Paul had followed his original idea of modeling the tune with Ray Charles in mind.

The following day the Beatles ran through most of the songs that they had been working on during the sessions, including "The Long And Winding Road." The first attempt at the song broke down after the first verse. Paul then began singing the second verse and led the band through the rest of the song. After Paul comments that John is a bit heavy on the bass, he requests that they do the song again with John playing softer.

On previous performances, Paul had been singing the line "Anyway you'll never know the many ways I've tried" during the bridge. This time he changed the lyrics to "Anyway you'll always know the many ways I've tried." Apparently Paul thought the change from "never" to "always" was an improvement as he sang "Anyway you've always known the many ways I've tried" for all subsequent performances during the sessions. (In concert, Paul sings "never" to match the released version of the song.)

The final set of rehearsals and performances of "The Long And Winding Road" took place on January 31 in Apple's basement studio. After Paul rehearsed parts of the song for fine tuning, he led the group through several recorded takes (designated Takes 13 through 19 to coordinate with the film's clapper board). Some clapper board takes consisted of multiple performances as there were some false starts and break downs. During the song's instrumental break, Paul provided scat vocals over Billy Preston's Hammond organ solo. Takes 13B, 15B, 16C, 16D, 18 and 19 are complete, with the final take being the best. Take 19 is featured in the *Let It Be* movie, as well as the *Anthology* video and *The Beatles 1* video. It was also selected for the *Let It Be… Naked* album.

In late January 1969, Glyn Johns took the session tapes to Olympic Studios and made a stereo mix of the best of the January 26 performances of "The Long And Winding Road." This was placed on an acetate of songs from the Apple basement sessions. On March 10, 1969, he once again made a mix of this performance. He made additional mixes of the song over the next two days. In all likelihood his mixes included Take 19 from January 31. After comparing these two performances, Johns gave the nod to the January 26 take of the song and included it on an acetate. When Johns compiled his version of the *Get Back* album on May 28, 1969, he once again went with the January 26 performance.

On April 1, 1970, Phil Spector, working with engineers Peter Brown and Richard Lush in Abbey Road's Studio One, augmented the Beatles sparse January 26 performance of "The Long And Winding Road" with 18 violins, four violas, four cellos, a harp, three trumpets, three trombones, two guitars, a choir of 14 singers and Ringo on drums. Richard Hewson arranged the score and conducted the orchestra and choir. During the song's instrumental break, Spector faded Paul's vocal out of the mix and replaced it with a heavy dose of strings and choir. This is the version of the song on the *Let It Be* album and on the single pulled from the LP.

Of all of Phil Spector's work on the project, "The Long And Winding Road" is by far the most controversial. Although some people believe Spector made necessary improvements to a dull and plodding song, others feel that he grossly overproduced the track. George Martin and Glyn Johns were shocked and disgusted. Paul was particularly upset with the use of the choir.

In his lawsuit to dissolve the Beatles partnership, McCartney stated that he received an acetate of the *Let It Be* album in early April 1970, along with a letter from Phil Spector which said that Paul should contact him if he wanted any alterations. After he was unable to contact Spector by phone, Paul sent Allen Klein a letter on April 14, 1970, requesting alterations be made to "The Long And Winding Road." He wanted Spector to bring down the volume of the strings, horns and chorus in the mix and bring up the volume of the band. He also wanted the harp completely removed from the mix. Although McCartney believed there was sufficient time to modify the track, the song was issued unaltered as re-produced by Spector on April Fools Day, 1970.

It has been argued that Spector needed to add orchestration to the song to cover up John's poor bass playing. This argument does not hold up as Paul may have been willing to overdub a new bass part. One also has to wonder why Spector went with the January 26 take of the song selected by Glyn Johns when there were superior performances recorded on January 31.

Although conversations taped during the sessions indicate that Paul was not against adding strings and brass to "The Long And Winding Road," Spector went way beyond what Paul had in mind. One can only wonder how the song would have sounded had George Martin been asked to score a subtle and tasteful orchestral arrangement similar to his enhancements to the "Let It Be" single.

For You Blue

Recorded: Jan 25, 1969 (Apple basement);
Jan 8, 1970 (Vocal overdub; Abbey Road Studios)
Mixed: March 25, 1970 (Phil Spector)

Producer: George Martin (January 25)
Engineers: Glyn Johns and Alan Parsons (January 25)

George: Lead vocal; acoustic guitar (Gibson J-200)
John: Lap-steel slide guitar (Hofner Hawaiian Standard)
Paul: Piano (Blüthner grand)
Ringo: Drums

George described "For You Blue" as "a simple twelve-bar [blues] song following all the normal twelve-bar principles except it's happy-go-lucky!" Harrison introduced the song to the band on January 6, 1969, by playing an instrumental version of the tune. Although he knocked off two more performances of the song on acoustic guitar the following day, the band showed little interest.

George's persistence paid off on January 9 when he reintroduced "For You Blue" to the others as his "folk/blues" song. After doing a few solo performances of the tune on acoustic guitar, he was joined by Paul on piano and John on electric guitar before the group moved on to other songs. When the band returned to the song later in the day, they were in the standard lineup of John and George on electric guitars, Paul on bass and Ringo on drums. The group managed a few complete performances of the song amid false starts and jamming on oldies. At this stage, the lyrics had not been finished.

On January 25, the Beatles were ready to record "For You Blue," which was initially titled "George's Blues" before temporarily being called "Because You're Sweet And Lovely." The song was recorded prior to Billy Preston's arrival and featured George on his Gibson J-200 acoustic guitar, Paul on piano, Ringo on drums and John on a Hofner Hawaiian Standard lap-steel slide guitar. Although the Get Back sessions had many dreary and uninspired performances, George's upbeat tune lifted the mood of the band. After a series of runthroughs, Glyn Johns rolled the tape to record Take 1. This performance, which opens with Paul on piano, is on Anthology 3. During Take 3, George mistakenly sings during the piano solo. When John lets George know of his error by yelling "piano," Harrison ad-libs "I've loved that piano from the moment that I saw you." Take 6 is featured in the Let It Be film.

Take 7 opens with a ten-second false start followed by the sound of rattling ice cubes in a glass. After another false start, John

yells "Quiet please" before George and the band knock out an excellent performance. Glyn Johns selected this take, starting with the rattling ice cubes, for the Side Two opener of both versions of the unreleased Get Back album. An altered version of this performance, details of which are discussed below, was used for the Let It Be album and the single.

Although everyone was satisfied with Take 7, the group recorded five more performances. The instrumental break from Take 9 was used as the lead-in to the portion of the Let It Be movie featuring the Apple basement recording sessions. During the piano solo of Take 12, George shouts out "Mr. Blüthner" as a salute to Paul's fine playing on the studio's Blüthner grand piano. At the end of the song, George comments "It felt nice." After listening to playbacks of Takes 7 and 12, George Martin wanted to edit the two performances to form the master take, but Harrison objected because he was satisfied with Take 7. Unlike the other songs recorded during the Get Back project, "For You Blue" was essentially started and completed in one afternoon session.

On January 29, the Beatles ran through many of the numbers previously rehearsed and/or recorded during the month-long sessions. The group's performance of "For You Blue" sounds a bit heavier than the earlier versions.

Glyn Johns made a stereo mix of Take 7 on March 10, 1969. This is the mix included on the unreleased Get Back album.

Nearly one year after "For You Blue" was recorded, George had second thoughts about his singing and redid his vocal on January 8, 1970. During the instrumental break, Harrison added some vocal ad-libs, including "Go Johnny go" and "Elmore James got nothin' on this baby," to give the impression he was singing live with the band. These references to Chuck Berry's "Johnny B. Goode" and blues guitarist Elmore James pay tribute to Lennon's fine guitar work on the song.

Prior to Phil Spector's involvement, former EMI engineer Malcolm Davies, with Peter Brown and Richard Langham serving as engineers, produced eight stereo mixes of "For You Blue" on February 28, 1970, none of which was ever released.

Phil Spector, assisted by engineers Peter Brown and Roger Ferris, mixed the song for stereo at Abbey Road on March 25, 1970. After obtaining a generally suitable mix on the first try, Spector went through seven mixes (numbered Remixes 2 through 8) of the song's introduction. The final master appearing on the Let It Be album and issued as the single is an edit of introduction Remix 5 onto Remix 1.

APPLE
An **abkco** managed company
presents

THE BEATLES "Let it be"

TECHNICOLOR® **United Artists**
Ⓖ Entertainment from Transamerica Corporation

70/169

Get Back

Recorded: January 23, 24, 27, 28 and 29 (Apple basement studio); January 30 (Apple rooftop concert)
Mixed: April 7 (mono & stereo) from Jan 27 & 28 performances

Producer: George Martin (Jan 27, 28, 29 & 30; maybe Jan 23 & 24)
Engineers: Glyn Johns; Alan Parsons (except January 24); Neil Richmond (January 24)

Paul: Lead vocal; bass guitar (Hofner)
John: Backing vocal; lead guitar (Casino)
George: Backing vocal; rhythm guitar (Telecaster)
Ringo: Drums
Billy Preston: Electric piano (Fender Rhodes)

"Get Back" was the first song released from the *Get Back* sessions. It was issued on a single paired with "Don't Let Me Down" in April 1969, more than a year ahead of the *Let It Be* album.

The genesis of "Get Back" dates to the morning of January 7, 1969. Prior to John's arrival, Paul begins messing around with a bass riff that leads him to sing bits of Ray Charles' "What'd I Say," "Carry That Weight" and the Isley Brothers' "Shout" (commenting "that's how Lulu would do it"). This is followed by a thumping bass riff jam that lasts for about two minutes, with Paul trying out some structure and words. It takes a little over a minute for Paul to come up with the melody and chord changes that would form the verses of "Get Back." As others are talking, McCartney starts up again, this time working out the song's "Get back, get back, get back to where you once belonged" chorus with George providing guitar riffs on his Telecaster and Ringo keeping time with his hands and snapping his fingers. This performance lasts about four minutes.

Paul's next attempt turns into an extended funky-sounding jam. It begins with Paul's galloping bass riff leading into the chorus, with George quickly joining in on guitar. Paul begins working out some lyrics that would later become the second verse of the song ("thought she was a woman...but she gets it while she can"). Ringo joins Paul on vocals for the chorus and a few scat verses. When Paul seems ready to end the song after about three and a half minutes, saying "I've got blisters on my fingers," George keeps things going with a wah-wah guitar solo. Paul starts up again and Ringo is soon behind his drum kit providing a steady beat. McCartney continues to work on the lyrics as George stays on his wah-wah pedal. Paul sings in the style of Apple recording artist Jackie Lomax, perhaps realizing that the "get back to where you once belonged" chorus is similar to the "get back to where you should be" line from Lomax's recording

of George Harrison's "Sour Milk Sea" (on which Paul played bass guitar). Paul acknowledges his Lomax imitation by shouting, "C'mon Jackie!" This performance, with George often using his wah-wah, extends beyond nine minutes when the tape runs out.

The group returned to the song two days later on January 9, this time with John present and accounted for. Early runthroughs once again sound more like a jam than a finished song, but elements of the story line, such as references to Arizona and California, begin to appear.

On later performances of the song that day, Paul switched direction by temporarily changing the lyrics to political satire aimed at Parliament member Enoch Powell, who was in the news at that time spouting his beliefs that too many nonwhite citizens of the British Empire were immigrating to England and taking away limited jobs. Before launching into this political version of the song, Paul sings "Don't want no black man. Don't dig no Pakistanis taking all the people's jobs." The song's improvised lyrics include references to Puerto Ricans and Mohicans for the United States verse, and Pakistanis for England. The group jams behind Paul, who shouts "get back" over and over again in an angry voice that mocks the hatred behind Enoch Powell's beliefs. After a few political versions of the song, the band returned briefly to the song's original story line, with Jo and Theresa serving as the principal characters.

The following day, January 10, the band spent a significant portion of the morning session working on "Get Back." Prior to the start of band rehearsals, Paul performed the song on piano. After McCartney switched to bass, he led the group through a raucous version of "Get Back." At Paul's suggestion, the song was rearranged to open with crashing guitars (somewhat reminiscent of the start to "A Hard Day's Night") and a building drum roll from Ringo. The band performed several rocking runthroughs, with some incorporating bits of the "No Pakistanis" lyrics from the previous day. One of the more spirited performances features John joining Paul on the verses, a jamming wah-wah guitar solo and a Ringo drum fill leading into a third verse, which was later discarded. This verse contains references to living in a council flat (government-subsidized housing) and statements from the candidate for Labour (one of Britain's political parties). The verse about Loretta is essentially complete, but serves as the first rather than second verse. The middle verse features Jo Jo, Arizona and California, but is not in final form.

Although the group's progress with "Get Back" gives the impression that things were finally coming together for the band, things were about to fall apart. Shortly after the group's break for lunch on January 10, George announced he was quitting the group and walked out of Twickenham.

On January 13, the three remaining Beatles returned to "Get Back," with Paul refining the lyrics. Loretta's last name alternated between Marsh and Marvin after Paul rejected John's "suggestion" of "Sweet Loretta Meatball." Although they completed a few rocking takes of the song, Ringo's drum fills during the breaks threw the band's timing off. John's guitar solos, which borrow elements from Dale Hawkins' "Suzie Q," range from passable to pitiful.

By the time the Beatles returned to "Get Back" on January 23, George had rejoined the band and the sessions had moved to the basement of Apple's Savile Row headquarters. In addition, Billy Preston was providing keyboards, which added depth to the band's recordings.

Most of the day's recording session was devoted to "Get Back." Although the group did not perfect the song, its structure, lyrics and instrumentation were taking shape, including Ringo's galloping snare drum part, George's chopping rhythm guitar, John's guitar solos and Billy Preston's electric piano fills and solo.

The group continued to rehearse the song on January 24, at first without Preston, who did not arrive until mid-afternoon. The most interesting version recorded that day has back-to-back performances of the song, complete with spirited improvisations from Paul during the final coda.

On January 27, the group ran through over 30 takes of "Get Back." During one of the early performances, Paul sings the first verse with Japanese characters and cities; however, most of the versions of the song recorded this day were serious attempts at a suitable master take.

The performances are fairly similar, with the main differences being the tempo, John's guitar solos and the codas. During one of the codas, Paul sings, "it's five o'clock, your mother's got your tea on." He ends another with the "One, two, three o'clock, four o'clock rock" opening line from Bill Haley's "Rock Around The Clock." On the take that would later be chosen for the single and the *Let It Be* album, the group fails to play a coda, causing Harrison to comment, "We missed that end, didn't we?"

Due to the flubbed ending of this performance, the group continued work on the song. The later recordings are entertaining, but do not match the perfection of the master. The most interesting of the bunch has Paul singing pseudo-German lyrics until he switches to pseudo-French for the final chorus. During an instrumental break, Paul once again acknowledges the Jackie Lomax influence on the song by saying, "Yah, that's good Jackie" in a German accent.

The Beatles recorded additional takes of "Get Back" on the following day. The extended coda from one of these January 28 performances was put to good use. A segment containing the first 35 seconds of the coda was edited to the end of the January 27 performance chosen for the single. A later segment of the coda was used as the "Get Back" reprise that ends both unreleased *Get Back* albums and the *Let It Be* film. The full coda runs 1:22 and ends with John singing: "Shoot me when I'm evil, shoot me when I'm good, shoot me when I'm hungry, and shoot me when I'm...." The later performances of the song are ragged and have Billy Preston on organ rather than electric piano.

On January 29, the Beatles rehearsed the songs slated for the rooftop concert, including "Get Back." Because Billy was not present, John vocalized Preston's piano solo.

The next day the Beatles, accompanied by Billy Preston on electric piano, gave their last public performance on January 30. The impromptu concert was staged on the roof of Apple headquarters and included three complete performances of "Get Back," two of which appear in the *Let It Be* film. The group's final take on the song was the closing number to the concert and the film. This historic performance, complete with Paul's ad-libbed reference to playing on the rooftops, is included on *Anthology 3*.

Towards the end of January 1969, Glyn Johns made stereo mixes of January 23 and January 27 performances of "Get Back." These mixes were transferred to an acetate for the Beatles to review.

On March 26, "Get Back" was mixed for mono at Abbey Road by EMI engineer Jeff Jarratt. The finished master combines the January 27 coda-less performance with the first 35 seconds of a coda recorded on January 28. An acetate of this mix was played on Easter Sunday (April 6) on BBC 1 by disc jockeys John Peel and Alan Freeman. Because Paul was not satisfied with the mix, the song was remixed for mono on April 7 by Glyn Johns and Jerry Boys at Olympic Studios. This is the mix used on the British single. Johns and Boys also prepared a stereo mix for the American single. Paul was the only Beatle who attended these sessions. George Martin was most likely not present. Phil Spector remixed the song for the *Let It Be* album on March 26, 1970, adding introductory banter. He did not add the coda. The 2003 album *Let It Be... Naked* contains a remix of the January 27 master without the coda.

Don't Let Me Down

Recorded: January 22, 27, 28 and 29 (Apple basement studio);
January 30 (Apple rooftop concert)
Mixed: April 7 (mono & stereo) from January 28 performance

Producer: George Martin (January 28, 29 & 30; maybe Jan 22)
Engineers: Glyn Johns; Alan Parsons (all except January 22)

John: Lead vocal; rhythm guitar (Casino)
Paul: Backing vocal; bass guitar (Hofner)
George: Backing vocal; lead guitar (Telecaster)
Ringo: Drums
Billy Preston: Electric piano (Fender Rhodes)

"Don't Let Me Down" was written by John as an expression of his love for Yoko Ono. In late 1968, he recorded a demo containing most of the elements of the finished song.

John introduced "Don't Let Me Down" on January 2, 1969, as his initial offering for the *Get Back* project. The first runthroughs, with John playing chords and George adding some lead guitar lines, took place without Paul. After McCartney arrived, he rearranged the song and suggested that it open with the title being sung twice. The group continued rehearsing the song the following day.

When the band returned to the song on January 6, much time was spent on the middle eight. The group experimented with different rhythms, lyrics, harmonies, falsetto voices and call and response vocals, none of which proved satisfactory. The only new idea to survive the day's extensive and frustrating rehearsals was John's decision to add a guitar introduction to the song. And while much of the time devoted to the song was unproductive, the group did work its way through a few near-satisfactory performances that showed the song's potential.

At this stage, the instrumentation of the song was still open to discussion, with consideration being given to adding piano. Although George was willing to play bass to allow Paul to move to piano, John wanted the song to have two guitars. During the initial rehearsals of the song, and for the next few days, George used a wah-wah pedal to alter the sound of his guitar.

On January 7, the group continued work on the middle eight. Performances from the next two days show the band making progress in spite of John's constant inability to remember the lyrics.

Prior to the start of rehearsals on January 10, Paul played "Don't Let Me Down" on piano. By the time the group returned to the song that afternoon, George had quit the band. The performance by the remaining Beatles was an embarrassing mess.

The group rehearsed "Don't Let Me Down" in Apple's basement studio on January 21. During one of the performances, John lapses into laughter and Little Richard improvisations. Another runthrough is tighter, but once again spiked with inappropriate vocal ad-libs. George is no longer using his wah-wah pedal and is playing his rosewood Fender Telecaster through a Leslie speaker.

Billy Preston joined the *Get Back* sessions on January 22. On his first take of the song, Preston starts tentatively, but quickly falls into a groove with his blues-sounding electric piano riffs. John plays organ on this performance, perhaps to help Billy learn the chords to the song. After a few rehearsals, the group performs a fairly solid rendition of the tune, although John has trouble with the lyrics to the first verse and gets a bit silly during the second bridge. As the song reaches what had previously been its end, John says "Take it, Billy" and the band starts up again with Preston taking a piano solo while John ad-libs "Can you dig it?" and "I had a dream this afternoon." When the song comes to a halt, John says the song's title and the band adds a brief coda. One of the later takes from this day was selected by Glyn Johns for the unreleased *Get Back* album.

When the Beatles returned to the song on January 27, they rehearsed specific sections and recorded two full takes. While the song was starting to come together, there were still vocal glitches.

By January 28, the band had finally mastered the song, turning in two near perfect performances. The best of these was selected to serve as the flip side to "Get Back," although part of John's vocal from another take was dropped in to cover up some flubbed lyrics during the first verse. In addition, some vocal ad-libs and screams by John and Paul from another take were added to the end of the song.

The following day the group, without Billy Preston, rehearsed "Don't Let Me Down" for the rooftop concert. To avoid straining his vocal chords, John sang in a deeper and more relaxed voice. Paul stopped the song early on to work on his harmony part with John. During some of the choruses, John sang the title to "Keep Your Hands Off My Baby," a 1962 hit for Little Eva that was recorded by the Beatles for the BBC. Towards the end of the song, John calls out, "Go Bill," and does a brief vocalization of the missing pianist's solo.

The group played the song twice during the rooftop concert. During the first, John forgot the opening lyrics to the second verse, forcing him to ad-lib some gibberish. When the group returned to the song later in the show, John muffed the lyrics to the first verse. The earlier take of the song is tighter and appears in the film. *Let It Be... Naked* contains an edit of the two rooftop performances.

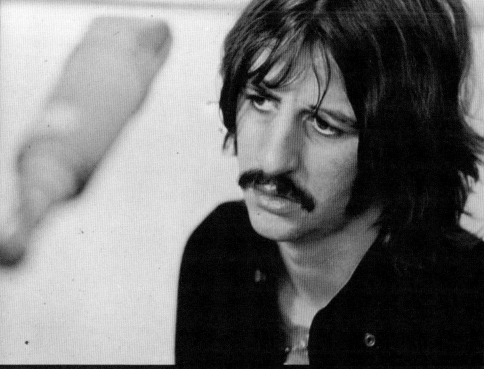

APPLE
An abkco managed company
presents

THE BEATLES "Let it be"

TECHNICOLOR® United Artists
Entertainment from
Transamerica Corporation

You Know My Name (Look Up The Number)

Recorded: May 17 & June 7 & 8, 1967; April 30, 1969 (Studio 2)
Edited: June 9, 1967; November 26, 1969
Mixed: June 9, 1967; April 30, 1969; November 26, 1969

Producers: Geoff Emerick (May 17); George Martin (June 7 & 8); Chris Thomas (April 30, 1969)
Engineers: Geoff Emerick & Richard Lush (1967); Jeff Jarratt & Nick Webb (1969)

John: Lead vocal; guitar
Paul: Lead vocal; piano; bass
George: Guitar; vibraphone
Ringo: Drums

Brian Jones: Tenor saxophone
Mal Evans: Gravel sound effects

Embellishments: Bongos; tambourine; hand claps; percussion; crowd noise; applause

While "Let It Be" is a tightly structured and serious ballad, the song chosen to serve as the single's B-side is the complete opposite—a free-spirited piece of nostalgic nightclub nonsense. "You Know My Name (Look Up The Number)" was recorded in several parts that would later be edited together. John lifted the title from a phrase appearing on the front cover to the 1967 London telephone directory: "You have their NAME? Look up their NUMBER." Although John envisioned the song as nothing more than the title repeated over and over again in the style of the Four Tops' "Reach Out I'll Be There," the end result was more reminiscent of Goon Squad lunacy or the Bonzo Dog Doo-Dah Band than Motown soul. In his Playboy interview, John described the song as "a piece of unfinished music that I turned into a comedy record with Paul."

The Beatles began work on Part One on May 17, 1967, during the time they were knocking out songs for the *Yellow Submarine* cartoon. The group recorded 14 takes consisting of Paul on piano and bass, John and George on guitars and Ringo on drums, supplemented by bongos, tambourine, hand claps and vocals. The group returned to the madness on June 7, adding overdubs to Take 9 and recording a separate rambling rhythm track that would not be used. The following evening the group recorded Parts Two through Five of the song. In addition to the usual instruments, the song contains George on vibraphone and Brian Jones of the Rolling Stones on tenor saxophone. The next evening (June 9) the song was edited together and numbered Take 30. The 6:08 rhythm track consisted

of Take 9 of Part One, Take 12 of Part Two, Take 4 of Part Three, Take 6 of Part Four and Take 1 of Part Five. The song was mixed for mono and left alone while the group moved on to a more important project—the recording of "All You Need Is Love."

After ignoring "You Know My Name" for nearly two years, John and Paul entered Abbey Road studio on April 30, 1969, to overdub vocals, percussion and sound effects, including crowd noise, applause and Mal Evans shoveling a bucket of gravel. To add to the nightclub atmosphere, John asks the crowd for a big hand for Denis O'Bell, a name obviously derived from Denis O'Dell, who produced the *Magical Mystery Tour* TV film. Paul then takes on the persona of fictional crooner Denis O'Bell for the lounge act segment of the song. "You Know My Name," still running 6:08, was mixed for mono at the end of the session.

Earlier that evening, George overdubbed a new improved guitar solo onto Take 27 of "Let It Be." At that time, the group had no idea that the two songs would be issued together as the Beatles last British single nearly one year later in March 1970.

In November 1969, John decided that if the Beatles wouldn't release "What's The New Mary Jane" (a *White Album* reject) and "You Know My Name," he would issue the songs as a Plastic Ono Band single. He booked a session at Abbey Road on November 26 (serving as co-producer with Geoff Emerick) to remix and edit the songs. Mono Remix 3 from April 30, 1969, of "You Know My Name" was copied and renamed Remix 4. It was then edited down to 4:19. "What's The New Mary Jane" was mixed for stereo and edited.

Apple made test pressings of a single containing the songs, assigned a British catalog number (APPLES 1002) and announced a rush release date in England of December 5, 1969. An Apple press release stated that the disc featured John and Yoko backed by "many of the greatest show business names of today." This, however, was not to be. The single was put on hold on December 1 and was never released because the recordings were really Beatles songs and the release of the single was objected to by the other Beatles.

While "You Know My Name" would have been difficult to program onto a Beatles album, it was interesting enough to merit release. John finally succeeded in getting the song issued when it was placed on the B-side to "Let It Be."

Anthology 2 contains a new version of the song that restores much of what John edited out in November 1969. For the first time the song is in stereo and runs 5:42. The additional running time exposes more of the song's infectious comedic aspects.

Teddy Boy

Recorded: January 24 & 28 (Apple basement)
Mixed: Mar 10, 1969 (Glyn Johns); Mar 25, 1970 (Phil Spector)

Producer: George Martin (January 28; maybe January 24)
Engineers: Glyn Johns; Neil Richmond (Jan 24); Alan Parsons (28)

Paul: Lead vocal; acoustic guitar (Martin D-28)
John: Square dance calls; whistling; acoustic guitar (Gibson J-200)
George: Lead guitar (Telecaster)
Ringo: Drums

"Teddy Boy" was started by Paul during the Beatles stay in Rishikesh, India in March 1968. The song was finished later that year in Scotland and London. Although he played a brief bit of the song at Twickenham on January 9, the band was not formally introduced to the tune until January 24 when Paul sang and played a mostly solo performance on acoustic guitar. After a brief rehearsal during which he taught the chords to John and George, Paul led the band through a complete performance. In order to liven things up (and perhaps out of boredom), John throws in square dance calls midway through the song: "Take your partner, dosey doe, hold her tight and don't let go, when you've got it, jump up...." Glyn Johns selected this take of the song for the first version of the *Get Back* album. In keeping with the original "warts and all" philosophy of the project, he even left in a bit of feedback squeal. As the song comes to an end, Paul can be heard saying "So goes that one for further consideration."

"Teddy Boy" was given further consideration on January 28 and 29, with Paul leading the way on acoustic guitar and vocal. During the first of these performances, Paul vocalizes instrumental solos midway through and at the end of the song and breaks into laughter during one of the verses. Ringo provides steady drumming, but John's guitar is at times erratic. Lennon also supplies brief vocal contributions and can be heard talking in the background. The January 29th take, which was not recorded by Glyn Johns, is the worst of the lot, ruined by John's poor guitar playing.

Although Phil Spector prepared two mixes of "Teddy Boy" (full length and edited 3:10 versions), the song was not included on the *Let It Be* album, most likely because Paul's recording of the song was included on his *McCartney* solo LP released a month earlier. In addition, the song was not featured in the *Let It Be* film. The song did not appear on a Beatles album until 1996's *Anthology 3*. The *Anthology* version is an edit of 1:15 from January 28 followed by 2:00 from January 24.

I'm Ready (Rocker)

Recorded: January 22 (Apple basement)

Producer/Engineer: Glyn Johns

Paul: Lead vocal; bass guitar (Hofner)
John: Electric guitar (Casino)
George: Lead guitar (Telecaster)
Ringo: Drums
Billy Preston: Electric piano (Fender Rhodes)

The Beatles spent a significant part of their first two days in their improvised Apple basement studio running through bits of oldies. Unfortunately the group's performances were, for the most part, substandard. Things did improve after the arrival of Billy Preston, who played electric piano on the songs. While most of the rehearsals and jamming on oldies was not properly recorded on the equipment borrowed from EMI, Glyn Johns captured some interesting if not polished performances.

One of the recorded segments opens with a brief performance of a Chuck Berry-style rocker that was identified by Paul on the tape box as "Rocker." At the tapes starts rolling, Paul can be heard singing "I'm ready and I'm able to rock 'n' roll all night, I'm ready," which is taken from Fats Domino's "I'm Ready." The song, written by Pearl King, Ruth Durand and Joe Robichaux, charted at 16 in the Billboard Hot 100 and at seven in the Billboard Hot R&B Sides chart. The song did not chart in the U.K., but its flip side, "Margie," was a number 18 hit. This bit of Beatles improvisation runs for 33 seconds.

Save The Last Dance For Me

Same recording session and personnel as I'm Ready (Rocker), but with John also contributing vocals

The jamming on "Rocker" is followed by the classic Drifter's song "Save The Last Dance For Me." The group clearly has fun on this one, with John and Paul sharing the vocals. After completing just the first verse ending with "Oh darling, save the last dance for me," they break into two lines of "Don't Let Me Down" before the song peters out. "Save The Last Dance For Me," written by Doc Pomus and Mort Shuman, was first recorded by the Drifters in a 1960 session with Ben E. King on lead vocals. The track was produced by Jerry Leiber and Mike Stoller. The song topped the Billboard Hot 100 for three weeks and the Hot R&B Sales chart for one week in 1960. It was a number two hit in the U.K.

Rip It Up/Shake Rattle and Roll

Recorded: January 26 (Apple basement)

Producer: George Martin
Engineers: Glyn Johns; Neil Richmond

Paul: Vocal; piano (Blüthner grand)
John: Vocal; bass guitar (Fender VI)
George: Guitar (Telecaster)
Ringo: Drums
Billy Preston: Organ (Lowrey DSO Heritage Deluxe)

The tape on this medley starts as "Rip It Up" is nearing its end. John and Paul sing the third verse a capella before being joined by the band for the chorus. During George's guitar solo, John and Paul begin singing lines from "Shake, Rattle And Roll," causing the spirited rocker to shift into the latter song. The group clearly has fun with this performance, with Paul pounding away on the keys. The medley is included on the Glyn Johns "Beatles Sunday" acetate and in the *Let It Be* film. It is included on *Anthology 3* in edited form.

"Rip It Up," written by Robert Blackwell and John Marascalco, was issued as a single by American singer/pianist Little Richard in 1956. The song topped the Billboard R&B Best Sellers in Stores chart for two weeks and peaked in the Billboard Best Sellers in Stores pop chart at number 17. It charted at 30 in the U.K. A cover version by Bill Haley and the Comets peaked at 25 in America and four in the U.K. Elvis Presley's version of the song peaked at 27 in the U.K.

"Shake, Rattle And Roll," written by Charles Calhoun, was recorded by Joe Turner in 1954. It topped the Billboard Most Played in Juke Boxes R&B chart for three weeks. Bill Haley's cover version was a million seller number seven pop hit in America and a number four hit in the U.K.

Miss Ann/Kansas City/Lawdy Miss Clawdy

Same recording session and personnel as Rip It Up, with George adding vocals

This entertaining medley has a bit of confusion at the start as Paul is ready to sing "Miss Ann," but John and George start playing "Kansas City." Paul joins in with them, but switches back to "Miss Ann" a minute into the performance. After a short instrumental jam, John breaks into "Lawdy Miss Clawdy" and is joined by Paul. Glyn Johns placed this medley on his Beatles Sunday acetate. An edit of the medley appears in the film.

All three songs are associated with Little Richard. "Miss Ann" was co-written by Little Richard (Penniman) and Entoris Johnson and recorded by the singer in 1957. It peaked at number six on the Billboard Most Played R&B chart and at 56 in the Billboard Top 100.

"Kansas City," written by Jerry Leiber and Mike Stoller, was first recorded by Little Willie Littlefield as "K.C. Loving" in 1952. Little Richard recorded the song in 1955, but it remained unreleased until 1959, when it was issued as a single to compete with a cover of the song by Wilbert Harrison. In America, Harrison's recording topped the Billboard Hot R&B Sides chart for seven weeks and the Hot 100 for two weeks. The Little Richard single stalled at 95. It was a different story in the U.K., where Little Richard's version peaked at 26 and Harrison's disc did not even chart. The Beatles recording of "Kansas City" from their *Beatles For Sale* LP is the Little Richard arrangement.

"Lawdy Miss Claudy" was written by New Orleans R&B singer Lloyd Price, who recorded the song in 1952 at Cosimo Mantassa's J&M Studio in New Orleans with Dave Bartholomew producing. The backing musicians included Fats Domino on piano and Earl Palmer on drums. The song topped the Billboard Best Selling Retail Rhythm & Blues Records chart for seven weeks during its 26-week run. It was named R&B Record of the Year for 1952 by Billboard and Cash Box. Both Elvis Presley and Little Richard recorded the song in 1956, with Presley's version charting at number 15 in the U.K.

Blue Suede Shoes

Same recording session and personnel as Rip It Up

This delightful take has John singing lead, with Paul joining him. Once again, the group is having fun with a song from their past, only this time they remember the words and chord changes. At Paul's request, Billy Preston provides an organ solo. Towards the end of the song, John switches one line from "blue suede shoes" to "brown suede boots." Glyn Johns included the song on his Beatles Sunday acetate. *Anthology 3* edited most of the song to the end of the "Rip It Up"/"Shake, Rattle And Roll" medley.

"Blue Suede Shoes" was written and recorded by Carl Perkins. When released on Sun Records in early 1956, the song peaked at number two on both the Billboard pop and R&B Most Played in Juke Boxes charts and at number one for three weeks on the Country & Western Most Played in Juke Boxes chart. The single peaked at number ten in the U.K. Elvis Presley's cover version peaked at number 20 in the U.S. and at number nine in the U.K.

IMPERIAL
★ ★ ★ ★ ★
Imperial Records, Inc.
Hollywood, U.S.A.
X5585
IM-1888
Post Music, Inc. and
Vanderbilt Music Corp.
I'M READY
(Lewis, Bradford & Domino)
FATS DOMINO

ATLANTIC
45 R.P.M.
A-4560
45-2071
VOCAL QUARTET
Ben E. King
Progressive, BMI
Time: 2:36
SAVE THE LAST DANCE FOR ME
THE DRIFTERS
Arranged & Conducted by STAN APPLEBAUM
A LEIBER-STOLLER PRODUCTION

Specialty
45 R.P.M.
Pub: Venice-BMI
Time: 2:20
XSP-579-45
RIP IT UP
(Blackwell-Marascalco)
LITTLE RICHARD
And His Band

ATLANTIC
45 RPM
A-1209
45-1026
VOCAL
Pub., Progressive, BMI
Time: 2:57
SHAKE, RATTLE AND ROLL
(Calhoun)
JOE TURNER
and his BLUES KINGS

Specialty
Publisher
Venice Music, Inc.
BMI - 2:20
LAWDY MISS CLAWDY
(L. Price)
LLOYD PRICE
And His Orchestra
SP 428 A

Specialty
Pub: Venice-BMI
Time: 2:05
45 RPM
MISS ANN
(Johnson-Penniman)
From the Album "Here's Little Richard"
LITTLE RICHARD
606
(5069)

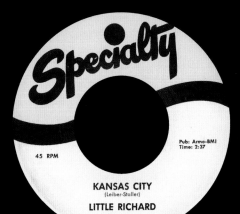

Specialty
45 RPM
Pub: Armo-BMI
Time: 2:37
KANSAS CITY
(Leiber-Stoller)
LITTLE RICHARD
664
(5200)

SUN
U 176 (BMI)
Hi Lo Music
2:14
Vocal
BLUE SUEDE SHOES
(Perkins)
CARL PERKINS
234
MEMPHIS, TENNESSEE

TAMLA
TAMLA RECORDS, DETROIT, MICHIGAN
45 RPM
Jobette BMI
Time 2:49
DM B-013301
Produced by:
Smokey
YOU'VE REALLY GOT A HOLD ON ME
(Wm. Robinson)
THE MIRACLES
T-54073

You Really Got A Hold On Me

Same recording session and personnel as Rip It Up, but with George and John on lead vocals

The Beatles ran through a loose and rough performance of "You Really Got A Hold On Me" with George and John on lead vocals. Unfortunately, John had trouble remembering the words and just about everything else about the song. George's admiration for Smokey Robinson comes through as he gamely tries to hold it all together. Glyn Johns mixed and included the song on his Beatles Sunday acetate. The *Let It Be* film has a brief excerpt of this 3:16 take.

"You Really Got A Hold On Me" was written by Smokey Robinson and recorded by Robinson with his group the Miracles. Released in December 1962, the Miracles version of the song rose to number one on the Billboard Hot R&B Singles chart and number eight on The Hot 100. The Beatles recorded the song for their second U.K. album, *With The Beatles*. In America, the song appeared on *The Beatles' Second Album*.

The Walk

Recorded: January 27 (Apple basement)

Producer: George Martin
Engineer: Glyn Johns; Alan Parsons

Paul: Vocal; bass guitar (Hofner)
John: Vocal; electric guitar (Casino)
George: Lead guitar (Telecaster)
Ringo: Drums
Billy Preston: Electric piano (Fender Rhodes)

During a break from rehearsing and recording "I've Got A Feeling" while Glyn Johns changed tapes, Billy Preston and the band messed around on a blues jam that led to Paul singing some of the words to "The Walk." John also joined in, but had even more trouble than Paul remembering the words. The new tape was in place for Johns to capture the end part of the performance. This 56-second fragment was mixed and included on Johns' January 1969 acetate.

"The Walk" was a dance song co-written (with Bob Garlic) and recorded by American blues singer/harmonica player Jimmy McCracklin. The song peaked at number seven in the Billboard Top 100 and at number five in the Billboard R&B charts when issued as a single on the Checker subsidiary of Chess Records in early 1958. The disc was issued in the U.K. on Decca's London Records subsidiary.

Cannonball/Not Fade Away/Hey Little Girl/ Bo Diddley

Recorded: January 29 (Apple basement)

Producer: George Martin
Engineer: Glyn Johns; Alan Parsons

George: Vocal; lead guitar (Telecaster)
John: Vocal; guitar (Casino)
Paul: Bass guitar (Hofner)
Ringo: Drums

This medley starts with the instrumental "Cannonball" and quickly shifts to George singing a few barely audible lines from "Not Fade Away" before his voice is given volume. After an instrumental break, John sings the first two lines from "Hey Little Girl" before moving on to "Bo Diddley." The group feels comfortable with the syncopated Bo Diddley beat, turning in another loose but entertaining performance. The medley was recorded by Glyn Johns on January 29, but was not transfered to any of his acetates. Abbey Road engineer John Barrett's mix of the medley has appeared on several bootlegs.

"Cannonball" is an instrumental song written by guitarist Duane Eddy and producer Lee Hazlewood. When Eddy's recording of the song was issued as a single in late 1958, it peaked at number 15 in the Billboard Hot 100 and at 22 in the Billboard Hot R&B Sides chart. The song charted at 22 in the U.K.

"Not Fade Away" was written by Buddy Holly (shown on the record's label as Charles Hardin, his first and middle names) and producer Norman Petty. The artist is listed as the Crickets. The song, which is in the same groove as the Bo Diddley beat, was the B-side to "Oh! Boy," which peaked at number ten in the Billboard Top 100 and was a number three hit in the U.K. The song also appears on the 1957 album *The "Chirping" Crickets*. The Rolling Stone's 1964 cover of the song charted at three in the U.K. and at 48 in the U.S.

"Hey Little Girl," written in 1959 by Otis Blackwell and Bobby Stevenson, was recorded by Dee Clark. The single peaked at number 20 in the Billboard Hot 100 and at two in the Billboard Hot R&B Sides chart. The disc was issued in the U.K. on EMI's Top Rank International label, but did not chart.

"Bo Diddley" was recorded by R&B singer/guitarist Bo Diddley in 1955. Bo, whose real name was Ellas McDaniel, wrote the song based on the lullaby "Hush Little Baby." The single topped the Billboard Most Played by Jockeys R&B chart for two weeks.

Mailman, Bring Me No More Blues

Same session, producer and engineers as Cannonball medley

John: Vocal; guitar (Casino)
George: Vocal; lead guitar (Telecaster)
Paul: Bass guitar (Hofner)
Ringo: Drums

The Beatles ran through several Buddy Holly songs on January 29, including "Not Fade Away," "Maybe Baby," "Peggy Sue Got Married," "Crying, Waiting, Hoping" and "Mailman, Bring Me No More Blues." For the latter song, John handles the lead vocal, doing his best to sound like Holly, backed by George. The group turns in a fine performance, clearly remembering this relatively obscure song recorded by Holly. *Anthology 3* contains an edited version of this performance.

"Mailman, Bring Me No More Blues," written by Ruth Roberts, Bill Katz and Stanley Clayton, was recorded by Holly in 1957 and issued in America as the B-side to "Words Of Love" (which was recorded by the Beatles in 1964 for their fourth U.K. album *Beatles For Sale* and issued in the U.S. on *Beatles VI* in 1965). Holly first issued the song in the U.K. on the 1958 album *Buddy Holly*.

Love Me Do

Recorded: January 28 (Apple basement)

Producer: George Martin
Engineer: Glyn Johns; Alan Parsons

Paul: Lead vocal; bass guitar (Hofner)
John: Backing vocal; electric guitar (Casino)
George: Lead guitar (Telecaster)
Ringo: Drums
Billy Preston: Electric piano (Fender Rhodes)

The Beatles mess around on a bluesy arrangement of the group's first single, "Love Me Do." Paul handles the vocals in a very loose manner, but does remember the words. John occasionally joins in at spots. Billy Preston's electric piano helps fill out the sound, which is missing the harmonica that was so dominant in the group's 1962 recordings of the song.

The idea of the Beatles recording a re-make of "Love Me Do" sounded intriguing at the time fans read about it in The Beatles Book in the summer of 1969. Unfortunatley, the performance does not live up to expectations.

Besame Mucho

Same session, producer and engineers as Cannonball medley

Paul: Lead vocal; Bass guitar (Hofner)
John: Backing vocal; guitar (Casino)
George: Guitar (Telecaster)
Ringo: Drums

Paul leads the band through the Latin standard "Besame Mucho." This is another performance where the group's enthusiasm makes up for their relatively loose playing. The group is shown running through the song in the *Let It Be* film.

"Besame Mucho," written by Consuelo Velazquez and Sunny Skylar, was a number one hit in 1944 for the Jimmy Dorsey Orchestra. The Beatles were familiar with the song through the Coasters two-part cover version issued in 1960. While "Part I" charted at number 70 in the Billboard Hot 100, the Beatles drew more from "Part II" and added a "Cha-cha-boom" refrain. The group recorded the song at their Decca audition on January 1, 1962, and at their EMI commercial test on June 6, 1962. The latter is on *Anthology 1*.

Bye Bye Love

Recorded: January 25 (Apple basement)

Producer: George Martin
Engineer: Glyn Johns; Alan Parsons

Paul: Vocal; acoustic guitar (Martin D-28)
John: Vocal; acoustic guitar (Gibson J-200)
George: Lead guitar (Telecaster)
Ringo: Drums

During a break from rehearsing and recording "Two Of Us," John and Paul returned to a song by the duo that inspired their vocal harmonies with a performance of the Everly Brothers "Bye Bye Love." The song charted in 1957 in the Billboard Top 100 at number two and in R&B charts at five. It peaked at number six in the U.K.

Going Up The Country

Same January 22 recording session and personnel as I'm Ready

Glyn Johns rolled the tape as Paul led the group through a brief performance of Canned Heat's current single "Going Up The Country." The song would later chart at number nine in the Billboard Hot 100 and at number 19 in the U.K.

THE WALK
(McCracklin-Garlic)

CHECKER

Arc Music
8619 BMI

JIMMY McCRACKLIN
And his Band
885

MANUFACTURED BY CHESS PRODUCING CORP., CHICAGO, ILLINOIS, U.S.A.

Jamie
PHILADELPHIA   HOLLYWOOD

UNBREAKABLE
45 R.P.M.

RECORD NO.
1111
DE-9

Gregmark (BMI)
Time 1:52

Produced by
Sill-Hazlewood

CANNONBALL
(L. Hazlewood & D. Eddy)
DUANE EDDY
his 'twangy' guitar and
THE REBELS

MARCA REGISTRADA · MANUFACTURED BY   BRUNSWICK RADIO CORP · NEW YORK · U.S.A.

Brunswick

RECORD NO.
9-55035
(103,104)+

Vocal Group
With Orchestra

NOT FADE AWAY
(Norman Petty-Charles Hardin)

THE CRICKETS

Abner
MADE IN U.S.A.

59-1111
Vocal-BMI

Time: 2:15
Obie Music

HEY LITTLE GIRL
(O. Blackwell - B. Stevenson)
DEE CLARK
Abner 1029

Checker
RECORD CO.

ARC
7788

VOCAL
B. M. I

BO DIDDLEY
(E. McDaniels)
BO DIDDLEY
814

MANUFACTURED BY CHECKER RECORD CO., CHICAGO, ILL.

CORAL

Vocal With
Instrumental
Accompaniment

RECORD NO.
9-61852
(102,256)+
(2:10)

MAILMAN, BRING ME NO
MORE BLUES
(Ruth Roberts-Bill Katz-Stanley Clayton)
BUDDY HOLLY

MARCA REGISTRADA · MF'D BY CORAL RECORDS, INC · NEW YORK, U.S.A. · SUBSIDIARY OF DECCA RECORDS, INC.

45 RPM

ATCO
Records

Vocal & Instrumental
60C-4294
Tenor Sax Solo
by KING CURTIS

45-6163
Pub., Peer
International, BMI
Time: 2:10

BESAME MUCHO
(PART II)
(Velazquez - Skylar)
THE COASTERS
Produced by LEIBER & STOLLER
Division of Atlantic Records, New York, N. Y.

Cadence

Acuff-Rose Publ.,
BMI
Time: 2:17
45 RPM
1315

Vocal With
Orchestra

ZTSP 26301

BYE BYE LOVE
B. Bryant - F. Bryant
THE
EVERLY BROTHERS

CADENCE RECORDS INC., NEW YORK, N. Y.

GOING UP THE COUNTRY
(Alan Wilson)
(From The Liberty Album "Living The
Blues"—LST-27200)

56077
LB-2648
Metric Music Co.
BMI — 2:30
Produced By
Canned Heat &
Skip Taylor

LIBERTY

CANNED HEAT

From *Get Back* to *Let It Be*: An Overview

The *Get Back/Let It Be* sessions and the resulting unreleased and released albums and bootlegged recordings are among the most interesting and confusing aspects of the Beatles recorded legacy. While there can be no doubt that the group recorded some incredible music during these sessions, the Beatles and Apple have struggled with how best to present it.

When the project shifted from its original vision of rehearsals for a planned concert featuring songs from *The White Album* to the development of new songs for a TV special and concert, Paul had a backlog of potential classic songs. He was ready with "Let It Be," "The Long And Winding Road," "Two Of Us," "I've Got A Feeling" and others. "Get Back" would evolve from a jam into one of the Beatles biggest hits during rehearsals at Twickenham and Apple. Other songs would be held over and end up on *Abbey Road* and solo releases.

Leading up to the sessions, John was more interested in being with Yoko than contributing to Beatles projects. His drug use was also affecting his creative abilities. He came into the sessions with "Dig A Pony," which he later dismissed as a piece of garbage, "Don't Let Me Down" and little else. His "Everybody Had A Hard Year" had already been joined together with Paul's "I've Got A Feeling." Three songs auditioned for *The White Album*, "Mean Mr. Mustard," "Polythene Pam" and "Child Of Nature," would be rehearsed during the sessions, but not recorded at Apple. His attempts to redo "Across The Universe" were dismal failures. He led the group through an improvised song, "Dig It," that was credited on the label as a group composition. In addition to "Don't Let Me Down," his finest moments were the resurrection of one of the first songs he ever wrote, "One After 909," his vocal harmony and acoustic guitar on "Two Of Us" and his guitar solos on "Get Back" and "For You Blue."

George came into the sessions with a backlog of wonderful songs, but with the realization that he would be lucky to get one or two taken seriously by the group. Although the band rehearsed "All Things Must Pass" for a few hours at Twickenham, they showed little interest in "Isn't It A Pity," "Let It Down" and "Hear Me Lord," songs he would later record for his *All Things Must Pass* LP. John waltzed with Yoko during rehearsals for "I Me Mine," though the song was recorded by George, Paul and Ringo a year later on January 3, 1970. "For You Blue" was the only George composition recorded at Apple.

Ringo, on piano, auditioned "Octopus's Garden" to George, who recommended chord changes and played acoustic guitar. They were joined by George Martin on vocals and John on drums. Although not recorded at Apple, the song wound up on *Abbey Road*.

The band ran through scores of oldies during sessions, with several being recorded as brief stand-alones or parts of medleys. These performances were often entertaining, but almost always marred by forgotten words and loose playing.

Although several of the tracks on *The White Album* received orchestral and other overdubs, the songs were, in most cases, basic recordings, often with the standard lineup of two guitars, bass and drums. The group was clearly moving away from its psychedelic phase that had dominated *Sgt. Pepper* and *Magical Mystery Tour*. For the January 1969 *Get Back* sessions, the group adopted a "no overdubs" policy. This shift was explained by John in the May 3, 1969, New Musical Express: "For me, the satisfaction of writing a song is in the performance of it. The production is a bit of a bore.... All I want to do is get my guitar out and sing songs."

While this "play it over and over again until we get it right" approach frustrated George Martin, Glyn Johns found it fascinating. He envisioned a record full of loose performances and studio banter, a "live in the studio" album. Johns made rough mixes of some of the performances at Olympic Studios on the evenings of January 24, 26 and 27 and cut an acetate on January 30 with the following tracks: "Get Back" (without the coda and followed by the start of "I've Got A Feeling" and a few guitar strums from "Help!") (recorded January 23); "Teddy Boy" (January 24) (an edited version of this mix was included on the *Get Back* album); "On Our Way Home" (early title for "Two Of Us" with two false starts) (January 24); "Dig A Pony" (January 22); "I've Got A Feeling" (January 22); "The Long And Winding Road" (January 26); "Let It Be" (January 26); "Don't Let Me Down" (January 22); "Because You're Sweet And Lovely" (alternate title of "For You Blue") (January 25); "Get Back" (January 27 with pre-song banter used on the *Let It Be* album and without the January 28 coda edited to the single) (this take was used for the single and the album); and "The Walk" (January 27). Although the "Rocker" and "Save The Last Dance For Me" into "Don't Let Me Down" segment from January 22 may have also have been mixed, it is not on the acetate.

Johns also cut a one-sided acetate of additional performances, all but one from the Sunday, January 26 session. The disc included "I've Got A Feeling" (Jan. 27); "Dig It" (8:30 edit); "Rip It Up"/"Shake, Rattle And Roll;" "Miss Ann"/"Kansas City"/"Lawdy Miss Clawdy;" "Blue Suede Shoes;" and "You Really Got A Hold On Me." One of these acetates, labeled "Beatles Sunday," was auctioned off in 1994.

These acetates were put together by Johns to give himself and the Beatles an idea of what type of album could be put together from the January 1969 sessions. Neither should be considered a proper attempt at or compilation for a *Get Back* album. Hoping that the group would embrace his concept for a "live in the studio" album, Johns gave copies of the acetates to the Beatles, most likely on January 31. His idea was quickly shot down.

On February 5, stereo mixes of the songs performed during the rooftop concert were made. This session took place at Apple Studios with Alan Parsons serving as engineer. It is not known if George Martin was present. Nothing further was done with the *Get Back* session tapes for over a month.

After traveling to the U.S. to produce a Steve Miller LP, Johns returned to England and engineered a February 22 session with the Beatles recording "I Want You." A few weeks later he received a call from Paul requesting that he meet John and Paul at Abbey Road. Upon his arrival, Johns was questioned about his idea to put together an album from the sessions. He was shown a big pile of tapes in the corner of the room and told "There are the tapes. Put them in your car. Take them away and do the album as you want to do it."

Johns was extremely excited about having the extraordinary opportunity to put together a Beatles album as he saw fit. On March 10, he began mixing songs for the new album at Olympic Sound Studios. The first day he prepared fresh mixes of several of the tracks previously mixed in January (as listed on the previous page).

On March 11, Johns continued his work on the project with new mixes of "On Our Way Home" and "The Long And Winding Road." He also made an unreleased mix of "Lady Madonna" from January 31. The next day he made mixes of different versions of "Let It Be" and "The Long And Winding Road," both from January 31. Neither of these mixes were released; however, the January 31 performance of "Let It Be" served as the basic master take for the single and all album releases of the song.

On March 13, Johns mixed a January 27 performance of "I've Got A Feeling" as well as two different versions of "Dig It" (January 24 and 26). He also mixed "Maggie Mae" (January 24), which would

find its way onto every version of the 1969 and 1970 *Get Back* and *Let It Be* albums. Finally, Johns remixed the rock 'n' roll songs that were on the one-sided acetate from January.

Realizing that no album from the January sessions would be ready for release any time soon, the Beatles requested that "Get Back" be mixed in mono for single release. On March 26, the song was mixed at Abbey Road, with an acetate of this mix being broadcast on BBC radio on Easter Sunday, April 6. The song was remixed at Olympic the following day, along with "Don't Let Me Down." The two songs were rush-released as the Beatles next single.

After listening to the mix of the January 31 version of "Let It Be," George realized that his lead guitar solo on the song was not up to his usual high standards. On April 30, Harrison entered Abbey Road Studio Three to overdub a new solo. While this was a violation of the "no overdubs, warts and all" concept behind the album, the new solo was a big improvement.

In early May, Johns put together a rough mix for a proper *Get Back* album (the contents of which are discussed in the next chapter). Johns prepared acetates of this mix, probably distributing them to the Beatles on May 5 or 6 at Olympic Studios, where the group was recording overdubs on "Something" and starting "You Never Give Me Your Money." It is believed that the group attended mixing and playback sessions held at Olympic on May 7 and 9, during which time they suggested that more studio banter be added.

Glyn Johns, assisted by engineer Steve Vaughan, did additional work on the *Get Back* album at Olympic on May 15 and was joined by George Martin on May 28 to create a stereo mix of "Let It Be" and complete the banding of the album. This first version of the *Get Back* album realized Glyn Johns' vision of presenting the Beatles "live in the studio" with loose "warts and all" performances mixed with studio banter. The lone exception to the "no overdubs" policy was George's guitar solo in "Let It Be."

Although the *Get Back* album captured the freshness and excitement of the sessions, it did not contain the best performances of many of the songs. Johns often selected recordings from the early sessions when the group was still learning the songs. "Don't Let Me Down," "Dig A Pony" and "I've Got A Feeling" were from the second day, January 22. The latter song comes to a halt before its final verse with Paul and John effectively trading lines from their separate contributions to the song. January 31 takes of "Two Of Us" and "The Long And Winding Road" were passed over for inferior early rehearsals. Johns sacrificed quality in his quest for fun and interesting takes.

The Beatles began having second thoughts about putting out an album of "warts and all" performances. While Mal Evans reported that the album presented the Beatles with their socks off, perhaps the group realized that most people's feet smell bad. Rather than continuing to record more songs to flesh out and improve the album, the Beatles decided to record a new album consisting of songs recorded after the end of the Apple sessions on January 31, 1969. The group returned to Abbey Road Studios on July 1 and spent the next two months perfecting their masterpiece album, *Abbey Road*. The *Get Back* LP would be put on hold and go through a series of rescheduled release dates.

Part of this change of heart was due to John's move away from his anti-production stance expressed earlier in the year. In an interview in the June 28 NME, John indicated that the group had gotten tired of "just strumming along forever" and "got a bit into production again." After the release of *Abbey Road*, George Harrison gave the following explanation: "We had *Get Back* in the can, but one day we just decided we'd like to do a newer album."

Shortly before the release of *Abbey Road*, radio stations in Canada and the United States began playing songs recorded during the *Get Back* sessions. The source of the Canadian air play and the subsequent broadcast of the songs by WKBW-AM in Buffalo, New York, was the early May 1969 acetate of the rough mix of the *Get Back* album prepared by Glyn Johns. It is believed that John Lennon gave a copy of the acetate to Canadian journalist Ritchie Yorke in London after Lennon returned from performing at the Toronto Rock 'n' Roll Festival. After a few Canadian radio stations, including Toronto's CHUM-FM and CJRN in Niagara Falls, began airing the *Get Back* songs, the program director from Buffalo's WKBW received a call from a Canadian man who offered to sell the station a tape of unreleased Beatles songs for a hundred bucks. The station obtained the tape and broadcast the songs on the evening of September 20. Unfortunately the tape only contained the left channel.

After learning that a Buffalo radio station had played what was purported to be the *Get Back* album, Steven Segal of WBCN in Boston broadcast songs from a tape of *Get Back* songs he had obtained months earlier from San Francisco underground radio disc jockey Tom Donahue, who had received his tape from Apple publicist Derek Taylor. This tape was sourced from the acetate prepared by Glyn Johns in late January 1969. When Segal played the songs on the evening of September 22, he was unaware that he was playing something different from what had aired in Buffalo.

A number of underground radio stations in the U.S. obtained tapes of the *Get Back* tracks from one of these sources. Although they were quick to broadcast the songs, the stations were forced to stop after receiving cease-and-desist letters from Northern Songs.

The fledgling rock bootlegging business also got into the act with a cassette of *Get Back* tracks pulled from the WBCN tape going on sale in New York in October 1969. In late December, a bootlegger began pressing vinyl copies of an album titled *Kum Back*, which was also sourced from the stereo WBCN tape of the January 1969 acetate. During the first few months of 1970, additional bootlegs were issued with songs from the WBCN broadcast and/or tracks from the WKBW broadcast sourced from the May 1969 acetate.

As 1969 drew to a close, the *Get Back* album still had not been issued, being pushed back again to coincide with the release of a feature length film covering the recording sessions. Because the movie had sequences of the group performing "I Me Mine" and "Across The Universe" at Twickenham, it was decided to add the songs to what would now be called a soundtrack album. Although the Beatles had already recorded the latter song in February 1968, "I Me Mine" was neither rehearsed nor recorded at Apple. This problem was solved on January 3, 1970, when George, Paul and Ringo taped the song at Abbey Road. On January 5, Glyn Johns compiled a second version of the *Get Back* album, adding the two songs and dropping "Teddy Boy," perhaps because it was not featured in the film.

Although Beatles manager Allen Klein had nothing to do with the recording of the songs or the original concept behind the *Get Back* project, he clearly left his mark. It was Klein who convinced the Beatles that they would earn significantly more money by releasing their documentary film as a movie rather than broadcasting it on television as originally planned. He thought it would be stupid to waste the show on one-time broadcast deals when a movie would generate money for years to come.

Allen Klein approached United Artists with the proposition of having the documentary movie count as the third and final film owed by the Beatles under their 1963 agreement with United Artists. (Although the group expected *Yellow Submarine* to fulfill its contractual obligations with United Artists, the company refused to accept the cartoon as a Beatles film, but did agree to distribute the movie.) According to David Picker, who was then serving as president of United Artists, the company agreed to accept the documentary as the third film because it was clear that there would be no more movies like *Help!* or *A Hard Day's Night*.

Under their film agreement with United Artists, the Beatles also owed the company a soundtrack album. This is confirmed by the group's January 26, 1967, contract with EMI, which acknowledges that the Beatles "have a commitment to United Artists whereunder one LP record of a film of the [Beatles] shall be made available for United Artists for the U.S.A. only." During the film negotiations, Klein told United Artists that they would get the distribution rights for the soundtrack album in the United States.

As a result, Capitol lost what was then known as the *Get Back* album. To ease the blow, Klein arranged for Capitol to manufacture the records. Thus, while the album was not part of the Capitol catalog, the company received substantial income for pressing the discs. Because the soundtrack LP agreement was limited to the U.S.A., Capitol Records (Canada) and Discos Capitol de México were not affected. The *Let It Be* album was distributed by Capitol's subsidiaries in Canada and Mexico.

While Klein was confident that the documentary film would be a huge success, he had concerns about the album. Abkco's Allan Steckler observed that "The Beatles had shown a marked progression in their writing, playing and production values. *Get Back* was a drastic throwback. It didn't fit in. Particularly when compared to *Abbey Road*, which was the group's most sleek production. *Abbey Road* was very slick. It slid over the speakers. By comparison, *Get Back* didn't sound finished." According to Steckler, Klein felt the same way. He wanted to bring in his old friend Phil Spector to fix it.

Phil Spector was one of the top record producers of the early and mid-sixties, best known for his famous "wall of sound" that turned pop records into mini-symphonic operas. Spector got his start in the music business as a member of the Teddy Bears, a vocal trio that had a number one hit in 1958 with his song "To Know Him Is To Love Him." The Beatles included a gender-altered version of the song, "To Know Her Is To Love Her," in their early stage show and recorded the song at their 1962 Decca audition and for the BBC.

In May 1960, Spector began serving an apprenticeship under famed songwriters and producers Jerry Leiber and Mike Stoller, during which time he attended sessions with acts such as the Coasters, the Drifters and Ben E. King. He learned production techniques at these sessions, often contributing his ideas. Spector also played guitar on a few songs, including "Thumbin' A Ride" by the Coasters (later recorded by Apple artist Jackie Lomax and released on Apple 1807) and "Saved" by LaVern Baker. His most memorable moment was his guitar solo on the Drifters' "On Broadway."

Spector's biggest success came with Philles Records, formed with Lester Sill in 1961. The label's early hits included: the Crystals' "He's A Rebel" (#1 in November 1962), "Da Doo Ron Ron" (#3 in June 1963) and "Then He Kissed Me" (#6 in September 1963); "Zip-A-Dee-Doo-Dah" by Bob B. Soxx and the Blue Jeans (#8 in January 1963); and "Be My Baby" by the Ronettes (#2 in October 1963).

Spector flew to London on January 24, 1964, for a promotional visit coinciding with the Ronettes British tour. Because Philles was distributed in England by London Records, a Decca subsidiary, Decca promotion manager Tony Hall helped arrange Spector's itinerary, setting up a meeting with the Rolling Stones. Spector attended a few of the sessions for the band's first album, co-wrote "Little By Little" with the group and reportedly played maracas on "Not Fade Away."

Famed British journalist Maureen Cleave reported in The Evening Standard that Spector "heard the Beatles months ago and loved them. Thought they were a great Canadian outfit. 'I would love to have a crack at recording that group,' said Mr. Spector longingly."

Hall also arranged for Phil and the Ronettes to meet the Beatles at his London home (see photo below with Phil surrounded by the Ronettes and George Harrison). Spector was on the plane with the Beatles when they flew to New York for their first U.S. visit.

The mid-sixties saw Spector's greatest triumph and failure. Working with Barry Mann and Cynthia Weil, he co-wrote "You've Lost That Lovin' Feeling" specifically for the Righteous Brothers (Bill Medley and Bobby Hatfield), who were known for their "blue-eyed soul" style of singing. The Spector-produced epic ballad topped the charts for two weeks in February 1965.

Spector tried to repeat the magic in 1966 with Ike and Tina Turner, who he had signed to his Philles label. He co-wrote "River Deep–Mountain High" with Jeff Barry and Ellie Greenwich, with whom he collaborated on "Da Doo Ron Ron," "Then He Kissed Me" and "Be My Baby." He reportedly spent over $22,000 laying down the song's dense thundering rhythm track. When released in the U.S. in May 1966, the record charted for four weeks, peaking at number 88 before falling off the charts. Although the song was a number two hit in England, Spector was crushed by the song's failure in the U.S. and began a self-imposed exile from the music business.

In 1969, Spector attempted a comeback under a deal with A&M Records. His biggest success was his production of "Black Pearl" by Sonny Charles and the Checkmates, Ltd., which reached number 13 that summer. On September 13, A&M released Ike and Tina Turner's "River Deep–Mountain High" album for the first time in the U.S. The cover to the record came with a sticker proclaiming "River Deep–Mountain High is a perfect record from start to finish. You couldn't improve on it." The quote was followed by the signature of George Harrison.

When Spector's association with A&M ended shortly thereafter, he began planning a serious return to the record business, prompting a page-one story in the December 13, 1969, issue of Billboard. It was around this time that Allen Klein came up with the idea to have Phil Spector work his magic on the *Get Back* album. Rather than directly approach the Beatles about having Spector redo their album, Klein went for a more subtle approach. He arranged for Phil to meet with John and Yoko.

On January 27, 1970, John wrote a new song titled "Instant Karma (We All Shine On)." He wanted to record the song that evening and quickly recruited a version of the Plastic Ono Band with George Harrison on lead guitar, Klaus Voormann on bass, Billy Preston on electric piano and Alan White on drums. At Harrison's suggestion, John had Phil Spector, who was in London at the time, produce the record.

Spector's successful handling of the session led to him being invited by John and George (with Klein's blessings) to reproduce the *Get Back* album. Spector began his work on the project on March 23, 1970, at Abbey Road. He was assisted by engineer Peter Bown. Many of the sessions were attended by Harrison and Klein. Ringo played drums for the orchestral overdub session held on April 1. Spector completed his mixes for the album the following day.

Because the album had to be completed quickly to coincide with the release of the movie, Spector most likely did not wade through the multitude of tapes recorded at Apple during January 1969. He probably limited his review to the *Get Back* album, other recordings previously mixed by Glyn Johns and the film itself. Although Spector added orchestration to three of the songs, he followed Glyn Johns' concept of giving the album a live-in-the-studio feeling by mixing in bits of studio chatter between the tracks.

When the *Let It Be* album was first issued in May 1970, the reviews were mixed. While Billboard and other establishment-type publications focused on the quality of the songs, the more hip magazines lambasted Spector's heavy handed production. Rolling Stone lamented that Spector had "whipped out his orchestra and proceeded to turn several of the rough gems on the best Beatles album in ages into costume jewelry."

George Martin was astonished and sickened by the final product. "It was always understood that the album would be like nothing the Beatles had done before. It would be honest, no overdubbing, no editing, truly live...almost amateurish. When John brought in Phil Spector he contradicted everything he had said before. When I heard the final sounds I was shaken. They were so uncharacteristic of the clean sounds the Beatles had always used."

Glyn Johns, who was proud of his original *Get Back* album, was Spector's harshest critic. "He totally and utterly wrecked the album. I really think he crucified what was a bloody good record."

Paul McCartney was particularly upset with Spector's schmaltzy production of "The Long And Winding Road." In his lawsuit to dissolve the Beatles partnership, McCartney cited Spector's addition of strings, voices, horns and drums to the song as "an intolerable interference" with his work.

John Lennon, on the other hand, praised Spector's efforts. Lennon felt the *Get Back* album had been "badly recorded...with a lousy feeling to it." John believed Spector "made something out of it" and "did a great job." In his Rolling Stone interview with Jann Wenner, Lennon remembered "When I heard it I didn't puke, I was so relieved after hearing six months of this like black cloud hanging over, that this was going to go out."

Let It Be remains the group's most controversial album among critics and fans. Many believe Glyn Johns' mix is charming and superior to the post-session production work of Phil Spector. They vilify Spector for his orchestral and choir additions, claiming that he made the entire album unlistenable. Others believe that Spector turned an amateurish-sounding collection of songs into a polished album that enables the listener to appreciate the quality of the songs.

The truth is somewhere in between. A comparison of the Glyn Johns mix and the Phil Spector production reveals that both have brilliant moments and flaws. Johns' decision to let well enough alone with Paul's ballads, "Let It Be" and "The Long And Winding Road," was certainly appropriate. His inclusion of the free-wheeling performance of "Save The Last Dance For Me" into "Don't Let Me Down" is a treat. But his choice of rough runthroughs from the early days of the sessions over tighter performances from January 30 and 31 is unfortunate.

Phil Spector chose better takes of "Two Of Us," "Dig A Pony" and "I've Got A Feeling." He wisely stayed with Johns' selections for "One After 909," "For You Blue" and "Maggie Mae." His edit on "I Me Mine" was clever, but his lush orchestral and choir overdubs onto "The Long And Winding Road" turned a simple and reflective ballad into a schmaltzy, sappy piece of muzak. His mix on the song "Let It Be" is horrendous. But as bad as his work is on the latter two songs, one should not let them ruin what overall is a very good album with some terrific songs and performances.

Twenty-six years later, on October 29, 1996, Beatles fans finally got to hear more of the "Beatles with their socks off" performances from the *Get Back/Let It Be* sessions with the release of *Anthology 3*. The album contains a dozen tracks from the sessions.

"She Came In Through The Bathroom Window" was recorded on the first day (January 21). Neither this nor any other perfromance of the song was included on any of the *Get Back* or *Let It Be* albums. The song would later be recorded as part of the *Abbey Road* medley. "Dig A Pony" is also from January 21. It has some interesting banter at the end after John shouts "Shabbat." As Glyn Johns has encouraging words for the take, Paul says "Ah, you see, you see. We improve with time like a fine wine, really." Lennon is skeptical, commenting in the background, "You're not talking to Ricky and the Red Streaks, you know" (referring to Paul's suggestion that the Beatles go on the road booked under that name). Paul continues with the wine analogy, "I'll put us down as Beaujolais '62." "I've Got A Feeling" is from January 23. It was selected by Johns for the *Get Back* LP.

"Two Of Us" is a charming performance from January 24, complete with Paul's nod to the Everly Brothers ("Take it, Phil"). *Anthology 3* contains an edit of "Teddy Boy" mixing parts of takes recorded on January 28 and 24. "For You Blue" is the first recorded take of the song from January 25.

"Let It Be" is represented with an early take from January 25 surrounded by dialog from the January 31 session. The track opens with John asking, "Are we supposed to giggle in the solo?" followed by Paul's "Yeah," and John's "OK." The song is preceded by Paul announcing, "This one, this is gonna knock you out." Even at this early stage with only two completed verses, the song is starting to gel with Paul's graceful piano and soulful vocal. The background vocals are in place, although John and George sound tentative on bass and guitar. Billy Preston did not attend this session. The added dialog at the end has John saying, "I think that was rather grand. I'd take one home with me...OK, let's track it. You bounder, you cheat!"

Anthology 3 also contains some of the oldies recorded during the sessions, including an edit adding "Blue Suede Shoes" to the end of a medley of "Rip It Up"/"Shale, Rattle And Roll," all from January 26. Also included is John singing lead on an obscure Buddy Holly tune, "Mailman, Bring Me No More Blues," from January 29.

Anthology 3 has the same January 26 take of "The Long And Winding Road" found on the *Get Back* and *Let It Be* albums, but without the orchestra and choir added by Phil Spector. Also included is a 4:07 edit of another song that would later be recorded for *Abbey Road*, Paul's "Oh! Darling." This January 27 performance features both Paul and John on vocals. When the song appears to end, John announces that he's just heard that Yoko's divorce has gone through and states "Free at last." As John sings "I'm free...this morning, Baby told the lawyer it's OK," the band falls back into the song.

The performance of "Get Back" that ends the rooftop concert and the *Let It Be* film is included in unedited form, complete with the guitar amps being temporarily turned off and Paul's coda ad-libs about Loretta "playing on the roofs again" and her mommy getting angry, with Paul warning Loretta, she's "gonna have you arrested."

Although not recorded until January 3, 1970, "I Me Mine" was included on the *Let It Be* album. *Anthology 3* has the unedited 1:34 take of the song, without Spector's orchestral embellishments.

The inclusion of these songs on *Anthology 3* gave fans a better understanding of the sessions. It also gave those inclined the opportunity to put together yet another version of the *Get Back* album.

During the summer of 2003, word began filtering through Beatle fandom that Apple was going to release a "de-Spectorized" version of the *Let It Be* album. Many people assumed that the "new" disc would be the unreleased Glyn Johns *Get Back* album. Others speculated that the album would have the same running order as the *Let It Be* LP, but would use the pre-Spector versions of "Across The Universe," "I Me Mine," "The Long And Winding Road" and "Let It Be" that appeared on *Anthology 3*. Few gave any thought to the possibility that Apple would issue an entirely new version of the album. But that's exactly what happened.

In early 2002, Apple's Neil Aspinall contacted Allan Rouse at Abbey Road about redoing the *Let It Be* LP. Rouse had served as project coordinator for *Anthology* and *Yellow Submarine Songtrack*. He brought in Paul Hicks and Guy Massey to engineer and mix the new album. The trio was given the freedom to select which versions of songs to include and to remix the songs as they saw fit.

Because the objective was to produce an album of great songs that would fit in with the rest of the Beatles catalog, the trio decided to drop the throw-away tracks "Dig It" and "Maggie Mae" as well as all studio banter. The album includes "Don't Let Me Down," which was on the unreleased *Get Back* album but not on *Let It Be* (although the song was included on the *Hey Jude* collection). The album's running order bore nothing in common with previous incarnations, opening with "Get Back" and closing with "Let It Be." While the trio listened to all 30 reels of tape recorded at Apple during January 1969, most of the tracks on the new album use the same master take as the previously released LP.

At the suggestion of Ringo, the new collection of songs was titled *Let It Be... Naked*. The album was released on November 17, 2003. It peaked at number five in the U.S. and sold over one million copies (platinum certification). In the U.K., the disc peaked at number seven and was certified gold.

Sonically, *Let It Be... Naked* is spectacular. The Abbey Road trio took full advantage of current technology to add clarity and depth to the recordings. They selected the best performances of the best songs, made appropriate edits and brought forth previously buried vocals and instruments to the front of the mix. On the down side, the album has none of the humor or freshness of the Glyn Johns *Get Back* album. While the disc is not the Beatles with their socks off, it is an album that fits in comfortably with *The White Album* and *Abbey Road* as a well-produced collection of great songs played by a great rock 'n' roll band.

After the announcement of the release of the Peter Jackson film of the *Get Back* sessions scheduled for September 4, 2020, Beatles fans speculated that Apple would also release an anniversary box set for the *Let It Be* album along the lines of the anniversary editions for *Sgt. Pepper's Lonely Hearts Club Band*, *The White Album* and *Abbey Road*. Speculation was that the *Let It Be* set would be released simultaneously with the film and a special *Get Back* book. Fans were hoping for a multi-disc set containing performances from the Twickenham and Apple rehearsals.

If such a product was to be part of the *Get Back* film campaign, this book would have covered the vinyl/CD/Blu-ray audio products and the new film. However, it was announced shortly before this book was set to go to press that the release of the *Get Back* film would be pushed back nearly a year to August 27, 2021, due to Covid-19, leading to yet another delay in the long history of delays associated with *Get Back* and *Let It Be* as chronicled in this book.

The title of this book is ironically titled *The Beatles Finally Let It Be*. Its publication date was set to coincide with the release of the Peter Jackson film, a time for Beatles fans to rejoice as the Beatles would finally release the *Let It Be* film. Despite the delay of the new film, Bruce Spizer and 498 Productions, LLC decided to proceed with the publication of this book because it is primarily an historical overview of the *Get Back /Let It Be* project commencing with its conception in September 1968 and running through the *Let It Be... Naked* album issued in November 2003. Information pertaining to the new *Get Back* film and any possible set of new audio releases would only comprise a relatively small part of the book.

That said, Bruce Spizer's Beatles album series books are intended to be as complete as possible, covering all releases up to the date the book goes to print. So while this book cannot cover something not yet released, 498 Productions will publish a special addendum called *The Beatles Finally Finally Let It Be* covering the *Get Back* film and any other product that may be released preceding or simultaneously with the film. The digital edition of the addendum will be available for **free download** at www.beatle.net. Or you can order a printed copy from the same website to insert into your hardcover book. We will notify all customers who purchased directly from beatle.net once it is available. If you are reading this *after* the release of the Peter Jackson *Get Back* film, visit beatle.net today to download. Thanks for reading. We hope to see you soon!

The Glyn Johns *Get Back* Albums

While serving as balance engineer and, at times, unofficial producer during the *Get Back* sessions at Twickenham and Apple, Glyn Johns got the idea to prepare an album of loose performances and studio banter. "One night I took a couple of reels of the eight-tracks away with me to Olympic Studios and mixed two days of rehearsals with a lot of chat and humor and so on. I thought it would make the most incredible Beatles album ever, because it was so real." He gave copies of his rough mixes to each of the Beatles. The following day the group told him that his concept for the album was a terrible idea.

A month or so later, when the Beatles could not be bothered to come up with a better idea, Johns was handed the tapes and told to do the album the way he wanted to. He prepared an acetate in early May that served as the basis for the *Get Back* album, although his rough mix was tweaked a few weeks later after receiving input from the group. At the time the mixing and banding of the album was completed under the supervision of George Martin on May 28, 1969, all of the Beatles except George Harrison were out of the country. Whether the group was ever enthusiastic about the results is not known, but Apple kept promoting the LP's upcoming release.

The initial concept for the album's cover was to "get back" to the image and design of the group's first album, *Please Please Me*. The Beatles arranged for Angus McBean, who took the picture featured on their first album cover, to photograph the group in the same pose in the same interior stairwell at EMI's Manchester Square headquarters. The text on the cover was supposed to mimic that of the *Please Please Me* album, with "THE BEATLES" in tall yellow letters towards the upper left corner and the title track ("Get Back" instead of "Please Please Me") in red towards the bottom followed by additional information in blue ("with Don't Let Me Down and 12 other songs" instead of "with Love Me Do and 12 other songs"). No printer's proof of the first version of the *Get Back* LP cover has surfaced; however, bootleggers have created the cover (see next page).

The *Get Back* album opens with sounds of the band getting ready to start their rooftop performance of "One After 909" (which is identified on EMI tape boxes as "The One After 909"). As the tape begins to roll, a chord from Billy Preston's electric piano and a few stray guitar notes are heard. This is followed by a member of the film crew shouting "All cameras four" (indicating Take 4), the crack of the clapperboard and John's count-in to the song. The Beatles then play an inspired performance with John and Paul sharing lead vocals. George's lead guitar and Billy Preston's piano riffs highlight the tight musical backing. At the end of the song, John sings what sounds like "Oh Danny boy, the old Savannah's calling." (The correct lyrics to "Danny Boy" are "Oh Danny boy, the pipes, the pipes are calling.") This leads into a bit of dialog taken from the end of the rooftop concert, with Paul saying "Thanks Mo" to Ringo's wife Maureen (because she was clapping the hardest) and John's classic line "I'd like to say 'thank you' on behalf of the group and ourselves. I hope we passed the audition."

"One After 909" is followed by a link track featuring a segment of the Beatles and Billy Preston jamming on two oldies. As the tape from January 22 begins to roll, Paul can be heard singing "I'm willing and I'm able to rock 'n' roll all night, I'm ready." Although the lines are from the Fats Domino song "I'm Ready," the 33-second improvisation is identified by Paul on the session tape box as "Rocker." After Paul says "Just a minute boys," the group discusses what to do next. They then launch into the first verse of the Drifters' "Save The Last Dance For Me," which segues into John and Paul singing the first two lines of "Don't Let Me Down." After this breaks down, John says "This time it's serious." He then jokingly gives members of the band separate instructions on the song's tempo: "Now remember, you're waltz, you're 3/4, I'm 5/6." George is heard in the background playing riffs from "Don't Let Me Down" and saying "There's a letter for you John." After Lennon laughs and says "It's Doris," Paul shouts "Do your thing man," to which John replies "I can't keep off it."

John then counts in for the start of "Don't Let Me Down," which quickly breaks down when George asks, "Oh no, what are we doin'?" (This is a bit confusing as George should certainly be aware that the group is about to perform "Don't Let Me Down," having just practiced its riffs. The explanation is that Glyn Johns selected this false start from a recording of "Don't Let Me Down" taped later that day.) After George is told the song title by Paul, Paul says "I was just into" and plays the bass riff from "Dig A Pony." John then instructs Ringo to "Do a nice big 'cooshhh' [sound of a crashing cymbal] for me, you know, to give me the courage to come screaming in."

After another count-in, the group performs a bluesy full take of "Don't Let Me Down." This version, also from January 22, is at a slower tempo than the single and is full of vocal ad-libs, including John's "goody, goody, goody, good" following the line "she done me good." Prior to the start of Preston's electric piano solo, John shouts "Hit it Bill" and continues with vocal ad-libs over the solo.

"Don't Let Me Down" is immediately followed by more studio banter, starting with John saying "Well ladies and gentlemen I'd like to change the [begins quickly strumming his guitar] tempo a little." Upon completing his rhythm guitar improvisation, Lennon adds "OK, let's do the next song then." After George asks "Is he [Glyn Johns] tapin' then?," John replies "Yeah, we'll do "Dig A Pony" straight into "I've Got A Fever" [meaning "I've Got A Feeling"]."

Glyn Johns used the above dialog to lead into the album's next selections, "Dig A Pony" and "I've Got A Feeling," which were recorded back-to-back later that day. The segment starts with George practicing riffs from the song and John saying "OK...You never changed drumming now. Yeah, that's OK. OK. Alright Glynis, we're off again." In the background Paul is practicing his bass and George is singing the first song's "All I want is you" introduction over matching guitar notes. After John's count-in, a deliberate three note false start and John's second count-in, the group launches into acceptable but somewhat ragged performances of both songs. At the end of the first tune, the "All I want is you" vocal line is followed by John singing "Yes I do" just before the band goes straight into "I've Got A Feeling."

This performances is a spirited take, but the song breaks down at the 2:40 mark (just before the final verse) when Lennon realizes he's playing too loud. As the music stops, John admits "I cocked it up tryin' to get loud." After Paul says "Yeah," John retorts with "Nothin' bad though."

Immediately prior to the start of the *Get Back* album's next song, Glyn Johns edited in the following segment involving Ringo: "Glyn [sound of Ringo hitting his tom-tom twice], what does that sound like?" This dialog took place after the January 27 "I'm so ashamed" take of "I've Got A Feeling" mixed by Johns for the March 13 acetate. This insert was not included on the early May acetate.

Side One closes with the title track, "Get Back." Johns uses the same stereo mix as the single released in America, which is a January 27 performance edited with a coda from the next day. The early May acetate uses the same January 27 take, but without the coda. It ends with John saying "It's just different every time we do it."

Side Two opens with the sound of rattling ice cubes in a glass, followed by George's "OK?" This leads into a false start of "For You Blue." After John yells "Quiet please," the band turns in an excellent performance of the song (Take 7 from January 25, 1969). The early May acetate uses the same performance, but without the rattling ice cubes. Phil Spector used the same performance for the *Let It Be* album, but without the pre-song banter and false starts. In addition, it used George's rerecorded vocal from January 8, 1970, with its shout-outs to John.

The album's next song, "Teddy Boy," is another fun but ragged performance. This take is from January 24 and has square dance calls from John. In keeping with the original "warts and all" philosophy of project, Glyn Johns even left in a bit of feedback squeal. As the song comes to an end, Paul can be heard saying "So goes that one for further consideration." The song was dropped from the lineup for second version of the *Get Back* album and was not included on the released *Let It Be* LP.

For the *Get Back* LP, Johns selected a slow, plodding version of "Two Of Us," which was also recorded by the group on January 24. There's nothing really wrong with this take, but it is clearly inferior to the crisp upbeat version of the song recorded on January 31 that Spector selected for the *Let It Be* album.

"Two Of Us" is immediately followed by Paul saying "And so we leave the little town of London, England." This leads directly into another link track, "Maggie Mae," which returns the group to its Liverpool skiffle roots. This 38-second track, recorded between takes of "Two Of Us" on January 24, also appears on the *Let It Be* album.

For his early May acetate, Johns prepared a 5:06 edit of the group's extended January 26 improvisational performance of "Dig It." As the song comes to an end, Johns added another 12 seconds to the track by tacking on the end of a January 24 take of the song, where an electric guitar riff is followed by John saying "That was 'Can You Dig It' by Georgie Wood. And now we'd like to do 'Hark, The Angels Come.'" This selection was further edited down from a total running time of 5:18 to 4:10 for the *Get Back* album. Spector thought even less of the song, editing it down to 58 seconds for the *Let It Be* album. Had the song not been in the film, he probably would have dropped it all together.

John's "introduction" to "Hark The Angels Come" is no doubt a take off on Mendelsohn's "Hark The Angels Sing." It is a perfect link to the album's next song, the religious hymn-sounding "Let It Be."

184

The song is preceded by a film crew member announcing "Take 27" and the sound of a clapperboard. After someone says, "Uh no, I've lost me little paper," the crew member says "Take 27, sync to second clap." After the clapper, Paul follows with "Sync to second clap, please" before starting the performance used as the basic master for the single and all album versions of the song. This stereo mix of the song, made on May 28, has George's rerecorded guitar solo from April 30, as does the mix used for the early May acetate. At the end of the song, Paul comments in a barely audible voice, "Reload our stomachs, too," apparently in response to an off-mike crew member saying to reload a camera. As discussed in the Recording History chapter and the following chapter on the *Let It Be* album, Take 27A would sound different for both the "Let It Be" single and the *Let It Be* album.

Prior to "The Long And Winding Road," John asks, "Are we supposed to giggle in the solo?" to which Paul replies "Yeah." This insert, which actually occurs before Take 23 of "Let It Be," was added for the *Get Back* album and is not on the early May acetate.

Johns selected a January 26 take of "The Long And Winding Road" even though better performances were available from the January 31 session. At the end of the song, Paul adds a brief coda of stray melodic piano notes. Phil Spector used the same take for the *Let It Be* album, but added numerous embellishments.

The *Get Back* album ends with a 39-second reprise of "Get Back" taken from the latter part of the same January 28 coda edited onto the January 27 master take of the song. This little bit of fun, complete with "Oh, we got to get together" and "ho, ho, ho, ho, ho" faked laughter, was also tagged to the end of the film.

During the summer of 1969, Capitol Records was preparing its release of the *Get Back* album complete with the full-color book. This special package would have listed for $10.98, which was slightly less than *The White Album*. Although this version of the *Get Back* album was scheduled and re-scheduled for release numerous times by Apple, it was not issued. One has to wonder if the group would have approved its release had Glyn Johns selected better performances of some of the songs. The *Get Back* album has been available on bootleg CDs for many years in excellent quality.

As 1969 drew to a close, Allen Klein decided to convert the planned television special on the recording of the album into a feature-length film. As the *Get Back* LP would now have to serve as a soundtrack album for the movie, alterations to the album's lineup were needed to better match the content of the film.

Director Michael Lindsay-Hogg's cut of the film contained a charming sequence of John and Yoko waltzing to George's "I Me Mine." It also featured the group working through John's "Across The Universe." As neither song was recorded at Apple during the *Get Back* sessions, this posed some practical problems which were solved within the first few days of January 1970.

On January 3, 1970, George, Paul and Ringo recorded "I Me Mine" at Abbey Road with George Martin serving as producer. As John was on a month-long vacation in Denmark, he did not attend. The 1:34 finished master was mixed for stereo by Glyn Johns at Olympic Studios on January 5, 1970. In keeping with the spirit of the other tracks on the *Get Back* album, Johns edited in Paul fooling around on bass and brief studio banter before the start of the song. After George says, "Alright. Are you ready, Ringo?," the drummer replies, "Ready, George." Phil Spector would extend and embellish the song for the *Let It Be* album.

Johns altered "Across The Universe" to make it sound different than the version released on the *World Wildlife Fund* LP by eliminating the song's opening sound effects and creating a fresh stereo mix with the tape running at its proper speed. He left in a brief bit of studio chat that precedes the start of the song on the master tape (Lennon's "Are you alright, Ritchie?").

Because Johns was proud of his original *Get Back* album, he made only minor changes when he compiled and banded the soundtrack version of the album on January 5, 1970. Side One was, for the most part, left intact, with the primary difference being the addition of "Let It Be" to the end of the side. Johns reportedly shorted the intro to "Save The Last Dance For Me" by 29 seconds.

The first four songs on Side Two are in the same order as on the first version, but there are two deletions and two additions. "Teddy Boy" was dropped from the lineup because it was not shown in the film. "Let It Be" was shifted to Side One, thus destroying the effectiveness of Lennon's "and now we'd like to do 'Hark, The Angels Come'" remark at the end of "Dig It." The two new songs, "I Me Mine" and "Across The Universe," were placed towards the end of the side just before the "Get Back" reprise. Johns removed the rattling ice cubes and false start that preceded "For You Blue" and later incorporated parts of George's January 8, 1970, vocal overdub.

The album's cover was changed to "GET BACK with Let It Be and 11 other songs" (see page 128). Although Johns had dutifully compiled an album reflecting the film, his soundtrack version of the LP suffered the same fate as its predecessor. It was never released.

Let It Be as Reproduced for Disc by Phil Spector

More than 15 months after the conclusion of the *Get Back* sessions, an album containing recordings from the January 1969 Apple basement and rooftop sessions was finally released in May 1970. By this time the *Get Back* single was a year old, so both the album and the film were renamed *Let It Be* after the group's latest hit single. The Beatles were never quite pleased with the Glyn Johns warts and all version of the album, nor was Allen Klein, who orchestrated John's hiring of Phil Spector to fix the recordings.

Spector decided to keep and run with the "live in the studio" feel of the album, utilizing some of the existing studio banter and adding more lifted from the *Let It Be* movie. He also retained the brief return to skiffle, "Maggie Mae," and the improvisational "Dig It" (albeit severely shortened). During five mixing sessions held from March 23 through 30, 1970, Spector selected tracks for the album (sometimes choosing different takes than Glyn Johns) and mixed and edited ten tracks. All but "Teddy Boy" would appear on the album.

But Spector couldn't let it be when it came to songs that he thought would benefit from his trademark "wall of sound" production that had served him so well in the early to mid-sixties. On April Fools Day 1970, he added orchestral and choir embellishments to two of the songs, "Across The Universe" and "The Long And Winding Road," and strings to "I Me Mine." The orchestra consisted of 18 violins, four violas, four cellos, a harp, three trumpets, three trombones, two guitars and drums played by Ringo. The choir had 14 singers. The orchestral score was arranged and conducted by Richard Hewson, who had arranged Mary Hopkins' "Those Were The Days" and would later arrange Paul's orchestral version of his *Ram* album, *Thrillington*. During the session, Spector's weirdness and paranoia took hold, threatening to bring the proceedings to a halt. Ringo had to pull him aside and tell him to "cool it." The session lasted well past midnight.

The following day, April 2, Spector mixed the three augmented tracks. The album was finally in stores five weeks later.

The released album, as reproduced for disc by Phil Spector, opens with dialog from John: "'I Dig a Pigmy' by Charles Hawtrey and the Deaf-aids. Phase one in which Doris gets her oats." Lennon's remark is immediately followed by Ringo hitting his snare drum. This segment, which appears in the film, was taped during rehearsals

for "Dig A Pony" held on January 21. Charles Hawtrey was a British actor, and deaf-aids is slang for hearing aids, although the group often used the term when referring to their amplifiers. Doris pops up elsewhere during the sessions and may have been an inside joke.

The album's first song is "Two Of Us." While Glyn Johns chose a somewhat sluggish performance of the song from January 24, Spector selected Take 11 from January 31. This up-beat rendition is clearly the best version of the song recorded by the Beatles. It was used in the film and shown on the March 1, 1970, Ed Sullivan Show. Spector became aware of this version of the song from watching an advance of the film and recognized that it was vastly superior to the January 24 performance picked by Johns.

Spector's mix of "Two Of Us" is superb: the acoustic guitars are bright and crisp; the vocals are clean and up front; George's bass part on the upper strings of his guitar is in the background, but clearly audible; and Ringo's drumming is given emphasis at the appropriate times. Spector was able to bring out the beauty of the song as performed live by the Beatles and wisely chose not to add any embellishments.

Spector also played it straight with the album's next song, "Dig A Pony." Rather than using the ragged January 22 runthrough selected by Johns, Spector chose the superior January 30 rooftop performance. Just as the song is about to begin, Ringo calls out "Hold it," so he can blow his nose. This is followed by Lennon's count-in leading into the song. At the end, John says, "Thank you brothers...me hands gettin' too cold to play the chords." Spector's mix of "Dig A Pony" completely removes the "All I want is you" vocal line that opens and closes the song.

"Across The Universe" is the first song on the album heavily produced by Spector. Phil, like George Martin and Glyn Johns before him, started with Take 8 from February 8, 1968. But while Martin sped up the song and Johns left its speed alone, Spector slowed it down so that the song dropped from D to D flat and ran nine seconds longer. On March 23, he made eight mixes, none of which were used. Then, on April 1, he made a reduction mixdown from Take 8 (designated Take 9) onto an eight-track tape. Separate tracks were provided for the following elements of Take 8: (1) the reduction mix of Take 7; (2) John's vocal recorded on February 8;

LET IT BE

and (3) maracas, George's wah-wah guitar and McCartney's piano recorded on February 8. That left five open tracks for overdubbing an orchestral backing, a choir and fresh acoustic guitars. Later that day, Spector recorded the orchestra and choir.

Spector mixed "Across The Universe" the following day. The song opens with John's acoustic guitar, which is heard as part of the reduction mix of Take 7. John's guitar disappears during the chorus and other parts of the song where the reduction mix of Take 7 is faded out. Similarly, George's tamboura is heard only when the reduction mix of Take 7 is brought to the front of the mix. By using John's February 8 vocal from Take 8 and acoustic guitars recorded on April 1, Spector was able to fade out the reduction mix of Take 7 during the chorus, thus eliminating the backing vocals of Lizzie Bravo and Gayleen Pease. He also mixed in maracas and Harrison's wah-wah guitar (second and third refrains only) from Take 8 during the chorus. McCartney's bass piano notes, also from Take 8, appear towards the end of the song. With the exception of John's acoustic guitar intro, the mix is dominated by Spector's trademark wall of sound, though Lennon's lead vocal is prominently featured.

George's "I Me Mine" was also given the wall of sound treatment. On March 23, Spector made his initial mix of the song from Take 16. He eliminated one of George's two lead vocals to free up a track for later overdubs and extended the song by 51 seconds with a clever edit. At the 1:21 mark, just after the line "flowing more freely than wine," the song jumps back to the :31 mark to the line "all though the day." This leads back into the hard-rocking "I I me me mine" segment and continues past "flowing more freely than wine" until the end of the song. Hewson's orchestral score was superimposed over the extended edit of the song on April 1. Spector's April 2 mix of "I Me Mine" keeps the orchestra in the background, allowing the Beatles rocking performance to shine through.

While Spector extended "I Me Mine" from 1:34 to 2:25, he chose to shorten "Dig It." The Glyn Johns edit was just under four and a half minutes long. Spector thought 51 seconds was enough. He faded up the song as John begins singing "Like a rolling stone" three times, followed by "Like the FBI, and the CIA, and the BBC, B.B. King, and Doris Day, Matt Busby, dig it...." He copied Glyn Johns' link from "Dig It" to "Let It Be" by crossfading into Lennon's "That was 'Can You Dig It' by Georgie Wood. And now we'd like to do 'Hark, The Angels Come.'"

Although Spector did not record any additional orchestral parts for "Let It Be," his mix of the song was a drastic departure from both the Glyn Johns mix and the George Martin-produced single. One can't help but wonder why Spector tinkered with the single version of "Let It Be," which was riding high on the charts at the time he remixed the song on March 26. Perhaps he wanted to create the illusion that the album contained a different performance.

Martin embellished the piano ballad with subtle orchestration and backing vocals recorded on January 4, 1970. Although Harrison recorded an additional guitar solo that same day, Martin chose not to use the raunchy-sounding new solo, instead opting for Harrison's more laid back solo recorded on April 30, 1969.

There is nothing subtle about Phil Spector's mix. Although the first verse and chorus sound similar to the other mixes, the remainder of the song has a totally different feel. During the second verse, Ringo's hi-hat is given a distracting echo effect. The next chorus has the brass blaring away. For the instrumental break, Spector mixed in Harrison's January 4 distorted solo, which, while brilliant, is too heavy-handed for the ballad. The percussion once again becomes a distraction during the third verse with awkward drumming from Ringo and over-emphasis of the maracas. Spector extended the song from 3:50 to 4:01 by splicing in an additional chorus after the third verse. The concluding choruses have Paul's vocal fighting for attention with blaring brass and George's raunchy lead guitar. Even John Lennon, who championed Spector's work on the album, admitted that Phil got "a little fruity" on "Let It Be."

Side one concludes with "Maggie Mae." Spector's mix is very similar to Glyn Johns' mix of the song.

The second side of the album opens with "I've Got A Feeling." Spector passed on Glyn Johns' selection of an incomplete January 22 runthrough of the song, instead opting for the first of two rooftop performances, which appears in the film. He included John's post song banter, "Oh my soul...so hard."

The album's next track, "One After 909," is another rooftop performance. This is the same take that Glyn Johns selected for the *Get Back* album; however, the mix is different. Spector retained Lennon's brief rendition of "Danny Boy" that follows the song.

Although Spector has access to the near-perfect January 31 performance of "The Long And Winding Road" appearing in the *Let It Be* film, he elected to go with the same January 26 recording selected by Glyn Johns. He augmented the Beatles sparse rendition with lush orchestration and a choir. During the song's second middle eight (later an instrumental break), Spector faded Paul's vocal out of the mix and replaced it with a heavy dose of strings and choir.

188

All of the Beatles were sent acetates of the album a month prior to its scheduled release. According to Paul, the disc came with a note from Allen Klein saying he thought the changes to the album were necessary. Paul was not pleased with what Spector had done to his ballad, particularly his use of a women's choir. He sent Klein a letter on April 14 stating that in the future, "no one will be allowed to add to or subtract from a recording of one of my songs." Paul indicated that he had considered orchestrating the song, but decided against it. He requested the following alterations: "(1) Strings, horns, voices and all added noises to be reduced in volume; (2) Vocal and Beatles instrumentation to be brought up in volume; (3) Harp to be removed completely at the end of the song and original piano notes to be substituted; and (4) Don't ever do it again."

Although McCartney thought there was time for his requested changes to be made, nothing was done. In all likelihood, Klein never even contacted Spector about McCartney's requested changes.

In the *Anthology* video, George Martin summed it up: "That made me angry – and it made Paul even angrier, because neither he nor I knew about it till it had been done. It happened behind our backs because it was done when Allen Klein was running John. He'd organized Phil Spector and I think George and Ringo had gone along with it."

Spector has always maintained that his actions were needed to salvage a poor recording. In a 2008 interview published in the Mirror, Spector said: "'The Long and Winding Road' was a terrible recording when I first heard it. John was playing bass on it with all the wrong notes. There was no snare drum on it – I had to get Ringo in to play. It was really awful. Paul was singing like he didn't believe it, he was kinda mocking it. And John didn't like the song. That's why he played bass on it, and he didn't know the chord changes so he was guessing. It was a farce and I had to do everything I could to cover up the mistakes."

While some people agree that Spector salvaged a plodding performance full of bad bass notes and an uninspired vocal, others believe he ruined a beautiful simple ballad that was best left alone. It remains his most controversial work on the album.

Spector played it straight with George's "For You Blue." He selected the same take as Glyn Johns, but eliminated the rattling ice cubes and false start. The other main difference is his use of George's recorded vocal from January 8, 1970, which obviously was not available for Johns when he compiled the first *Get Back* album in May 1969. The new vocal is easily identifiable. During the

instrumental break, Harrison contributes some vocal ad-libs, including "Go Johnny go" and "Elmore James got nothin' on this baby," adding to the illusion he was singing live with the band. The first call out also serves as a nod to Chuck Berry's "Johnny B. Goode." The second compliments John's excellent playing on the lap-steel slide guitar by favorably comparing him to blues guitarist Elmore James, King of the Slide Guitar.

The album concludes with the same performance of "Get Back" that was issued for the single (and selected for the *Get Back* album), but with sufficient modifications to trick the listener into thinking it is a different take of the song. Spector starts the track with the instrumental and vocal warm-ups and banter that precede the January 27 performance selected for the single. This includes John's parody of the lyrics, "Sweet Loretta Fart, she thought she was a cleaner, but she was a frying pan," along with Paul mumbling "Rosetta" and practicing his "Sweet Loretta Mar..." opening notes, and George readying his guitar for the song's choppy rhythm guitar intro. ("Rosetta" was a jazz standard written in 1928 by Earl Hines and William Woode. Paul produced and played piano on the Fourmost's 1969 recording of the song.) To further add to the live feel of the track, Spector did not mix out Billy Preston's stray electric piano notes hit during the build-up instrumental intro.

At the end of the performance, Spector did not cut to the January 28 coda used on the single, but rather added the post-song clapping and remarks from the end of the rooftop concert. The album concludes appropriately with Paul's "Thanks, Mo" (to Ringo's wife Maureen for clapping the loudest) and John's "I'd like to say 'Thank you' on behalf of group and ourselves. I hope we passed the audition." John's closing comments were a fitting way to end the last album of new recordings issued by the Beatles. The group had passed the audition long ago and given so much to the world.

Most of the millions who purchased the *Let It Be* album in 1970 were unaware of the Glyn Johns *Get Back* album and all the differences between the two. To them, *Let It Be* was just the next Beatles record and the soundtrack to the new Beatles film.

For George Martin, the revamped album was a sore subject. In *Anthology*, he explained: "EMI came to me and said, 'You made this record originally but we can't have your name on it.' I asked them why not and they said: 'Well, you didn't produce the final thing.' I said, 'I produced the original and what you should do is have a credit saying: "Produced by George Martin, over-produced by Phil Spector".' They didn't think that was a good idea."

The Beatles Get Naked: No Strings Attached

On November 17, 2003, Apple released a new collection of songs from the *Get Back/Let It Be* sessions titled *Let It Be… Naked*. It was a freshly remixed collection of the best takes of the best songs associated with the *Get Back/Let It Be* project. It was packaged with a 32-page booklet full of pictures taken during the sessions and a 22-minute bonus disc containing studio chatter and bits of songs.

Let It Be… Naked opens with the same January 27 performance of "Get Back" released on the single and all previous versions of the album, but with greater clarity. George's chopping rhythm guitar, Ringo's galloping snare drum part, Paul's bass and lead vocal, Billy Preston's electric piano fills, and John's lead guitar and backing vocal all leap through the speakers with a force not previously heard. The only drawback to the new mix is that it is missing the January 28 coda that was tacked on to the end of the single.

The album has the same January 31 rooftop concert version of "Dig A Pony" selected by Phil Spector, although parts of the song sound different than *Let It Be* LP version.

"For You Blue" is the same basic take with George's re-recorded vocal that was on the *Let It Be* LP. The new mix brings out the unique sounds of Paul's plucking piano and John's lap-steel slide guitar.

All previous releases of "The Long And Winding Road" are from the same January 26 take of the song. *Let It Be… Naked* has the final January 31 take of the song that appears in the film. During the earlier recordings of the song, including the previously released version, Paul sings "Anyway you'll never know the many ways I've tried." By the end of the sessions, Paul had changed the lyrics to "Anyway you've always known the many ways I've tried." Paul gives a stellar performance on both piano and vocal, John hits his bass notes and Billy Preston provides a soulful organ solo.

The album uses the same upbeat January 31 version of "Two Of Us" as the *Let It Be* album. The new mix improves upon what was already a great sounding song. The acoustic guitars and harmonies of Paul and John are so crisp and clear that it sounds as if the two of them are in the room with the listener.

Although most of the songs on the album are from a single take, "I've Got A Feeling" is an edit using the best bits of the two rooftop performances of the song. Although this breaks the "no edits or overdubs" rule, the new version showcases the fun spirit of the concert and is superior to all previous mixes.

Let It Be… Naked has the same rooftop performance of "One After 909" selected by Glyn Johns and Phil Spector. The new mix gives the song added punch, with Billy Preston's piano riffs and George's guitar ripping through the speakers.

"Don't Let Me Down" is also a splicing of two performances from the rooftop concert. This was necessary as John botched the lyrics to different verses in the song. The new version showcases strong vocal harmonies by John and Paul not present on the single.

"I Me Mine" is the same Phil Spector edit, but without his orchestral score. The new mix brings out the swirling organ, acoustic guitars and distorted electric guitars with stunning clarity.

Let It Be… Naked uses the same take of "Across The Universe" found on the *No One's Gonna Change Our World* charity album and the *Let It Be* LP, but prior to its embellishments. Take 7 has John's vocal and acoustic guitar, George's tamboura and Ringo's drums. The song starts out with no reverb and minimal separation. As the song moves forward, the tamboura is spread across the mix. Progressive amounts of reverb are then added, with the song ending in a massive flood of reverb. It is the only track on the album that deviates from the dry mixes, but fits in well with the rest of the LP.

The disc appropriately closes with "Let It Be." This is the same Take 27A used by Glyn Johns, George Martin and Phil Spector, but without any of the enhancements found on the single and official album. Rather than choose between the two later recorded guitar solos, this version edits in Harrison's solo from the second Take 27, which appears in the film. The new mix also has the backing vocals, John's bass and Billy Preston's organ more towards the front.

The bonus disc is a "fly-on-the-wall" view of the sessions. It opens with the group arriving at Twickenham and then alternates between discussions and rehearsals of songs. To make up for the dropping of "Dig It" and "Maggie Mae" from the new album, the bonus disc has bits of different versions of each. Other songs include "Back In The U.S.S.R.," "All Things Must Pass" and a country version of "Get Back." The dialog provides insight into what the members of the group were thinking during the sessions. George observes that "The things that have worked out best for us haven't really been planned anymore than this has." Towards the end of the disc, Paul says "Goodnight and thank you very much for having us. It's been wonderful working with you." Wonderful indeed.

LET IT BE... NAKED

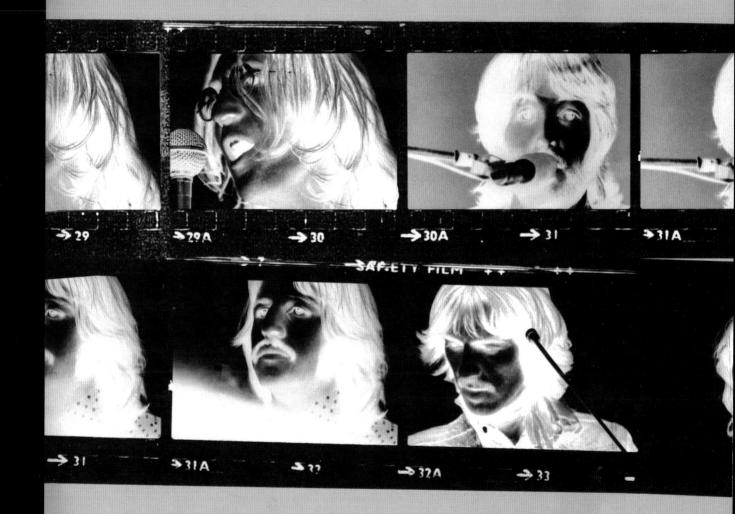

THE BEATLES

And The Band Played On

During the rehearsals that took place at Twickenham and Apple during January 1969, the Beatles played a wide variety of songs. Some were complete performances, but often they quickly fell apart because no one could remember the words. Other times, just a fragment was played or sung. And while at times the sessions resembled a sinking ship, the band played on. Below is a representative and fairly complete list of the songs.

All but five of the 17 songs later recorded for *Abbey Road* can be traced back to the *Get Back* sessions, including "Sun King," "Maxwell's Silver Hammer," "Oh! Darling," "Carry That Weight," "Octopus's Garden," "Mean Mr. Mustard," "She Came In Through The Bathroom Window," "Golden Slumbers," "Her Majesty," "Polythene Pam," "I Want You (She's So Heavy)" and "Something." George also introduced "Old Brown Shoe," which would be recorded in March 1969 and serve as the B-side to "The Ballad Of John And Yoko."

Other songs would later appear as solo releases. Songs performed by George include "All Things Must Pass," "Let It Down," "Hear Me Lord" and "Isn't It A Pity," all of which would be recorded the following year for his *All Things Must Pass* LP. Paul performed "Teddy Boy," "Junk," "Every Night" and "Hot As Sun," which would be on his first solo album, *McCartney*, "Another Day," which would be his first single, and "The Back Seat Of My Car," which was held over for his second LP, *Ram*. John's "Gimme Some Truth" would be recorded for his *Imagine* LP, while "Child Of Nature" (a/k/a "On The Road To Marrakesh") would get new lyrics and become "Jealous Guy."

The group also tried out other songs and improvisations that would not later be recorded. John sang songs identified as "A Case Of The Blues," "Madman" (a piano song in the same vein as "Mean Mr. Mustard"), "Suzy's Parlour" (a risqué rock 'n' roller with 'rat-tat-tat' backing vocals featured in the film), "The Teacher Was A-Lookin'," "Watching Rainbows," "Annie" and "Shakin' In The Sixties."

Paul often knocked out tunes on the piano before the others arrived, including "Woman," a song he wrote for Peter & Gordon in 1966. Other solo piano tunes are identified as "The Day I Went Back To School" and "Song Of Love." On acoustic guitar Paul played "There You Are, Eddie" and "Pillow For Your Head." Paul and John sang the political-themed "Commonwealth" and "Enoch Powell" and "La Penina." They also improvised "Negro In Reverse" and "Get Off!," as well as several jams identified only by a few sung words.

George Harrison played "Window, Window," "How Do You Tell Someone" and the Dylan-influenced "Ramblin' Woman." Ringo sang bits of "Taking A Trip To Carolina" and "Picasso."

The Beatles also revisited some of their earlier recordings, including a bluesy versions of "Love Me Do" and "Please Please Me." Other songs played in full or in snippets included "Lady Madonna," "Martha My Dear," "You Can't Do That," "I'm So Tired" (sung by Paul), "Ob-La-Di, Ob-La-Da," "Run For Your Life," "Strawberry Fields Forever" (on piano and sung by Paul), "I'll Get You," "Help!," "She Said She Said," "Norwegian Wood," "Every Little Thing," "When I'm Sixty-Four," "Lovely Rita," "The Inner Light," "Back In The U.S.S.R.," "All Together Now," "Hello Goodbye," "Hey Jude" and "Revolution."

In addition to "One After 909," the Beatles ran through bits of several early Lennon-McCartney tunes, including "I Lost My Little Girl," "Because I Know You Love Me So," "I'll Wait Till Tomorrow," "Thinking Of Linking," "Won't You Please Say Goodbye," "Too Bad About Sorrows," "I've Been Thinking That You Love Me," "My Words Are In My Heart" and "Just Fun." The song "I Fancy Me Chances" may also be an early Lennon-McCartney tune. "Suicide" was written by Paul when he was 14. He later included a bit of it on *McCartney*.

The Beatles also played several songs that were part of their stage show. Most were not recorded by the band for EMI or the BBC. Songs previously recorded are noted below by "(EMI)" and "(BBC)."

During the *Get Back* sessions, the Beatles performed more songs by Chuck Berry than any other artist. These included "Brown-eyed Handsome Man," "Little Queenie," "Sweet Little Sixteen" (BBC), "Almost Grown," "Johnny B. Goode" (BBC), "Thirty Days," "I'm Talking About You" (BBC), "Rock And Roll Music" (EMI & BBC), "School Days," "Maybellene," "You Can't Catch Me," "Around And Around," "I Got To Find My Baby" (BBC) and "Vacation Time."

The group also ran through several songs associated with Elvis Presley. In most cases, the Beatles would have been familiar with the original versions of these tunes as well as the Presley recording. The songs included "Don't Be Cruel," "All Shook Up," "(You're So Square) Baby I Don't Care," "Milk Cow Blues" (Kokomo Arnold), "My Baby Left Me" (Arthur Crudup), "That's All Right" (Arthur Crudup) (BBC), "Good Rockin' Tonight" (Roy Brown), "Lawdy Miss Clawdy" (Lloyd Price) and "Shake, Rattle And Roll" (Big Joe Turner). (The Beatles also played Turner's "Honey, Hush" during the sessions.)

Little Richard was another important influence on the Beatles, with the group recording his "Long Tall Sally" in 1964. During the *Get Back* sessions, the group played several of his recordings, including "Jenny, Jenny," "Slippin' And Slidin'," "Lucille" (BBC), "Miss Ann," "Send Me Some Lovin'" and "Kansas City" (EMI).

Buddy Holly was a favorite of the Beatles, with the group performing several of his songs during the *Get Back* sessions, including "Well, All Right," "Not Fade Away," "Maybe Baby," "That'll Be The Day," "Peggy Sue Got Married," "Crying, Waiting, Hoping" (BBC), "Mailman, Bring Me No More Blues" and "Early In The Morning."

The Beatles recorded three Carl Perkins songs for EMI. During the *Get Back* sessions they played "Blue Suede Shoes," "Your True Love," "Sure to Fall (In Love With You)" (BBC), "Tennessee" and "Gone, Gone, Gone." The group also recorded three Larry Williams songs for EMI. During the January 1969 sessions they performed two of these songs plus another: "Dizzy Miss Lizzy" (EMI & BBC), "Bad Boy" (EMI) and "Short Fat Fannie."

Arthur Alexander was a favorite of John, with the Beatles recording "Anna" for their first album. During the *Get Back* sessions they played "A Shot Of Rhythm And Blues" (BBC), "Soldier Of Love" (BBC) and "Where Have You Been (All My Life)."

Shortly after George Harrison's late November 1968 visit with Bob Dylan in Woodstock, NY, the Beatles ran through numerous Dylan songs, including "Blowin' In The Wind," "I Want You," "Rainy Day Women #12 & 35," "Positively 4th Street," "Mighty Quinn (Quinn The Eskimo)," "Please Mrs. Henry," "Mama, You've Been On My Mind," "I Threw It All Away," "I Shall Be Released," "All Along The Watchtower" and "Stuck Inside Of Mobile With The Memphis Blues Again." The last three songs added a touch of irony with George wanting to be released from the bad vibes of the Twickenham sessions. "All Along The Watchtower" opened with "There must be some way out of here." For the latter song, George and Paul replaced "Memphis Blues" with "Twickenham Blues." The group also played a bit of the Band's "To Kingdom Come" and a few notes of "The Weight."

The group also played some Jerry Lee Lewis songs, including "Great Balls Of Fire," "Whole Lotta Shakin' Goin' On," "High School Confidential" and "Fools Like Me." Gene Vincent was recognized with "Be-Bop-A-Lula" and "Lotta Lovin'" as was Eddie Cochran with "Twenty-Flight Rock," "Somethin' Else" and "Hallelujah I Love Her So" (although the group was familiar with the Ray Charles original). During the January 25 session for "Two Of Us," the group paid tribute to the Everly Brothers by recording "Bye Bye Love." Earlier that month they played parts of the duo's 1960 hit, "Cathy's Clown,"

as part of a medley. They also performed Hank Williams' "You Win Again," Buck Owens' "Act Naturally" (EMI), "Five Feet High And Rising" by Johnny Cash and the standard "You Are My Sunshine."

The Beatles also ran through some Motown tunes, including Barrett Strong's "Money (That's What I Want)" (EMI & BBC), Marvin Gaye's "Hitch Hike" and the Miracles' "You Really Got A Hold On Me" (BBC & EMI), "Tracks Of My Tears" and "I've Been Good To You."

In addition to "Maggie May," the Beatles played another song by the Vipers Skiffle Group, "Hey Liley, Liley Lo." They also ran through several skiffle songs associated with Lonnie Donegan, including "Rock Island Line," "Take This Hammer," "Lost John," "Diggin' My Potatoes," "Michael Row The Boat" and "Midnight Special."

Other songs included "It's Only Make Believe" by Conway Twitty, "Queen Of The Hop" by Bobby Darin, "Three Cool Cats" and "Besame Mucho" by the Coasters, "Bo Diddley" and "Crackin' Up" by Bo Diddley, "What I'd Say" and "Don't Let The Sun Catch You Crying" by Ray Charles, "What Am I Living For" by Chuck Willis, "Bring It On Home To Me" by Sam Cooke, "Stand By Me" by Ben E. King, "Hi Heel Sneakers" by Tommy Tucker, "Let's Dance" by Chris Montez, "The Walk" by Jimmy McCracklin, "Hey Little Girl" by Dee Clark, "Right String But The Wrong Yo-Yo" by Dr. Feelgood, "Little Demon" by Screaming Jay Hawkins, "Papa's Got A Brand New Bag" by James Brown, "Watch Your Step" by Bobby Parker, "New Orleans" by Gary U.S. Bonds, "Shout" by the Isley Brothers, "Some Other Guy" (BBC) by Ritchie Barrett, "Hippy Hippy Shake" (BBC) by Chan Romero, "Singing The Blues" by Guy Mitchell, "Mack The Knife" by Bobby Darin, "Devil In Her Heart" (EMI) by the Donays, "Move It" by Cliff Richard, "The Lonely Sea" by the Beach Boys, "Daydream" by the Lovin' Spoonful and "The Third Man Theme" by Anton Karas.

The Beatles also did some contemporary songs, including "Going Up The Country" by Canned Heat, "I'm A Tiger" by Lulu, "A Quick One While He's Away" by the Who and "Speak To Me" and "Little Yellow Pills" by Apple artist Jackie Lomax.

Some of the stranger songs performed were "Baa, Baa, Black Sheep," "Hello Dolly," "Rock-A-Bye Baby," "Turkey In The Straw," "Hava Negeilah," "The Peanut Vendor," "Adagio For Strings," "Tea For Two," "Chopsticks" and "Todgy, Todgy, The Battery Boy."

The amazingly diverse repertoire displayed by the Beatles during the *Get Back* sessions was partly due to the group getting back to its roots when its stage shows ran the full gamut of musical styles. It also highlights the breadth of their musical knowledge and influences that made the Beatles the greatest band of all time, appealing to audiences all over the world.

Let It Bootleg

by Scott "Belmo" Belmer

Prior to the release of the official *Let It Be* album in May 1970, several bootlegs of the January 1969 *Get Back* sessions were available in head shops and record stores throughout America. The content of these bootlegs can be traced back to two primary sources — January and May acetates compiled by Glyn Johns.

Towards the end of the January Apple sessions, Johns made rough mixes and prepared an acetate for the Beatles containing the following songs: "Get Back" (alternate take without a coda, followed by the start of "I've Got A Feeling" and a few guitar strums from "Help!"); "Teddy Boy;" "Two Of Us" (with two false starts followed by Paul saying "And so we leave the little town of London, England"); "Dig A Pony;" "I've Got A Feeling;" "The Long And Winding Road;" "Let It Be" (alternate take); "Don't Let Me Down;" "For You Blue;" "Get Back" (take selected for the single with pre-song banter and without the coda edited to the end); and "The Walk."

Apple's Derek Taylor obtained either an acetate or tape copy of the above songs. Apparently he gave a pair of 10-inch reel-to-reel tapes of the songs to his friend, San Francisco underground radio disc jockey Tom Donahue, who in turn gave copies of the tapes to his friend and fellow disc jockey, Steven Segal, then working at Boston underground station WBCN-FM. As these tapes were likely transferred with the understanding that they were not to be broadcast, neither disc jockey initially played any of the contents on the air.

In early May 1969, Johns put together a rough mix for a proper album. This banding, with minor tweaks, would soon become the first unissued *Get Back* LP. Once again, Johns gave copies of this acetate to the Beatles.

On September 17, 1969, Australian journalist Ritchie Yorke, then living in Toronto, interviewed John at Apple's London offices shortly after John & Yoko's return from the Toronto Rock 'n' Roll Revival. It is believed that Lennon gave his copy of the early May acetate to Yorke, who, upon his return, made a tape copy of the acetate, capturing only the left channel. Yorke then sold the tape to Toronto's CHUM-FM, which in turn sold tape dubs to Windsor's CKLW and Niagara Fall's CJRN. The stations broadcast these new Beatles songs, described as being from the upcoming *Get Back* LP.

WKBW-AM in Buffalo, New York purchased a tape of the songs broadcast in Canada from a Canadian man. The station played the tracks for a few days starting on the evening of Saturday, September 20. WKBW's tape was most likely dubbed off Canadian radio station CJRN, as a "Play 'Break the Bank' on CJRN" promo spot is heard during "The Long And Winding Road."

Upon learning that tracks from the yet-to-be-issued *Get Back* LP had been played by a Buffalo radio station, Steven Segal decided to broadcast his tape of *Get Back* songs on WBCN in Boston on the evening of September 22. Segal did not know that his station was actually playing something that differed from the Buffalo broadcast.

New York's WBAI-FM obtained and played a copy of Segal's tape of the January acetate, while stations in Cleveland, Cincinnati and Detroit began broadcasting recordings traced back to the May acetate. Stations in other cities also got into the act, airing *Get Back* songs sourced from one of the acetates. In most cases, air play of the illicit recordings quickly stopped due to threatened legal action.

It didn't take long for bootleggers to enter scene. By October 1969, a cassette of *Get Back* songs taped off the WBCN broadcast was being sold in New York City. This contraband tape was later sold at the Miami Rock Festival over the weekend of December 27.

The first Beatles vinyl bootleg was titled *Kum Back*. The disc was sourced from the WBCN tape of the January acetate. Legend has it that the disc (WCF, Kum Back #1) was pressed in Los Angeles in December 1969. The record had blank labels and was packaged in a white cardboard sleeve with "KUM BACK" stamped in either blue or red ink. The stereo disc has fairly decent sound quality, although it runs a bit fast. The initial pressing was 300 copies.

Side One contains "Get Back" (single version without coda); "The Walk," "Let It Be," "Teddy Boy" and "Two Of Us." Side Two contains "Don't Let Me Down," "I've Got A Feeling," The Long And Winding Road," "For You Blue," "Dig A Pony" and "Get Back" (alternate take followed by the start of "I've Got A Feeling" and a few guitar strums from "Help!"). The album went on sale in Boston and by early 1970 had spread to other parts of the country, including Minnesota and Milwaukee.

The *Kum Back* album was reviewed by Jane Scott in the January 23, 1970, edition of The Plain Dealer, Cleveland's daily newspaper. She reported that the contraband Beatles album began showing up in record stores a few days earlier, priced at $6.98. (Although this was the same as the list price for *Abbey Road*, most record stores discounted legitimate releases by a dollar or more.) Scott incorrectly reported that the authentic Beatles album was due in February and would be a double LP packaged with a 160-page book. She stated that "On some tracks it's hard to believe that these are the fab four." The best track on the album was "Let It Be," which was slated to be the Beatles next single. Other good songs included "Get Back," "Don't Let Me Down" and a funkier "I've Got A Feeling."

The *Kum Back* bootleg may have been played by radio stations as early as late 1969. Beatles author Bruce Spizer recalls taping songs matching the content of the album off a station in the New Orleans area on Christmas Eve 1969. A tape of Houston's KRBE-FM from late January has disc jockey Dan Diamond playing the *Kum Back* album starting at about 2:00 AM.

Other bootlegs of *Get Back* songs were being sold across the country, with varying quality dependent on who taped the broadcasts and the quality of the equipment used. Some were stereo and others were one-track or mono. And, of course, some bootleggers bootlegged the bootlegs. There were even 8-track *Get Back* boots.

A Studio Recording contained most of the songs on *Kum Back*, but with only one version of "Get Back" and neither "The Walk" nor "The Long And Winding Road." The disc ended with "Across The Universe" from the *Nothing's Gonna Change Our World* charity LP.

The Beatles Get Back To Toronto opens with "John & Yoko's Peace Message," an interview with the couple talking about their "War Is Over" campaign and plans for the Toronto Peace Festival. This is followed by "Get Back," "Teddy Boy," "Two Of Us" and "Dig A Pony." Side Two features "I've Got A Feeling," "Let It Be," "Don't Let Me Down," "For You Blue," "Get Back," "The Walk" and *The Beatles Fifth Christmas Record* "Christmas Time (Is Here Again)" from 1967.

Nearly all Beatles bootlegs pressed in late 1969 and early 1970 featured songs sourced from the January acetate; however, some titles had tracks from the later May acetate. The mega-rare *O.P.D.* contains the entire May acetate, but only the left channel. Its white cover has "O.P.D." stamped in the lower right corner.

Silver Album Of The World's Greatest has a blank silver cover. Initial pressings had "Dig A Pony," "For You Blue," "Two Of Us," "Dig It," "Let It Be," "The Long And Winding Road" and "One After 909" from the May acetate plus both sides of the "Get Back" single and "Across The Universe." Later pressings of the LP replaced "Don't Let Me Down" and "Two Of Us" with the January versions on *Kum Back*.

The *Get Back* bootleg on Immaculate Conception Records has a paste-on sheet with an image of a naked pregnant woman on its cover and blue labels with black text. It has "Get Back," "The Walk," "Let It Be," "One After 909," Teddy Boy" and "Two Of Us" on Side One, and "Don't Let Me Down," "I've Got A Feeling," "The Long And Winding Road," "Dig It," "For You Blue," "Dig A Pony" and "Get Back" on Side Two. This rare Beatleg primarily pulled its tracks from the January acetate, but added two songs from the May acetate that were not on the January acetate: "One After 909" and "Dig It."

The Lemon Records bootleg of *Get Back* also featured tracks from both acetates. Side One contains "One After 909," "The Walk," "Don't Let Me Down," "Dig A Pony," "I've Got A Feeling" and "Get Back." Side Two has "For You Blue," "Teddy Boy," "Two Of Us," "Dig It," "Let It Be," "Long And Winding Road" and "Across The Universe." The last track was taped off the radio by the bootlegger. The Lemon Records album was pressed in greater quantities than the other *Get Back* boots and is one of the more successful of these illicit releases.

Because these bootlegs were pressed prior to the release of the official *Let It Be* album, the bootleggers had to guess at the song titles and frequently got them wrong. "Two Of Us" often appeared as "On Our Way Back Home" on labels and jackets. "Dig A Pony" was sometimes called "All I Want Is You" or "Everything You Are." "For You Blue" appeared as "Sweet And Lovely Girl" or "I Love You (Yes I Do)." "Dig It" was identified as "Can Ya Dig It" or "If You Want It You Can Dig It," while "The Walk" was called "When You Walk" or "When Ya' Walk." "The Long And Winding Road" was sometimes titled "Don't Leave Me Waiting Here." One disc identified "One After 909" as "Move Over Honey." Many of these errors could have been avoided had the bootleggers read the description of the *Get Back* album in the September 20, 1969, Rolling Stone.

The *Get Back* bootlegs continued to be pressed and sold after the *Let It Be* LP was released. The demand remained as Beatles fans were curious to hear what the songs sounded like prior to Spector whipping out his orchestra. Although some estimates of the number sold of these various versions of the *Get Back* bootlegs are as high as 100,000 copies, sales were most likely between 15,000 to 20,000.

A few years later, additional Beatles performances from January 1969 surfaced with the release of two double albums, *Sweet Apple Trax Volume One* and *Sweet Apple Trax Volume Two*. These 1973 releases featured some of the group's rehearsals taped at Twickenham Studios. These high-quality recordings came directly from the sync soundtracks of unused film reels for the *Let It Be* film. The material for *Sweet Apple Trax* was purchased from someone within the bootleg industry for a reported $300. A thousand copies of each were pressed and quickly sold out.

In addition to early runthroughs of tracks appearing on the *Let It Be* album, these discs included other songs such as "Tennessee," "House Of The Rising Sun," "The Commonwealth Song," "Hi Ho Silver," "Ba Ba Blacksheep," "Suzy Parker," "Be Bop A Lula," "High Heeled Sneakers," "Norwegian Wood," "Shakin' In The Sixties," "Good Rockin' Tonight" and "Momma You've Been On My Mind."

Numerous knock-off versions of the albums soon followed. Some of the more notorious titles included *Watching Rainbows*, *Renaissance Minstrels*, *Hot As Sun*, *Get Back Session* and *Cinelogue 1*.

However, it wasn't until the early 1980s when *The Beatles Black Album* was released that fans were treated to a professional and highly desirable repackaging of the rehearsals previously released on the *Sweet Apple Trax* collections. The album cover was a take-off of *The White Album*, complete with raised letters on its all-black cover. The songs were listed inside the gatefold cover along with photos of the Beatles. It came with a full-color poster featuring a collage of pictures of the group. The album contained three vinyl discs. Sales in the United States were said to be around 3,000 copies.

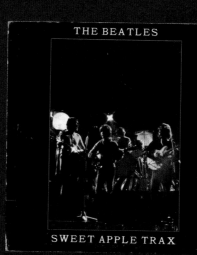

In 1987 the bootleg label TMOQ (Trademark of Quality) out of California released an 11-LP box set of *Get Back* rehearsals titled *Get Back Journals*. It is one of the more highly sought after Beatlegs. The music and rehearsals can be plodding at times; however, for those patient enough, there are a number of gems hidden within. Highlights include "Almost Grown," "Mad Man A Comin'," "Gimme Some Truth" and "Every Night."

In 1993 Vigotone released an 8-CD version of this set, *Get Back Journals*, featuring excellent mono and stereo tracks. The discs are housed in a hard case film box with metal corners and held together with two black vinyl straps (similar to the vinyl edition). The set includes a reproduction of the *Get Back* book that came with the British and several foreign pressings of the *Let It Be* album. Some of the more memorable tracks are "Fool Like Me," "You Win Again," "Thirty Days," "Dig It" and "Soldier Of Love." A later issue of the set came in a gold tin container. Only the first thousand or so copies of this collection came with the deluxe packaging and *Get Back* book.

Get Back Journals II came out in 1996 and picked up where the first volume left off. Again, this was a beautifully packed collection with 8 CDs, this time packaged in a white cardboard box inside an attractive full-color slipcase. These discs focus on the Twickenham recording sessions from January 6 through the 10th. Highlights include rehearsals of "All Things Must Pass," "Hear Me Lord," "Don't Let Me Down," "I Me Mine" and "Across The Universe." All are excellent stereo. The packaging includes a 28-page 10" x 10" book with black & white and color pictures, a history of the *Get Back* bootlegs and an overview of the Twickenham sessions.

In 2000 Vigotone issued another collection packed full of *Get Back* rehearsals titled *Thirty Days with Don't Let Me Down and 187 other songs*. The set is packaged in a slipcase with a cover mimicking the cover intended for the unreleased *Get Back* LP. There are 16 CDs of rehearsals and an additional CD housed in a cardboard jacket of the unreleased 1969 version of the *Get Back* album. A 48-page book details the contents and contains a couple of essays on the sessions. The set does not include any performances from the first day of the sessions (apparently because they were already covered on earlier releases). The last two days have near complete coverage with one CD of the rooftop concert and two CDs of the final January 31 studio sessions featuring multiple performances of "Two Of Us," "Let It Be" and "The Long And Winding Road." In between are countless interesting gems.

That same year Yellow Dog issued 38 2-CD volumes of its *Day By Day* series that include all available *Get Back* rehearsals. In 2004 Purple Chick began posting the rehearsals in its series *A/B Road – The Complete Get Back Sessions*. A current 83-CD Japanese collection is just what its name implies — *The Complete Get Back Sessions*.

Those wanting to hear the original unreleased *Get Back* album in high-quality full stereo got their wish in 1987 when a handful of bootleggers issued the album in vinyl. In 1992 Yellow Dog issued the CD *Get Back And 22 Other Songs*, which included the entire album plus performances of songs such as "I Lost My Little Girl," "Take This Hammer," "Schoolday (Ring! Ring! Goes The Bell)," "Good Rockin' Tonight," "Forty Days," "Too Bad About Sorrows" and "Fancy Me Chances."

For those preferring the Glyn Johns final mix of the album, Vigotone issued a CD in 1999, *Get Back with Don't Let Me Down and 9 Other Songs*, simulating the unreleased LP by dropping "Teddy Boy" and adding "I Me Mine" and "Across The Universe."

A recent limited edition 4-CD set, *Get Back Complete Edition (The Glyn Johns Compilations 1969 - 1970)*, includes: (1) the January acetates; (2) the early May acetate; (3) the first unreleased *Get Back* LP; and (4) the final *Get Back* line-up. Unfortunately the disc of the May acetate only has the left channel, making it an uneven listening experience. On the plus side, the disc contains several bonus tracks, including Glyn Johns and Phil Spector mixes of "Teddy Boy" and several John Barrett mixes of rock 'n' roll songs and medleys.

The rooftop concert can be found on the Yellow Dog's 1992 CD *The Complete Rooftop Concert* and Vigotone's 1994 CD *As Nature Intended*. The former disc has the concert plus rehearsals, including a longer version of "The Walk" and previously unheard versions of "She Came In Through The Bathroom Window," "Oh Darling!," "Across The Universe" and "Maxwell's Silver Hammer." The Vigotone disc has the entire rooftop concert plus the unissued *Get Back* LP.

Yellow Dog's *WBCN Get Back Reference Acetate* CD has the entire September 22, 1969, WBCN broadcast of the *Get Back* tracks plus 34 minutes of dialog recorded during the filming of *Let It Be*.

One of the more fascinating *Get Back* bootlegs is a fantasy item that purports to be a promotional copy of the unreleased *Get Back* album. The contents came in a white envelope with a green Apple logo and green text proclaiming "The Beatles as nature intended." This 1980s release has a simulated cover of the unissued *Get Back* album containing a vinyl record with green Apple promotional labels with the titles and other information in black type.

The package also includes a folded 22" x 33" "Fresh Beatles!" promo poster and an Apple memorandum dated July 17, 1969. The poster features an alternate picture taken during the *Get Back* LP cover session with the Beatles wearing different clothing. The memo reprints Mal Evans' report on the *Get Back* album from the July 1969 edition of The Beatles Book (issue No. 72).

Each of the envelopes for this release has a mailing label addressed to someone associated with the Beatles, such as Klaus Voormann, Billy Preston, Mary Hopkin or photographer Ethan Russell. Although the package is authentic looking and has fooled many excited fans and collectors, the bootlegger left an obvious clue to its dubious origin — despite having an "Abbey Road Station" postmark, the canceled stamps are from foreign countries such as Germany, Spain, Austria and Italy. Still, this well-made fantasy piece is highly collectible and worth seeking out. Just don't think you're getting Billy Preston's personal copy of a legitimate Apple promotional album!

This has been a quick overview of the *Get Back* Beatlegs of the last 50 years. What began innocently enough with *Kum Back* in late 1969 soon evolved into a worldwide phenomenon grossing hundreds of thousands of dollars with thousands of records and CDs full of Beatles performances, most of which are not available on legitimate releases.

Beatlegs of the *Get Back* material far outnumber those of any other period in the Beatles recording history. Admittedly, the music on many of these underground recordings is at times painful to listen to; however, hearing so many unpolished "diamonds in the rough" is well worth the effort.

Can you dig it?

GET BACK • THE BEATLES

stereo

THE BEATLES

GET BACK
with Don't Let Me Down
and 9 other songs

**The Beatles
as nature intended.**

Fresh Beatles!
BACK

KLAUS VOORMANN
Postfach 73-06
2000, Hamburg 73
Germany

I'M BACKING
BRITAIN
N.W. 8

ABBEY ROAD STATION
31. JULY
1969

GET BACK
THE BEATLES

■ GEORGE HARRISON (lead guitar)   ■ JOHN LENNON (rhythm guitar)
■ PAUL McCARTNEY (bass guitar)   ■ RINGO STARR (drums)

PCS
7080

SIDE ONE

1. ONE AFTER 909
(Lennon-McCartney)
2. DON'T LET ME DOWN
(Lennon-McCartney)
3. DIG A PONY
(Lennon-McCartney)
4. I'VE GOT A FEELING
(Lennon-McCartney)
5. GET BACK
(Lennon-McCartney)

SIDE TWO

1. FOR YOU BLUE
(Lennon-McCartney)
2. TEDDY BOY
(Lennon-McCartney)
3. TWO OF US ON OUR WAY HOME
(Lennon-McCartney)
4. DIG IT
(Lennon-McCartney-Harrison-Starkey)
5. LET IT BE
(Lennon-McCartney)
6. THE LONG AND WINDING ROAD
(Lennon-McCartney)

PRODUCED BY GEORGE MARTIN

EMI Records Ltd.

LONG PLAY 33⅓ R.P.M.   **APPLE RECORDS LIMITED**
No. 3 SAVILE ROW LONDON W1 ENGLAND
Made and Printed in Great Britain

"GET BACK"

TT: 20:11   PCS 7080-A

1. ONE AFTER 909   3:03
2. DON'T LET ME DOWN   3:50
3. I DIG A PONY   4:15
4. I'VE GOT A FEELING   2:58
5. GET BACK   3:16

"GET BACK"

TT: 24:17   PCS 7080-B

1. FOR YOU BLUE   2:52
2. TEDDY BOY   3:49
3. TWO OF US   3:38
4. DIG IT   4:06
5. LET IT BE   4:23
6. THE LONG AND WINDING
ROAD   3:52

Get Back **OUT NOW** on EMI / Apple Records (PCS 7080)

VISIT
www.beatle.net
for more books by Bruce Spizer

SUBSCRIBE TO BRUCE'S EMAIL LIST

FOR MORE EXCLUSIVE BEATLES ARTICLES AND CONTENT

THE BEATLES ALBUM SERIES ALSO AVAILABLE IN DIGITAL, HARD COVER AND SPECIAL COLLECTOR'S EDITIONS

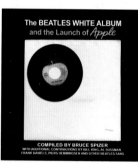
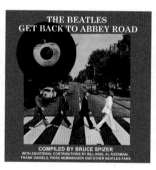

OTHER TITLES: DIGITAL EDITIONS, FIRST EDITION HARDCOVER AND SPECIAL COLLECTOR'S EDITIONS

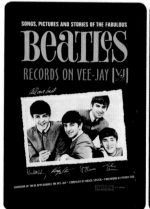

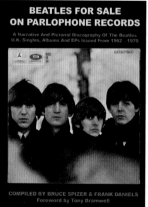